# Praise for
# *SWAY*

"Rather than prattling on about products and obsessing over sales leads, Christina shows you how to build a powerful go-to-market approach. The G.R.I.T. Marketing Method is your ticket to joining the C-suite as the leader of company strategy."

**–DAVID MEERMAN SCOTT,** *Wall Street Journal*
Bestselling Author of *Fanocracy*

"Whether you are in marketing or sales, *Sway* provides a framework and practical guidance for gaining trust within your company, allowing for a more collaborative and successful implementation of the corporate strategy."

**–CHRISTOPHER SINNOTT,** Business
Development, Amazon Web Services

"*Sway* has been one of the best marketing books I've read in a while. It's a combination of outstanding depth, step-by-step concepts, advice, and, of course, Christina's incredible wit. You'll find yourself having aha moments throughout and laughing along the way."

**–MISTY MEGIA,** CEO-Creative Producer,
The Theater of Marketing, and former Global Head
of ProAdvisor Program and Education, Intuit

"*Sway* takes the mystery out of marketing, breaking it down into manageable concepts and clear to-do lists. Whether you've been grinding out demand-gen campaigns for years or just starting out, Christina's lighthearted vibe breathes new life into how marketers can—and must—market themselves."

—ABIGAIL TULLER, Director of Communications, Autodesk

"This book is your golden ticket to understanding how to build influence for yourself and your organization. After reading *Sway*, I was able to better understand where I could make an impact in my company by delivering effective and efficient marketing strategies. All of a sudden, I was seen as the marketing superstar I knew I always was."

—JENNIFER KLEIN, Marketing Consultant, Klein Marketing Consulting

"Christina is inspiring and full of knowledge that can help all marketers. In *Sway*, she dives deep into the tactics, tools, and strategies that anyone can use to build influence in their organization and grow their careers."

—SABRINA RICCI, Author and Podcaster, *I Know Dino*, and Publisher, *Digital Pubbing*

"Christina Del Villar is the go-to expert on marketing that increases company revenue and grows brand impact. In *Sway*, she breaks down complicated marketing strategies into a clear, step-by-step method any marketer or CMO can implement for success—all with whip-smart humor that would make even the most marketing-budget-averse CEO smile. *Sway* should be on every marketer's bookshelf! Highly, highly recommend."

–**STACY ENNIS,** Best-Selling Co-Author,
*Growing Influence: A Story of How to Lead with Character, Expertise, and Impact*

"*Sway* will empower you to take your marketing strategy, and your career, to the next level. Christina's G.R.I.T Marketing Method lays out all the steps needed, in a way that's easy to understand and execute."

–**JESSICA MCINTYRE,** Demand Generation Manager, Clarify Health Solutions

"*Sway* is both a practical and strategic guide for marketing professionals. *Sway* teaches you not only how to be great at marketing but also how to be a great marketing professional."

–**ROB MCGRORTY,** Vice President of Product, OSARO, Inc.

# SWAY

Implement the G.R.I.T. Marketing Method
to Gain Influence and Drive Corporate Strategy

## Christina Del Villar

AN INC.
ORIGINAL

An Inc. Original
New York, New York
www.anincoriginal.com

This work is being published under the *An Inc. Original* imprint by an exclusive arrangement with *Inc. Magazine*. *Inc. Magazine* and the *Inc.* logo are registered trademarks of Mansueto Ventures, LLC. The *An Inc. Original* logo is a wholly owned trademark of Mansueto Ventures, LLC.

Distributed by River Grove Books

Design and composition by Greenleaf Book Group
Cover design by Greenleaf Book Group
Cover images used under license from ©Shutterstock.com/Rob Hyrons

Publisher's Cataloging-in-Publication data is available.

Hardcover ISBN: 978-1-7360283-2-2

Paperback ISBN: 978-1-63909-059-4

eBook ISBN: 978-1-7360283-3-9

First Edition

*This book is dedicated to any marketer who ever thought, "Why the heck am I even here if no one is going to listen to me or understand the amazing impact I am having on the company's revenue." I hope this book makes it easier for you to show your impact, increase your influence, and sleep better at night.*

# CONTENTS

# CHAPTER 1

# "This Is Your Life"

O ver the past thirty years as a marketing professional, I have seen *a lot*—in various stages of good, bad, and ugly. At this point, I have enough content to create a ten-season sitcom called *Silicon Valley: Marketlandia*. Or, at minimum, a book or two.

I've seen advances in technology that make it easier for marketing professionals to do their job and measure results. I've seen new types of marketing programs and channels pop up out of our innovation and desire to provide value. I've seen new areas of focus emerge—such as content marketing, customer marketing (what a novel concept), and growth marketing—while entire channels become obsolete or shift to survive. And I've seen marketing roles and professionals transform.

It's been a wild ride. But through it all, one thing has remained consistent: Marketing and marketing professionals are still misunderstood, undervalued, and considered nonessential instead of recognized as the backbone of the company we are. I sometimes feel as if we're invisible. Marketing organizations are thought of as a cost center, not a revenue center, so their budgets are often the first to get cut when companies become concerned about hitting revenue targets and meeting goals. We as marketing professionals are often some of the first to get laid off when downturns occur.

Let's face it: In the words of P!nk, we are "mistreated, misplaced, misunderstood." And frankly, it's sad.

But it doesn't have to be this way. It is up to marketing professionals, mavens, and gurus to help sway the rest of the organization—the executives, our managers, our manager's manager, the board, the world at large, heck, even our own parents—into understanding the value we bring to a company and its overall performance. We need to show the significance of our roles, our programs, and our organizations, as well as our impact. Marketing professionals need to make clear that the marketing organization not only is a revenue center but should be thought of as *the* Revenue Knowledge Center—the one-stop shop where everyone can turn to figure out how the company will meet its revenue targets, where the company is on those goals, and options to implement if the company is behind. In other words, marketing professionals know what it will take to grow the company twofold, fivefold, or even tenfold, and we can guide the company there. Marketers are nimble, smart, and adaptable, even when overwhelmed and under extraordinary circumstances.

In an effort to help marketing professionals become more effective and empowered, grow trust and influence within their organization, be truly impactful, and sway the naysayers, I developed the G.R.I.T. Marketing Method™. This is the framework I have used successfully for decades with individuals and companies. Applying this methodology will help you show others you are an amazing marketing professional full of grit and a lot more.

In these pages, you will learn how to have greater influence and strategic visibility in your company, establish the importance of marketing, demonstrate the value and impact you bring using data (not a bad word), build trust with executives, and develop a plan to boost revenue growth. By the end of this book, you will have the tools you need, and feel empowered, to establish yourself as a thought leader in your company—so that you'll never have to worry about your job again.

But first, I want to explore the current issues we face as marketing professionals, how we got here, and what things could look like when marketers are truly valued—and how we can get there.

## CURRENT STATE – THE DARK AGES

Several factors hinder the overall success of marketing organizations and marketing professionals. The first is that—let's face it—we are completely misunderstood, by our executives and company leaders as well as our company at large. (No, we don't just make cute T-shirts and plan cocktail parties.) In addition, we often do not have enough—or the right—data to show the value we bring. And finally, sadly, marketing is seen as nonessential or not seen at all. Marketing and marketing professionals are often invisible. But while I did just paint a pretty bleak picture, all hope is not lost. Once we recognize the problem, we'll be able to either solve it or find a work-around. 'Cause that's what marketing professionals do! We solve problems. We fix things. We get shit done.

## Misunderstood

It's one thing to say, "Executives just don't get us," but it's another to understand it. Why don't they get us? Are they just dumb? I don't think so. I think there are several factors at play.

But first, a story. A story I like to call "17,000 leads, please." #storyofmylife

I was once in a board meeting where the topic was how much money to invest in marketing programs and my team. I went into the meeting with solid go-to-market strategy, clearly showing our lead-generation programs, conversions, and estimated revenue numbers, and the corresponding budget we would need to implement the plan. I generally work backward from the revenue goals to determine

which programs we should invest in based on their return on invest-
ment (ROI), conversion, and time and ease to close. To be honest, I
was pretty pleased with what I had developed. Not cocky, just sure of
myself and the plan.

Imagine my surprise when one of the board members cut off my
presentation very early on with a sweeping hand (I might be embel-
lishing here—but that's how I remember it) and said, "We need you to
bring in 17,000 leads!" Um, okay. What exactly do you mean? "You
need to go find 17,000 leads. Yep, that's what we need."

My first reaction? Put in your own eye-rolling-dumbfounded-
look-string-of-cuss-words-ending-with-a-sigh combo, and you'll
get the idea.

What I wanted to say was "Did you hear anything I just said? Did
you see my amazing funnel slide showing you what we need, how we
will get there, and the result it will likely bring? 17,000? Did you pull
that number out of your, um, head?"

I actually said (potentially with a wee bit of snark), "I can get us
17,000 leads today, by buying a list. And it will cost us $6,000. But
they will be shit leads that will need to be nurtured for a long time,
will convert poorly, and will cause our sales team to pretty much hate
marketing." (Pro tip: In general, I do advise a more delicate approach
when calling out your board members.)

What the board had asked for was vastly different from what
I had presented to them. As pleased as I was with what I'd put
together, I had gone into the meeting unprepared for what *they* were
expecting. I failed to understand what they were looking for, I didn't
understand where they were coming from, and I lacked empathy
for what they were dealing with. In the case of the "17,000 leads,
please" example, we ultimately made some progress in a follow-up
conversation with the sales team and some board members. I shared
our current definition of a true lead, and together we all agreed on
that definition. That way, the next time I shared information about

our lead count and status, we would be on the same page. And when the board made future requests, they did so with a clearer understanding of their ask. We also spent some time defining and agreeing on what our targets and company goals really were (revenue versus a random number of questionable leads). Finally, we established how marketing would enable sales to sell better, with content, scripts, and more sales training.

It's super easy for us to get annoyed with executives, leaders, and board members and say, "They don't get us." And I mean, they usually don't. But we also have to ask: Do we really get them?

First off, executives are incredibly busy people, with full schedules. They're focused on the bigger picture (i.e., *everything* that is going on in the company), as they should be. And unlike us, marketing is not their day job. They do not have the luxury of thinking about marketing 24/7 like we do (you know you do). And company executives are likely not as passionate about marketing as marketing professionals are. Think about a small business owner who owns a dog biscuit bakery (don't ask, just go with it). This owner is passionate about bringing wholesome, quality natural dog biscuits to all of our furry friends. Do you think they got into the business of making dog biscuits because they love marketing (or accounting, or even shipping)? I'm guessing not.

While some executives are passionate about marketing, even these rare breeds have a whole slew of other things to focus on. While we as marketing professionals are focused on a specific demand-gen program, they are focused on the entirety of the company, its success, and its survival or growth. Marketing is just one (albeit big) piece of the puzzle, and marketing professionals need to help executives understand where we fit into the overall company strategy.

What marketing professionals need to understand is that the data and results we think are cool and amazing (and totally nerd out on) might be less exciting and useful to executives. And because marketers are essentially storytellers, we may be taking too long to get to the punch line. We like to have an introduction, explain our thesis (with pretty graphics), lay the groundwork, postulate a bit, and build some momentum and excitement for the big reveal. Have I lost you yet? Well, now put yourself in the shoes of someone who doesn't have a lot of time and just wants the punch line. Marketers either need to adjust what we present or help others better understand why we choose this data to look at. Don't worry, I have a whole chapter on how to do this. But it's coming later, after I lay the groundwork. (Just trying to build momentum and excitement for the big reveal.)

## Data Is Your Frenemy

Next, let's consider the data itself. If you are like most marketing professionals, data, not sales, is your nemesis. You usually (1) don't have any, (2) don't have enough, (3) don't have the right kind—that is, quality data, (4) have it, but don't have the tools or people to analyze it, (5) can't find it (a personal favorite), and so on and so forth. You get the point. For marketing professionals, good, quality data is more elusive than Bigfoot.

I remember starting a job at a new company once (but really, this has happened at almost every company I've been at). I was going to be responsible for spinning up the go-to-market and marketing programs for reaching a new channel and new, different target market the company wanted to penetrate. During the interview process, I had specifically asked about any leads, programs, systems, and tools in place. It sounded like nirvana, based on the interviewer. "Oh, yeah, for sure, we've got leads. We just don't know what to do with them. We've got Marketo, SFDC, and as much coffee and smoothies as you can drink." Sounded too good to be true. That should have been my tip-off.

What I pictured was a well-thought-out marketing and lead workflow that carried across the entire customer journey—systems and mechanics in place for a seamless experience, and automation everywhere. Everything in its perfect little place. Lead-workflow nirvana. Something a little like this:

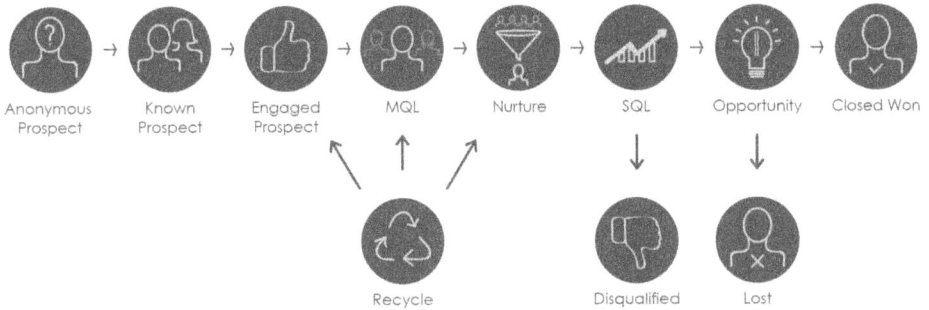

Lead Lifecycle Nirvana

I accepted the job with much glee.

Wow. The honeymoon did not last long. What I came to find with the systems, workflows, leads, data, and more was a complete clusterfuck.

All oh-so pretty on the outside, but everything was totally useless once I dug into it. There were no lead sources, so I had no information on how programs performed and what their potential was. There was no industry (professional services, food and beverage, government) or title (CFO, accountant, finance manager) information included, so I couldn't segment the list accordingly or build an effective contact-management strategy. And as these were small to mid-size company leads, I couldn't easily have them appended through a data or email appending service like Dun & Bradstreet. With a lot of the leads—are you ready for this?—the prospect's name hadn't even been collected, just their email address. So much for personalization. To be fair, there was a lead-scoring mechanism in place, but it was ineffective because the information was disastrously incomplete (garbage in = garbage out). If you are reading this section and it doesn't resonate with you, consider yourself lucky, or a unicorn, and you can skip the chapters on measurement and intention. But I'm guessing you are either laughing or crying right now, glad you're not the only one whose data is a shit-show. So please, read on.

In my example about the board meeting, it was me not telling the right story; in this case, it's the *data* that isn't telling the right story, to the right people, at the right time. It's similar to a product manager who comes into a new company and finds that the product code on the back end has been jerry-rigged together for years. Marketing professionals are in the same boat. We are inheriting systems that have been duct-taped together over the years. During this time, workflows have changed, marketing programs have changed, and buyer behavior has changed, but systems and workflows were never updated to reflect any of this. For example, why bother attaching a score to a product feature that is no longer available? Let's just say, you shouldn't.

Also, let's face it, beautiful data is expensive. The systems you need aren't cheap. You need to continually update the flows and monitor everything closely. It's a bit of a catch-22 for marketing professionals. We need data to show our value to get funds to build a better data machine.

While having good, clean, beautiful data is costly, it is exponentially more expensive to have bad data. Not only is bad data costly to your company; it does nothing to help you show the results, the impact, and your value, because you either don't have the correct data to pull from or no one believes the data. Bad data also does not help you make good recommendations on where to invest (or divest). Google "bad marketing data" and check out the results. One article estimates that poor "marketing" data costs online businesses alone $611 billion a year. That's a *b* for billion. Imagine if you were able to save your company millions by having good data, and bring in millions more in revenue with better data-driven strategy and programs.

Data should be at the forefront of every decision you make as a marketing professional, yet you often can't find it or trust it. Inaccurate, incomplete, outdated, and entirely absent data is your enemy.

So what happened in that great new job I took? Did I find the magical, mysterious, amazing unicorn leads? Was I able to accurately project our revenue based on the success and ROI of our programs? Could I say with certainty what our conversion from marketing-qualified lead (MQL) to sales-qualified lead (SQL) to closed-win rate was? Did I find the coffee and smoothies? No, no, no, and yes. After doing an audit of the data, leads, tools, and systems, I decided to scrap two-thirds of the database. I then rebuilt the workflows and scoring and updated our systems (we'll get into the MarTech stack in a later chapter). I added more fields on forms (you know, things like "name" and "company"), and with the marketing automation system I had in place, I set up progressive forms so we weren't asking for the same information over and over again from repeat visitors. Instead, we progressively asked for more information. Eventually, I was able to leverage the data to more accurately show results and impact, and make better decisions that helped the company grow. But that took time. Almost a year, to be inexact.

## The Invisible Corps

Now let's talk about us, the marketing professionals. As much as it hurts me to say this, most people think of marketing as nonessential. My goal here isn't to make you feel like crap. But if we as marketing professionals don't know where we're starting from in terms of how people in companies view us, and why (which I'll cover in the next chapter), it will be hard to rise above it. I promise you, though, there is hope.

What do I mean by nonessential? In this context, I mean that others in the organization don't know what we do, don't understand the value we bring, and think their corporate world would still chug along pretty darn well if marketing suddenly didn't show up. If you look up *nonessential* in the dictionary (which of course I just had to do), it lists synonyms such as *dispensable, gratuitous, unnecessary*. I don't know about you, but that is how I have felt before.

There have been several times in my career when I left a company not by choice but because I was (pick your descriptor) laid off, let go, downsized, riffed, or separated. Usually this was due to an overall reduction in costs and budgets. In my role as marketing leader, I am usually the one defining the strategy, developing the programs, and managing the team that is implementing, evaluating, reporting out results, and ultimately owning a revenue target. In almost all these instances of "separation," members of my team were asked to step into my shoes to fill that gap once I was gone. While my teams were amazing, they were hired for a specific reason or area of focus, which didn't include my job. I have decades of experience defining the needs of, purchasing, and implementing marketing systems; if I go away and someone with little experience in MarTech is put in charge of the overall integration process—well, let's just say, it's not the best idea. That person replacing me wasn't hired, nor do they have the knowledge, to identify and implement systems, and they will likely not be set up for success.

There is a pervasive sense that marketing professionals are interchangeable, which I think has contributed to the belief that we are not essential.

"Hey, we need to switch our eighty thousand in-person event to a virtual event, but we let go of our events person because we can't do in-person events right now. Go grab Mary on the content team; put her in charge of the virtual event. She's a good writer," says random company executive. Facepalm. Seriously, folks, just as engineers have specialties, marketing professionals do as well. While we are flexible, agile, fast-learning, problem-solving geniuses, we are not completely interchangeable.

The other issue marketing professionals often have is that people—besides not really knowing exactly what we do—think we are "just having fun." Sure, we tend to be happy-go-lucky people who like to come to work, smile, and try to bring good cheer. That doesn't mean we aren't also working on valuable programs that bring in revenue for our company. As marketing professionals, we aren't just working on designing clever T-shirts all day. And if we are designing T-shirts, it's not for shits and giggles. It's likely for a larger, well-thought-out marketing campaign, like the biggest industry event of the year, where sales members from our company move prospects through their own customer journey with demos, workshops, and sessions. This might be a VIP event where the company brings in the biggest volume of leads for the year. But before they are handed over to sales for follow-up, marketing needs to continue to qualify and nurture the leads. So, yes, we might create the occasional T-shirt, hat, or sticker, but it's for a larger purpose.

To sum it up succinctly, people throughout the organization, executives in particular, don't know what marketing professionals do, often because we lack quality data to convince them of our worth. We need to help people understand what marketing does, the impact we have, and what it takes to develop and deliver amazing marketing programs. We need to provide context around these programs so others within our organization and company can see we are developing with intent and predictability. And then we need to underscore the value we add and the impact we bring to the table by sharing and explaining results, as they relate to overall company performance.

## HOW THE *&^% DID WE GET HERE?

How did marketing professionals get to be undervalued and "invisible"? We need to take a step back and figure that out, as it will help set the stage for what we look at next—how to break the cycle and recognize areas that can be fixed, optimized, and changed.

As I was preparing for this book, I took a long look back on my illustrious career as a marketing professional and leader. I did a little soul searching. And I realized several common themes that got us to where we are today. One factor is what I like to call the revolving door of marketing managers, a reality that often disrupts momentum, from both a programming standpoint and an individual career trajectory standpoint. Another factor is our own individual lack of a marketing plan. In other words, while we marketing professionals are amazing at developing and implementing a marketing plan for our company, we generally fail to do something similar for ourselves. Yet another factor that got us into this mess is that the sales *cycle* is not our friend; because of the time it takes leads to go from top of the funnel to closed and won, measuring and showing the effectiveness of that lead could take years. Where else did we go wrong? Ah, yes— while marketing professionals are flexible and agile, we are not as interchangeable as people want us to be. This unfortunately leads to our failing to build trust within the organization by not setting proper boundaries and establishing more realistic expectations. And finally (ish), we have not empowered ourselves and each other to function at the highest level possible and have even more impact.

Let's dig a little deeper into these so you can recognize them in your own experience and do some course correction.

## Revolving Door Manager Syndrome

I cannot tell you—literally I cannot—how many times I have had to rebuild teams, programs, and trust because of the never-ending shifts in management. Some changes were good; some not so much. But at the end of the day these continual shifts in personnel almost always had some negative impact.

When I was at Oracle, I had no less than eight different managers. Eight! In a three-and-a-half-year period. Every time a new manager came in, I would have to go through the process of (1) explaining my job and my team's job, (2) walking through all of the campaigns and programs and why I chose them, (3) trudging through the data and explaining to New Manager Steve what the data means and how I got it, (4) then going back and redoing charts because New Manager Jill likes circles instead of triangles and blue tones instead of orange. Sigh. Basically, I would have to explain my and my team's existence. *Eight times!* Of course, New Manager Tim had his own goals and agendas, so I would generally have to shift everything around, build a new strategy, and then implement it. My team and I lost momentum every time this happened. And then six months later (give or take a manager or two—Keith, Richard, etc.), I would have to start the process all over again. I had to learn New Manager Fatima's processes and personality. Not to mention, my career trajectory was total crap. I once had a new manager who had to give me a review in his first week on the job, with no background on what the heck I had been doing all year.

This wasn't an ideal situation for me to be thrown into. But what I see now when I look back is that I didn't establish myself as a leader within the organization. I didn't build enough influence and trust with the right folks to make the transitions easier—for me, for New Manager Stacy/Lisa/Rob, for my team, and for the marketing organization as a whole. Ultimately, I did a really shitty job of marketing myself. I thought it was enough to just do my job and do it insanely well. Had I spent time marketing myself and my team, it would have been easier for New Manager Sally to have a sense of my capabilities and trust me to continue down the established path without wanting to reroute everything and break our momentum.

I'm guessing most of us fall into the trap of not marketing ourselves. It's like the cobbler's kids' shoes. But we need to change this.

You need to focus on developing some sort of plan to build trust and influence whatever is falling apart around you. By the time you finish this book, you will have a foundation in place to do so.

## The Long (and Winding) Sales Cycle

Another big problem marketing professionals have to deal with, especially if you work for a company with a B2B offering to large and enterprise-sized clients, is the overall sales cycle. Marketing can bring in tons of leads (17,000, for example—in one day, no less!), but if the sales cycle is long, then it will take a long time to see the results from your marketing efforts. In other words, if your company's sales cycle is twelve to eighteen months, that's the minimum it will take for your lead to turn into a sale. The lead first needs to be acquired, then marketing will likely retain and nurture the lead, which could take months, depending on the quality of lead and the channel it came through. Then, once the lead is qualified and heads over to a salesperson, it could take an additional twelve to eighteen months for sales to work and close the deal. So, yay, a lead turned into a closed-won deal twenty months later. And let's be honest, by then all of us—sales, marketing, executives—have all moved on (either with other programs or possibly other jobs). So the felt impact of the program that brought in the lead is completely lost.

Let me illustrate my point. When I was at Udacity, I was focused on the B2B and enterprise space with an offering that consisted of a prescriptive curriculum to help large companies bridge a technical skills gap. Selling into this new market was a huge endeavor on the part of our sales team, and the sales cycle lasted about twelve months. That meant that once the leads my team brought in were SQLs, the lead would then transfer over to sales. As part of a launch campaign for an upcoming degree on artificial intelligence, I had planned a thought leader webinar featuring Udacity's CEO and

Kai-Fu Lee, the father of AI. The webinar was going to kick off our overall marketing campaign for the new AI course, and who better to help us do that than the freakin' father of AI, Dr. Kai-Fu Lee himself? The day comes, and we do the webinar live, in studio. And it was a major success—we had over eighty thousand people view the webinar!! Holy crap! Whoot!

The next day, admittedly, I'm still basking in the glory of this epic event. The GM of our division congratulates me. Job well done. Amazing turnout. And then he says—I shit you not—"How much revenue did the webinar bring in?" Not even twenty-four hours later! (Imagine a deflating sound here as my basking-glory day came to a sudden halt.) I boldly replied, "Well, considering it takes about twelve months for our sales cycle, why don't you check back with me then?" He chuckled and said something like "Fair enough." I just sighed, knowing that twelve months from then, the data would show that a closed-won lead came from this amazing webinar. But in the meantime, people would wonder if the webinar and thought leader program were successful. They would wonder if my team and I were doing a good job. And when you add in the problem of revolving managers . . . it's really hard for people to see the impact our programs can have.

So we have to do better. We have to help people understand not only what we're implementing, but when we'll be able to show the *impact* and results of our amazing efforts. I wish I had a magic wand or some pixie dust or some Tarot cards to show the impact looking forward. But I don't. We don't. But we as marketing professionals can do a better job setting expectations. Later in the book, I'll take you through how to forecast out your programs and the potential leads and revenue generated from them. Having a forecast can help in setting expectations for the actual results of a program.

## Market the Marketer—Trust Me

As I've mentioned—and will continue to mention throughout the book—marketing professionals don't spend enough time marketing themselves. We don't take the time to understand our audience (sales, product, executives, etc.), and we don't spend enough time building trust. These two should go hand in hand. What are the goals of the executives, our managers, and our peers in other departments, and how do those goals fit into ours? Or better yet, how do our goals roll up neatly into their goals and the overall goals of the company?

If you think about a marketing funnel, what is the persona of the audience we need to build trust with? What are the pain points of this internal audience? First you have to educate them, make them aware of who you are and what you do. Then you have to engage them. Once you've "hooked" them, how do you nurture them and build enough trust so that they "buy in" to your programs and budget and believe your forecast and results? Does this sound familiar? Treat sales, product, executives, and leaders—everyone in your company—as a potential customer of yours, one that is loyal to you. Once they believe in you, how do you onboard them—or, in other words, get them to adopt your mindset? Now how do you expand that "account"—get more commitment in the way of budget, empowerment, recognition, resources, bonuses, heck, maybe even a testimonial? We're trying to avoid unhappy, confused "customers" here, folks! Basically, what we need to do is learn to market ourselves!

Let's face it, there is no "Easy" button. But I know you know how to do this! As you go through this book, just think about yourself as your very own marketing campaign. What are your objectives (for example: to be seen as an influencer); what are your goals (budget for programs); who is your audience, specifically the audience persona (manager, CMO, CEO, CRO, sales); what types of "programs" will you run to be seen and heard (reports, presentations and slides, updates, and report outs); what content do you need (how about turning your weekly update into an infographic); what channels will you use to show your impact (weekly town hall); and on and on. You get the point.

While adjusting your thinking this way might add another step, it will help you formulate your plan for disseminating your results more effectively and impactfully.

## Trust the Process

Building trust is another area where marketing professionals could do a better job. We probably haven't built trust—or enough of it, or the right kind of it—with the right people. But we've got to do this, with colleagues and executives, to be empowered and given the resources we need. And then we've got to keep these people in our corner.

I define trust as someone having a firm belief in me, my team, our overall character, and the programs we are executing. Sure, most people "like" us, but they don't really know what we do, our data isn't helping us tell the story any better, and we're kind of invisible. So how can we ensure people have a "firm belief in our character"?

Think about it. Let's say you're a teenager and you want to go to the store and buy something (I'm being vague here on purpose). You go to your next-door neighbor and say, "Hey, I'm heading off to the store. Can I have your wallet?" No matter how nice of a kid you are, the neighbor is going to be hesitant. Now you tell them, "Don't worry about it. I'll bring your wallet back in about twelve months with double the cash. Trust me." Sorry, kid. Ain't gonna happen.

Sure, this is a little out there, but hopefully you get the point. You, amazing marketing professional, are asking your company to give you a bunch of money to implement programs you can't really say for sure will work, and you won't have solid results for another twelve months, and by then everyone will have moved on. It's hard to build trust when the cards are stacked against you.

I wanted to find some quotes on trust to add here. What I found were a bunch of "inspirational" posters depicting sunsets, mountains, and kittens that mostly made me want to buy some darts. But there was one good quote. "Without trust, there can be no loyalty—and without loyalty, there can be no true growth." –Fred Reichheld. And yes, there was a mountain behind it. (And for some reason I read it in Yoda's voice.)

My first thought was *Yep, true story. Makes sense.* My next thought was *Who the heck is Fred and what does he know?* Well, it turns out Fred is a *New York Times* best-selling author, speaker, and business strategist best known for his research and writing on the loyalty business model and loyalty marketing. He is the creator of the Net Promoter Score (NPS) system of management, which we will discuss in a later chapter. Ah, okay, I trust him.

I am often in the position, due to lack of data or even lack of previous programs to reflect back on, of saying, "Trust me, it's going to work." But I have thirty years of experience, so it's a bit easier for people to stomach my request for $10 million followed by a cavalier "Trust me." I have spent years building trust and influence, so it's easier for me. At this point in my career, my managers and company leaders have a firm belief in my strength and character, and they trust me, even if they don't fully comprehend the marketing strategy or program I am developing.

But how do you build that strength, character, and ability to sway if you are relatively young in your career path? Oh, such a nice segue.

## Empowered—Emboldened—Gritty

We as marketing professionals need to be empowered. We need to be emboldened. We need to have grit.

Empowerment is a process of becoming more confident, becoming stronger, and controlling your own destiny. It doesn't happen overnight—it's a journey, and one that's well worth it. Strength and confidence will help you build trust!

Pro tip: We as humans tend to wait for someone else to empower us instead of empowering ourselves. But no one is going to empower you. You have to empower yourself.

Give yourself permission to be empowered and have grit. Assume no one is going to give this to you. And if you do not feel comfortable granting yourself permission, I hereby give it to you. There, you are now on the journey of being empowered. Go forth and conquer.

So what does it mean for us marketing folks to conquer? Call it Fantasy Island, nirvana, your happy place—it's reaching all we aim to achieve in our jobs and careers.

Marketing professionals should be considered influencers within every aspect of the overall corporate business strategy and go-to-market strategy.

First off, when I talk about the business strategy, or corporate strategy, I'm talking about the overall strategy of the company. It defines what the overall corporate structure will be, defines what the product is or will be, and determines the resources needed to make it all happen. It's the framework guiding the decision-making process and what should keep (or get) the company on track. It looks at the long-term goals of the company and the products or solutions. Seems like a no-brainer that marketing should be involved in the development of the overall business strategy, but often marketing professionals enter the mix long after the business plan has been developed—even years later in some cases.

From here, I'll talk about the go-to-market strategy (and I talk about it *a lot*).

The go-to-market strategy executes on the business strategy. Once the business strategy is defined, the go-to-market strategy specifically asks how the company will take a product to market. What does the company need to do to meet its long-term business goals?

Who is the target audience, how is the company going to find and attract them, and what is our message to them? It's another no-brainer to me that marketing professionals should be involved in this strategy's development too. But once again, we are often called in late in the game to "simply" (when is marketing ever simple?) implement the strategy. It certainly makes sense that we would carry out the go-to-market strategy, but I feel strongly that marketing and marketing professionals should be brought in early to define the strategy in the first place. Okay, hopping off the soapbox—for now.

Executives should look to you and other marketing professionals not just to maintain the current growth momentum and revenue trajectory but to continue building momentum and help with hypergrowth. Marketing should be thought of as the company Revenue Knowledge Center. Again, the concept here is that marketing and marketing professionals can provide a one-stop shop for understanding where, when, how, and how much revenue will come in. If there is concern about meeting company targets, marketing can discern the right levers to pull and options to put into place.

My experience shows that marketing should actually own the go-to-market strategy, working closely with sales and product, to help guide the overall direction of the business and product strategy, as well as company performance. There, I said it. Marketing should be driving the process because we own the data and know what the industry wants and needs, how to package it, how to sell it to our target audience based on value, and how to nurture customers through the entire customer journey. But if we can't own it, we should at least be influencing it from the beginning.

Assuring the marketing organization is always operating at peak level is critical so companies can, at minimum, maintain momentum. Too many times, I've seen companies gut marketing in hopes of using those funds to stay afloat a bit longer. But in doing so they cut off their feet, legs, and probably even their head. Momentum is lost really fast, but it takes two to five times as long to rebound—kind of like weight management. It takes two months to lose ten pounds (okay, maybe six months) but about ten seconds of just looking at a piece of cake to put it all back on.

I was once hiking in the Grand Canyon with my family. We hiked down one day, spent the night at the bottom, and were planning on hiking out the next day. Climbing out of the Grand Canyon is tough enough, but it was projected to be really freakin' hot—around 104 that day. The rangers emphasized over and over that we needed to hit the trail early and carry *a lot* of water. My family and I left at 3 a.m., made the long, hot climb out, and got to the top around noon.

There were others on the trail with us that day: in particular, two friends hiking together, people we likely passed along the way somewhere. We might even have stopped to chat with them, as you do when you're on a grueling hike, looking for any excuse to stop for a few short moments. Unfortunately, these two hikers did not make it—somewhere along the way they both died of dehydration and exposure, which is ironic because they were found with plenty of water and food on them. Apparently, they were "saving" their food and water for when they might really need it instead of sipping water throughout their hike, or even drinking it all at the beginning of the hike to give them the fuel they would need. It was a tragic and unnecessary loss. But clearly in their minds they thought that by conserving water and food, eating and drinking only when it felt absolutely necessary, they would have a higher chance of making it to the top.

This example might seem extreme, but it struck me as something companies do. Executives and leaders often "save" their food and water (i.e., cash), probably for a rainy day. But in doing so, with no fuel—marketing budget, programs, and leads—they can devastate the overall growth and momentum of the company, potentially leading to its failure or death. Ouch, that was heavy. Unlike at the Grand Canyon, though, companies don't have signs posted along the way reminding people to drink plenty of water. We as marketing leaders can help fuel the company, keep it fed and watered, so it can survive and thrive.

Marketing is often considered, erroneously, a cost center, when in fact it should be thought of as a revenue center. After all, we know which programs work best and which levers to pull when we need to accomplish things or pivot quickly. We know how long it takes to nurture leads in specific segments from specific channels and programs. We know what the sales process, onboarding and expansion process, and flow should look like throughout the customer journey. We know what we need to do to get to a certain revenue. But we need the tools, resources, and trust to do this.

## Breaking the Cycle

The time is now to break this vicious cycle. Even though this book has been in my head for years, I'm writing it during a pandemic. On any given day, marketing professionals lose their jobs due to things I've mentioned so far: issues with data, lack of trust, not having shown our true impact and value, not cleverly marketing ourselves. But when there is a pandemic, natural disaster, terrorist attack, stock market collapse, pick your poison, the effect is exacerbated for marketing professionals. I have seen so many amazing marketers lose their jobs during times of uncertainty, when in fact, companies should have done everything possible to keep them, and keep the machine fed.

Who, you ask, is going to break the cycle? Well, you are. With some help from this book, some amazing industry experts, and yours truly.

In this book I will help you build influence and trust so that you can not only be empowered (because you crowned yourself Queen Empowerment already) but truly show your impact and value.

So how do you break this cycle? Through my tried-and-proven G.R.I.T. Marketing Method, which we will spend the rest of the book covering. The goal is to help you develop the right mindset and give you the tools needed to be a go-to-market strategy and marketing influencer.

## HOW TO USE THIS BOOK

This book is directed at anyone who considers themselves a marketing professional, covering specific topics for B2B organizations (from startups to small and medium-size companies to large enterprises). The book can also be leveraged by solopreneurs figuring out how to structure their go-to-market strategies, as well as VPs of marketing, CMOs, and salespeople.

I'll share examples of what should be done to help you build a solid go-to-market strategy and, more importantly, have the influence and grit to implement it as intended. Ultimately this book will help you as a marketing professional not only *be* of significant value but *show* your value.

I will share with you "stories from the field," both my own and that of other marketing leaders. I will present you with concepts that have worked for me and other successful marketing professionals. Through examples, tips, and tools, I will demonstrate not just the "what" but the "how" as well.

To gain influence and trust and to show your true value-add and impact is a lofty goal, but it's one I know we can reach together. Some of what I am going to ask you to do will be hard and time consuming, but your overall happiness, success, and career trajectory depend on it. Unless of course you want to continue wondering every time executives hop into an all-day meeting if you'll still have a job at the end of it. (Admit it, you think that, and too often.) This isn't going to be easy. You are basically going to build your own marketing program to market yourself. And it's going to take grit. But you've got this.

Thank you for joining me on this journey. We will learn together and grow together. After all, who better to market our talents and efforts than us?

Challenge accepted! Now let's get to work.

CHAPTER 2

# What Is G.R.I.T.?

O ver the years I have come up with a clear, concise framework for developing, building, and measuring marketing strategy and programs: the G.R.I.T. Marketing Method.

With the G.R.I.T. methodology, I want to help you reach marketing enlightenment—nirvana—or at least some semblance of it. My goal is that you take this methodology and build your own framework to increase the influence and control you have over the company strategy, go-to-market strategy, marketing strategy and programs, and ultimately overall company performance. This will lay the foundation for showing that marketing is essential and should be thought of as a revenue center, not a cost center—moreover, a Revenue Knowledge Center, where the leaders and executives of your company can seek your valuable insight and guidance to develop strategy, products and solutions, and programs that boost company revenue. This will allow you to demonstrate the value and impact you bring to the company, using data to show how you are marketing with intent. You will be equipped to build further trust with executives, enabling you to have more sway and be even more effective. And we'll also look at how you can develop and implement a plan to boost revenue exponentially year over year, and get credit for it (wouldn't that be great?), thereby establishing yourself and your role at the company as essential so you never have to worry about your job security again.

So, what the heck is the G.R.I.T. Marketing Method? What is this framework I want you to learn, understand, and apply in order to become a better and more influential marketing professional?

Well, it centers on building a foundation around the following:

> **G**o-to-market strategy—Defining the overall go-to-market strategy, with marketing as the foundation for executing the overall corporate strategy and with a focus on directly aligning the go-to-market strategy with stages of the customer journey. From here, marketing professionals can build a Map of Influence (ohhhh, sounds mysterious!).

> **R**PM—Building repeatable, predictable, and measurable marketing programs that show the effectiveness and impact of marketing and marketing professionals. Yes, please!

> **I**ntention—Building marketing strategy and programs, content, and messaging with intent and purpose, to better align with the customer needs and company goals and vision. (Well, when you say it like that . . .)

> **T**ools and technology—Implementing tools and technology to build more efficient workflows, increase performance, and enable marketing professionals to measure impact consistently and with ease.

The G.R.I.T. Marketing Method allows you to build trust and demonstrate value and impact, which leads to influence. Plus, it will help you build confidence that will extend well beyond your current role. Before we move on, I want to give you my definition of influence so that as you go through the book, you will have a clearer understanding of my intent. When I talk about influence, it means you have developed enough trust with peers, managers, and leaders that they not only understand your effectiveness but actually start looking to you for strategic answers. Revenue numbers are down for the company as a whole? Who are the leaders going to look to for answers? You and the marketing team. Company executives are looking to initial public offering (IPO) in the next eighteen months and need to figure out how to get there? Who are execs gonna call? Marketing professionals and owners of the Revenue Knowledge Center. You get the point. This journey of understanding the G.R.I.T. methodology and implementation will take time. But you will be building influence along the way. Trust me.

These four elements can change your world.

Let's unpack each one a little more below, and then in the following chapters, we will cover them in depth. We'll even cover how to begin implementing some of these elements.

## *G* IS FOR GO-TO-MARKET STRATEGY

The goal of a go-to-market strategy is to bring the company, a product, or a solution to market. It should start from the overall business strategy and then incorporate the marketing and sales strategy, as well as customer onboarding and engagement with the customer success team. Regardless of who owns the go-to-market strategy, various departments should be part of the larger go-to-market team, however you define "team." I think of this team as including all of the essential people that own components of the customer journey, including marketing, product, sales, and customer success, at minimum. To have these teams all coming under one organization is a critical shift. But to be as efficient, effective, productive, and successful as possible, these teams need to be on the same page. Call it the Go-to-Market Department or the Revenue Center, or some clever new name. G.R.I.T. Department, for example. The goal is to bring together all the right people from these departments so there is alignment and shared objectives, resulting in an easier path to market.

When the teams that define, develop, and ultimately execute a go-to-market strategy are not under the same roof, in the same room, sitting at the same table, breaking bread—pick your metaphor—we are not as cohesive and effective as we could be.

First and foremost, marketing needs to be part of defining the go-to-market strategy. Taking that a step further, marketing should *own* this process. It just makes sense. Think about the customer journey itself, from understanding the product to marketing to sales and finally to customer success; think about how that journey aligns with the go-to-market strategy. Now think about all the touchpoints marketing has in every phase of the customer journey. Touchpoints are all the different components, pieces, and areas of the entire customer journey that marketing, well, touches: everything from helping define feature sets from a product standpoint; to determining the personas, targeted audiences, and messaging; to developing sales scripts to nurture prospects; to making how-to videos that help familiarize customers with the product after they purchase. And of course, there are the standard programs marketing already owns, like lead gen, events, content, and so forth. Marketing already plays such a huge role in the customer journey, but that role isn't recognized by the rest of the organization. We need to fix that. You need to fix that. Up for it?

If the standard customer journey goes from product ideation and development, to marketing implementing lead-gen programs and content, to the selling phase, and finally to customer success, it makes sense that marketing be integrated with the product team long before the product is built, helping define the audience targets, customer needs, pricing, feature priorities based on customer and market input and feedback, and overall product roadmap. From there marketing would plan, build, and implement lead-generation programs for the top and the middle of the funnel. Then as part of the sales phase of the customer journey, marketing would nurture and qualify the leads before passing them to sales. Then marketing would help sales continue to nurture the leads through the sales cycle with content, scripts, and campaigns. Marketing would then help customer success by building content for onboarding and adoption, owning the knowledge base or customer community, and sharing best practices via case studies and guides.

Marketing professionals (well, everyone in the company really, but let's start with us) all need to shift away from the idea that marketing exists only to execute the lead lifecycle phase of the customer journey. We as marketing professionals first need to recognize how our programs are really the foundation of the entire go-to-market strategy. Once we understand it, we need to help others understand and support it. And we need to include all the right people in the planning conversations to ensure alignment.

## *R* STANDS FOR RPM: REPEATABLE, PREDICTABLE, AND MEASURABLE

Now let us consider the marketing plan itself. Marketing teams are often small and scrappy. For them to be effective at this (or any) size, the best way to develop the plan is to incorporate repeatable, predictable, and measurable programs and campaigns.

What I mean by incorporating repeatable programs is, first, take a look at current content and programs and see where they can be repurposed as is, or with some modifications. And as you create new content and programs, you need to think about how to design them to be reused in the future. Also consider the extendibility. For example, you can produce a webinar, transcribe the contents and turn it into a guide, and turn the guide into ten or more blog posts, with each post inspiring six to ten social media posts. Then you can turn the webinar into an on-demand webinar, extending its reach and life. And then add all of this to your nurture campaign, and so on and so forth. What was once one program has now been turned into a hundred touchpoints or more. You are using your time effectively, your content and resources have bigger impact, and you start to build consistency for your sales team and prospects. Oh, and you are building trust and having a lot more influence too. Yeah!

Next up, predictability. Wouldn't it be great if you *knew* exactly how a program would perform? "If we run this webinar, Bob from Big Company A will sign up for our Enterprise tier in exactly fifty-seven days on a three-year contract, making our ROI huge and our customer acquisition cost (CAC) pennies." Whoo hoo. I love Bob. Sigh. If only being able to predict people's behavior and the outcome of programs were that easy. But it never will be. Yet, having as much predictability in your programs as possible—around how the programs will perform, how the product will be received, how much revenue came in from your programs—will lead to more trust, more resources, and more opportunities to influence. And guess what is going to help build predictability into your programs? Building programs that are repeatable.

But then you must measure it. Easier said than done. Once you set workflows in place to measure everything, you need to show the right data to the right people at the right time to help build your influence and resources. Admittedly, this expanded discussion will be a hard one to get through for some—but a critical one. (Think of it as an organic sleep aid if you must.) I'll provide some tools and examples to help you through it when we get there.

# I STANDS FOR INTENTION

Marketing with intention, that is. When I say I want you to market with intent, what I mean is to know your audience and be very deliberate in the types of programs and content (heck, even product) you build for your audience, which channels and format you use to disperse information, and what the message is. This may seem obvious, but somewhere along the way, whether it's because we're busy or we don't have enough information, we might have gotten off track. If this is the case for you and your company, now's a great time to get back on track.

Currently, 50 percent of the leads marketing generates go untouched by sales. Wait! What!? At first, you might think . . . well, you know what you think. However, if you ask sales why they didn't follow up on what you think are awesome leads, it comes back to the lead not being a good fit. Okay, sales might not state it as eloquently as that. It might "sound" something more like "These leads suck!" But maybe, just maybe, they have a point.

We should ask, were we truly intentional with who we targeted and what we presented to them? In other words, did we potentially use spray-and-pray tactics, or were we mindful of the audience we were trying to address and what message would resonate with them? Did we have a purpose for directing them to that specific piece of content, especially at that point in their journey? I receive emails all the time from companies whose product I have already purchased asking if I want to become a customer. Great question, because this email has now brought up some doubt in my mind. Do I really want to be your customer? A better approach would be to segment me out of this email flow and into one that nurtures the relationship.

Another question we should ask around intent is, did we help educate our prospects and properly set expectations? For example, if the prospect is in a trial, is the trial truly representative of what they would get if they were a customer? Or maybe this person doing the trial and evaluating our product could have different features and functions after subscribing, depending on the level they go with. You need to clarify this so they aren't surprised (and pissed off) when they find out they don't get the cool features in the Basic package.

As we move to more sophisticated systems and tools, including incorporating AI into the mix, we'll be able to do more personalization and truly market 1:1. Customers' expectations are only going to rise. We've been witnessing this for years already. Now more than ever, we need to be mindful about what we are creating and why (i.e., tie it back to customer needs).

Another component of marketing with intention is shifting from developing reactive programs to developing proactive ones, as well as moving away from ad hoc campaigns to ones that can be reused throughout the customer journey. Reactive programs and content are developed quickly, and usually not very thoughtfully, in response to something specific that arises (this could be an internal demand from executives or forces in the market). Ad hoc campaigns are less reactive but still developed for one-time use. It's kind of like that kitchen gadget you thought was so amazing at the time, but since it really only has one purpose, like trussing up a turkey, you use it once a year (or maybe once total, since you forgot about it and now can't find it). Don't create programs and content with one-time use unless it's absolutely necessary.

Being intentional with your marketing programs will lead to more qualified leads, higher conversion, and more overall impact.

## T IS FOR TOOLS (AND TECHNOLOGY)

There are a lot of tools, systems, and technologies at the disposal of marketing professionals, from customer relationship management (CRM) tools and marketing automation solutions that are the foundation of our MarTech stack, to our website and knowledge base, to our social media platforms. And all of these need to work seamlessly together.

These tools help marketing teams and professionals define, implement, and measure programs. They help build better workflows where the lead lifecycle is virtually automated, with people moving from phase to phase in an orderly, predictable manner. The tools help you and your sales teams understand where your leads are in the funnel and help nurture the lead through to the next phase. There are tools to help you distribute and manage your content. Some tools help you foster relationships with your customers and prospects.

Tools and technology are the backbone of your go-to-market and marketing strategy. You need to understand how to implement these tools for success and how much time and resources the company should be investing in them. In some cases, you might not have the luxury of time or resources to implement the perfect technology stack, but at minimum you need to know your options.

That's it. That's the G.R.I.T. Marketing Method at its simplest. Next, we'll dive deep into how to use the framework to build a better marketing strategy. Not everything will be applicable to your situation (i.e., it might depend on your role and level of experience, company culture, or industry). In some cases, you might not have the resources needed to implement the G.R.I.T. methodology in its entirety, so, like a good fitness instructor, I will give you some modifications (but I really want you to go all in). And it won't happen overnight. It will take time and some brain power to begin implementing the G.R.I.T. Marketing Method, but the goal is total world domination. (Oops, I mean, the goal for you is to build trust, have more influence, really be able to show the value and impact you bring to your company, and have a predictable career path.) Luckily, since it's often more a matter of shifting your mindset and doing things more effectively and deliberately, you likely already have a lot of what you need.

And off we go.

# CHAPTER 3

# Go-to-Market Strategy

The G.R.I.T. Marketing Method starts with the go-to-market strategy—not because it starts with a *G* and was therefore super convenient (bonus!) but because it is the most critical element for marketing professionals to be a part of. Forget that it will also enable you to build trust and have influence (just kidding, don't forget that!); go-to-market strategy is everything to a company. If we think about the definition of the term—the strategy developed to bring a company's product or solution to market—it's clear there are so many pieces we as marketing professionals own, and many more pieces we should be influencing.

Some companies do not have a formal go-to-market strategy. Great! (Er, kind of.) That gives you plenty of room to help define it. Some companies do have a go-to-market strategy, but no one remembers who created it, or why, when, and where it is today, both figuratively and possibly literally. And in some cases, there might be a go-to-market strategy in use, but you and the rest of the marketing organization weren't involved in the creation of it. Regardless of where your current go-to-market strategy stands and how it was developed, it's important to pinpoint the areas you do own, should own, and could own. The next few chapters will walk you through just that, as we take a look at the go-to-market strategy as it aligns with the customer journey.

When it all goes right—that is, when marketing is involved in the creation and development of the go-to-market strategy—the strategy is more powerful, which usually translates into more success for the company, and you. A great example of this is the process we established at Oracle for developing and implementing go-to-market strategy. Before I started, marketing was brought in closer to the end of the planning cycle. There was an organization called Advanced Technology Solutions (ATS) where new products, solutions, and go-to-market strategy were born. But heck, I was new and feeling invigorated, so I kind of invited myself to be part of this team. Off I went to join the ATS go-to-market team from the start of the process. While we technically reported into our own departments, for the purposes of specific projects, we became one team (I'll call it the GTM team for short), which now included sales, product, engineering, marketing, customer success, operations, and even finance.

When starting a new project cycle, the newly formed GTM team would come together for an entire week in Reston, Virginia, of all places. Product managers would take us through ten to twenty different products, solutions, tools, or features concepts we could potentially focus on for the next cycle. The GTM team would sit in a big conference room for four and a half straight days walking through these concepts and ideating on them. By day four, the breakfast array got old ("Aren't those the same exact blueberry muffins from Monday?"), the coffee still tasted terrible — but no one cared anymore—and the room smelled like dried-out sandwiches. But we were in it together, making progress as a team. The goal was to select which features and solutions Oracle would focus on for the next twelve months based on customer needs and revenue targets, and prioritize them.

At the end of that kickoff week, the GTM team would go off with specific tasks to gather more information. Customer support needed to prioritize projects based on customer feedback. Which of these options were must-haves versus nice-to-haves for customers? Sales needed to consider if these solutions could be sold as part of the current offering as an upsell, sold as new products altogether, or rolled in as a product update. Marketing needed to consider the overall messaging, branding, pricing, content needed, and programs that would be developed for launch and beyond. Product and engineering needed to work together to understand the scope, requirements, and skills needed to successfully develop everything.

The GTM team would reconvene several weeks later, usually in the same sandwich-smelling, burnt-coffee-abounding, pretty-sure-those-are-*literally*-the-exact-same-muffins-I'm-seeing room in Reston, and finalize the overall direction and priorities. From here, tasks were assigned, timelines and milestones developed, and deliverables defined. In doing this, we were all on the same page, working toward the same goals, with all of the right information and people in place. We had clear objectives and were working in alignment to not just deliver the product but see it through the entire customer journey. And marketing was right there from the start for a change. Even though we did not own the process or the overall strategy, it made for a much better product development and sales enablement, and led to a successful launch.

Unfortunately, this experience was an anomaly. In most organizations, if a go-to-market strategy exists, it was developed without input from marketing. It's not that marketing is being intentionally left out of the process; it's just how go-to-market strategies have evolved over time.

It is time for another evolution.

There are three main issues with the way most go-to-market strategies are developed and implemented today. The first is that when these strategies are being conceived, the folks involved are not considering the entire customer journey. Rather, the strategies often look at just the buying phase of the journey, where the sales team comes into the picture. The second issue is that the strategies are focused on the tactical components once a product has been developed. Even though it is a go-to-market strategy, the focus is more on execution versus an actual *strategy*. The third issue, which we've touched on, is that marketing is usually not part of the conversation at the point of development yet is overwhelmingly responsible for—and held accountable for—the execution of the strategy.

And we as marketing professionals are not helping the situation. We need to stop thinking of ourselves as simply executioners of the go-to-market strategy and start thinking about it like this: marketing = go-to-market strategy.

Actually, forget evolution. It's time for a revolution. Please! Marketing is the foundation of the go-to-market strategy, and this needs to be recognized and addressed. Companies should consider having a marketing-led go-to-market strategy and team.

Work with me on this. Even if you are the only one in your entire organization thinking like this, that is okay. For now. The goal is to have enough influence to bring people along with you. This evolution/revolution will take time to shift people's mindset. I'll show you where you can persuade others in your organization—your peers and counterparts, managers, leaders, and other company executives. The process will be a phased approach, and a different journey for each of you, but we will get there.

In the rest of this section, I'll cover what go-to-market strategies look like today and the inherent problems with how they are developed. We'll look at the customer journey itself, from product ideation and development to the lead lifecycle that marketing owns to the buyer's journey that sales focuses on and finally to the customer engagement phase. We'll explore how to align all these phases with marketing to develop a comprehensive strategy aligned with the customer journey. Then we'll look at the areas marketing can influence and how *you* can identify specific touchpoints to begin the long voyage of influence. From there I'll show you how to build your own Map of Influence and put it into practice. The goal of all this is to help you understand what and whom you should influence, why you want to influence, and how to influence.

Then, story time, or show 'n' tell. I'll share examples from my own experiences and bring in stories from other marketing thought leaders that will make it even clearer why marketing should own the entire process of developing the go-to-market strategy.

A caveat before we continue: This section is going to be a bit heavier. My teams have joked that I actually have an "executive face" I put on when I really need them to hunker down and focus, and if you could see my face right now, that's the face you'd see. This section is long and complex, but the concepts it covers are crucial to understand and put into practice if you want to start building more influence.

Now, back to my story around the Oracle GTM team. Twelve months later, after a lot of burnt coffee and stale blueberry muffins, we finally launched two of the solutions we had started formulating in that room in Virginia. By then having *everyone* involved from the beginning was the norm. Marketing led the charge in terms of determining which solutions to go to market with, working closely with all the other stakeholders, including customers. The "team," as it got closer to launch time, had ballooned to about fifty people throughout the company. Marketing had helped define the product based on what customers needed and what could be sold, had enabled sales to be effective out of the gate, and had developed and implemented all of the launch and lead-gen programs. Then the GTM team all sat back (actually, if I recall, we were on the edge of our seats biting our nails) and watched these solutions go live.

One of the solutions launched was the first to be sold online at Oracle. At that time consumers were just getting used to buying things online. But to buy an enterprise solution with a price tag of $25,000 to $1 million was unheard of. We tried to call it a SaaS (software as a service) offering, but Larry Ellison hated that term at the time. (Later it would be an industry-standard term.) The day of the launch, I envisioned someone sitting at their desktop computer with a credit card in hand, deciding which package to buy. "Do I want the blue jeans for $75 or the all-inclusive enterprise resource planning software for $567,000? Decisions, decisions." And there were several purchases that first day, from $25,000 to $250,000. I might have cried tears of joy or exhaustion, or both.

The launch, and the solution itself, would not have been as successful had we not had the structure of an all-encompassing GTM team in place from the beginning, had we not all been in the same room on the same page developing the go-to-market strategy together—with marketing having tremendous influence from the beginning.

## GO-TO-MARKET STRATEGY

Go-to-market strategies (as they typically exist) fall short in many ways. The strategy itself usually starts with the sales cycle, skipping over marketing, and focuses on the tactical components of bringing a product to market after the product has been defined and built. The strategy ends up being more of a product-launch recipe for marketing to follow versus a true go-to-market strategy. And it's not as impactful.

Go-to-market strategies can be developed with different focuses depending on the product, the company, and where the company is in their business lifecycle, goals, and markets. But whatever the focus, the strategy should absolutely take into consideration the *entire* customer journey.

The customer journey is just that—the journey taken by the prospective customer, from top of the funnel lead to happy (hopefully) customer. I like to think of it in specific phases: product blueprint >>

lead lifecycle >> buyer's journey >> customer engagement. We'll cover all of these in depth over the next few chapters and dive deep into how marketing professionals can gain influence in all of these areas, including the ones they don't technically own.

This is worth saying again: The go-to-market strategy, since it represents a company's plan to bring a product to market and ensure the product is then adopted, is the underlying foundation of the company's overall direction, strategy, and ultimate success. Therefore the strategy needs to be complete and all-inclusive, not just focused on the marketing and buying phase of the customer journey. And marketing needs to be involved in the development. Thus, the revolution.

I once worked for a mid-size financial services company. When I started, they handed me a go-to-market strategy they'd spent a lot of time developing with product and sales, saying it wasn't working (which is why the last person in my role was gone, and I was sitting there). I looked at the strategy. It did cover a significant portion of the customer journey, but I had a gut feeling something wasn't quite right. They had determined their target audience was CFOs, as it was a financial tool for enterprises. I decided to dive deeper into the data we had.

What I found was that the individuals actually engaging with us were not CFOs; they were IT folks who would have to integrate the solution and finance managers who were the end users of the solution. These two audiences were the ones signing up for trials and webinars, with IT folks reading the competitive content on comparing features, functionality, and pricing and finance managers download- ing the white papers and e-books. Ugh. The go-to-market strategy was focusing on the wrong people! Even worse, it had already been in effect for two years. No wonder conversion was low and revenue was declining. In the words of Indiana Jones, "They're digging in the wrong place!"

Once I knew what the problem was, I knew I could bring data into the conversation, determine and communicate the real target, and rework the strategy to improve overall conversion rates and increase revenue. First, I had the marketing team reduce the number of programs targeting CFOs directly and instead had them develop a simple ROI case study campaign with the CFOs. This campaign was still significant but not the main focus. Then I had the marketing team develop collateral, like best-practice guides and competitive comparison sheets, that IT and finance managers could use internally to inform other stakeholders within their organizations about our solution—and so become knowledgeable champions of it.

By first recognizing and then evaluating our actual target audience and their pains, we were able to adjust the strategy accordingly and build better, more effective programs. This led to the marketing team boosting revenue by 50 percent the first year, then two times year over year for the next few years. Yep, by simply focusing on our true target audience and adjusting programs, marketing grew the company revenue by millions.

It is crucial for marketing to be involved in developing the go-to-market strategy. It's even better if we own it. And it is critical to think of the entire customer journey while developing and implementing it.

## HOW A FOUR-LEGGED CHAIR HELPS THE CUSTOMER JOURNEY

A good go-to-market strategy is like a four-legged chair that includes product, marketing, sales, and customer success. Without one of these legs, the chair simply cannot stand up. And it doesn't matter which leg is missing; without it, the chair does not have the structural integrity to stand on its own, er, four feet.

Now let's think about this chair in terms of the customer journey.

Let's start with product. The product department owns the product blueprint phase of the customer journey. This team is tasked with collaborating cross-functionally with other organizations, such as sales and engineering, to define what the product strategy and definition will be. Then the team needs to build a product roadmap that sets priorities, which might be based on the needs of marketing (for an opportunity to launch something at an upcoming event) or sales (for a feature to help them close more deals). Next, product must work in collaboration with engineering to deliver on the roadmap and build the product itself.

Then, marketing. Marketing is responsible for the funnel and lead lifecycle. At the top of the funnel, marketing is responsible for generating awareness of the company and its products, and bringing in quality leads. Then the department nurtures those leads through the middle of the funnel, providing useful information such as best practices in order to keep the leads engaged. And finally, at the bottom of the funnel, via targeted programs and campaigns, marketing turns leads into more qualified prospects that sales can better engage with.

Speaking of sales, that's next. It should go without saying that their role here is to sell; sales owns the buyer's journey, one significant subset of the customer journey. (One quick sidenote: Since they need to be able to sell the right product to the right people at the right time, sales should be involved in more than just this piece of the customer journey. They should also be involved in defining the go-to-market strategy and helping determine how the product is positioned and sold, as they are a wealth of information. Remember, sales is on the front lines every day, talking to prospects and customers.) The buyer's journey sometimes overlaps with marketing, depending on when sales gets involved in your sales cycle—for example, how to categorize leads that are in trial may vary from company to company. But in general, the buyer's journey starts at the trial or evaluation phase, progresses through the consideration and negotiation phase, and finishes with the sale or purchase phase. From here, there should be a transition to customer success that allows for successful implementation.

Which brings us to the final stage of the customer journey, and an essential leg of the chair: customer success. This team owns the customer engagement phase of the customer journey and is tasked with product implementation, customer onboarding, ongoing training, engagement, retention, and satisfaction. Customer success is usually the first point of contact when issues arise with customers; because of this, the team works closely with engineering to define and prioritize bug fixes. The customer success team should also be working closely with product on the roadmap, desired features and functionality, prioritization, and building better solutions, and they should be working with marketing on customer communications around releases, issues, and best practices.

From here, the customer journey gets a bit complicated. For the sake of simplicity, let's just say there is a realm of ongoing account management where the focus is on expanding accounts, renewals and retention, turning customers into advocates, and trying to reduce churn. Different departments often share responsibility for these components of the journey, and the division of labor will be different at each company. Whatever the precise (or imprecise) arrangement, marketing offers support throughout the process, providing content and a platform to showcase customer success.

So there you have it, the entire customer journey, from product ideation to happy advocating customer, with clearly defined owners. Ish? I noted some of the overlap above, but we all know there's even more, which is why we should all be working collaboratively and cohesively to achieve company goals—and why, since marketing clearly has a role to play in each phase of the customer journey, we should own the whole lot.

So how the heck does it all fit together, and how can marketing professionals gain more influence and ultimately own it? With something magical I like to call *touchpoints*.

## TOUCHPOINTS

Marketing is the ultimate cross-functional organization, with involvement spanning the customer journey and all other teams. Therefore, it is critical we have representation within these other teams. Not only does marketing represent a leg of the chair, we also define the style, color, material, and more. I call each of these additional places of involvement *touchpoints*. They're all the different pieces of the entire customer journey that marketing, well, touches, and has the opportunity to sway.

Just as the customer has touchpoints along their journey from top-of-funnel lead-to non-churning customer, marketing has touchpoints throughout the customer journey as well. From defining the market to prioritizing product features, from developing the personas and targeted audiences to messaging, from scripts for sales to "getting started" videos for customer success, and of course all of the standard programs marketing already owns, like lead generation, events, content, and so on. Anything and everything marketing comes into contact with. This includes all the programs, activities, initiatives, and tactics, as well as all the little day-to-day, seemingly endless requests marketing professionals receive.

It's mind-blowing (or -numbing) when you think about everything marketing professionals do on a day-to-day basis—how many touchpoints we have and thus how many opportunities we have to influence. Think about the interruptions you have on a day-to-day or even hourly basis. You know what I'm talking about. The "this will only take five minutes and I need it now" tasks. Sales guy Kevin needs a slide developed in the next twenty minutes for a meeting he's having with an important, multimillion-dollar prospect. Clare from customer success needs to know where to find that e-book on the website. The *Wall Street Journal* wants a quote from your CEO but needs it today. Are you starting to see all the various touchpoints marketing professionals have on any given day? And these are just the little things. If we think about the entire customer journey—the very first time we interact with a prospect through their lifetime as a customer—these touchpoints begin to pile up. These are all opportunities for marketing professionals to have influence.

In the next few chapters, we're going to go in search of these touchpoints and see which ones we can influence. I also recommend you start tracking all of these in your own company.

## Example: Customer Journey with Touchpoints

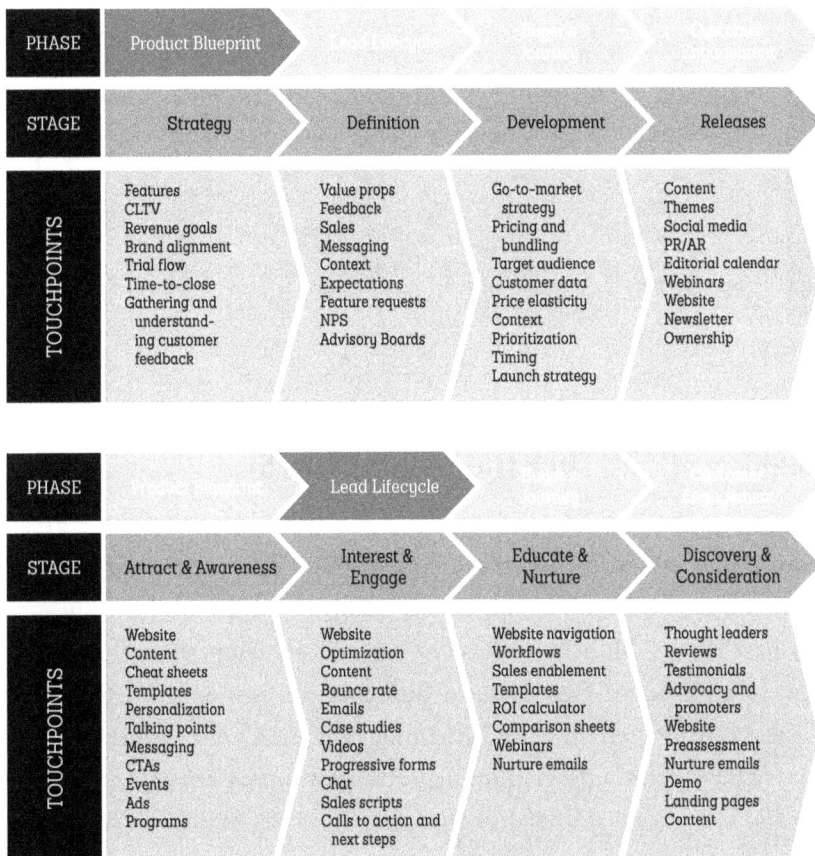

| PHASE | Product Blueprint | | | |
|---|---|---|---|---|
| STAGE | Strategy | Definition | Development | Releases |
| TOUCHPOINTS | Features<br>CLTV<br>Revenue goals<br>Brand alignment<br>Trial flow<br>Time-to-close<br>Gathering and<br>  understand-<br>  ing customer<br>  feedback | Value props<br>Feedback<br>Sales<br>Messaging<br>Context<br>Expectations<br>Feature requests<br>NPS<br>Advisory Boards | Go-to-market<br>  strategy<br>Pricing and<br>  bundling<br>Target audience<br>Customer data<br>Price elasticity<br>Context<br>Prioritization<br>Timing<br>Launch strategy | Content<br>Themes<br>Social media<br>PR/AR<br>Editorial calendar<br>Webinars<br>Website<br>Newsletter<br>Ownership |

| PHASE | Lead Lifecycle | | | |
|---|---|---|---|---|
| STAGE | Attract & Awareness | Interest &<br>Engage | Educate &<br>Nurture | Discovery &<br>Consideration |
| TOUCHPOINTS | Website<br>Content<br>Cheat sheets<br>Templates<br>Personalization<br>Talking points<br>Messaging<br>CTAs<br>Events<br>Ads<br>Programs | Website<br>Optimization<br>Content<br>Bounce rate<br>Emails<br>Case studies<br>Videos<br>Progressive forms<br>Chat<br>Sales scripts<br>Calls to action and<br>  next steps | Website navigation<br>Workflows<br>Sales enablement<br>Templates<br>ROI calculator<br>Comparison sheets<br>Webinars<br>Nurture emails | Thought leaders<br>Reviews<br>Testimonials<br>Advocacy and<br>  promoters<br>Website<br>Preassessment<br>Nurture emails<br>Demo<br>Landing pages<br>Content |

*continued*

| PHASE | Product Blueprint | Lead Lifecycle | Buyer's Journey | Customer Engagement |
|---|---|---|---|---|
| STAGE | Trial & Evaluation | Discovery | Nurture | Negotiation & Close |
| TOUCHPOINTS | How-to videos<br>Onboarding docs<br>Testimonials<br>Case studies<br>Best practices<br>Trial flow<br>In-app experience<br>Website<br>Expectation setting<br>Reviews<br>Webinars | Website<br>Scoring<br>Lead quality<br>Lead scores<br>Website content<br>Workflow<br>Videos<br>Next steps/CTAs<br>Progressive forms<br>Chat<br>Sales scripts<br>Prioritization | Nurture emails<br>Sales flow<br>Tools – ROI calc<br>Industry reports<br>Website<br>Sales scripts<br>Comparison sheets<br>Product webinars<br>Tips and tricks<br>Case studies | Proposals<br>Promos<br>Contracts<br>Templates<br>Signing bonuses<br>ROI calculators<br>Best practices<br>Easy to buy<br>Pricing strategy<br>Sales ops |

| PHASE | Product Blueprint | Lead Lifecycle | Buyer's Journey | Customer Engagement |
|---|---|---|---|---|
| STAGE | Onboarding & Adoption | Support | Retention | Expansion & Renewal |
| TOUCHPOINTS | • Training scripts<br>• How-to videos<br>• Product webinars<br>• Website/login flow<br>• Best practices<br>• Content review<br>• Customer strategy<br>• Communications<br>• Reporting<br>• Expectation setting<br>• Customer feedback | • Chat<br>• Community<br>• Knowledge base<br>• Best practices<br>• Training<br>• FAQs<br>• Surveys<br>• Website<br>• Case studies<br>• SLAs<br>• Product webinars<br>• ROI reports | • Best practices<br>• Newsletter<br>• Product releases<br>• Q&As, Ask the Experts, Ask Me Anything<br>• Webinars<br>• Client showcase<br>• Momentum press releases<br>• Thank-yous<br>• Surveys | • Advisory Boards<br>• Sneak peeks<br>• Advanced training<br>• Communications<br>• Nurture campaigns<br>• VIP events<br>• User groups and conferences<br>• Sneak peeks<br>• Meetups<br>• Feature guides<br>  • Surveys<br>  • Advocates<br>  • Thought leader programs<br>  • Affiliate and referral programs<br>  • Reward programs<br>  • Engage community<br>  • High touch outreach |

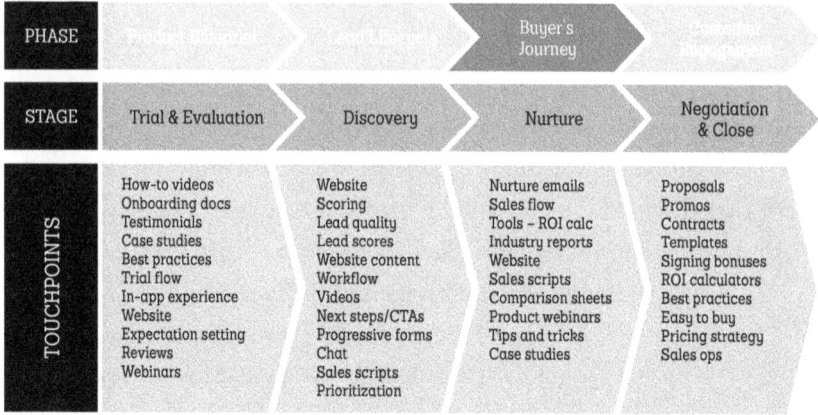

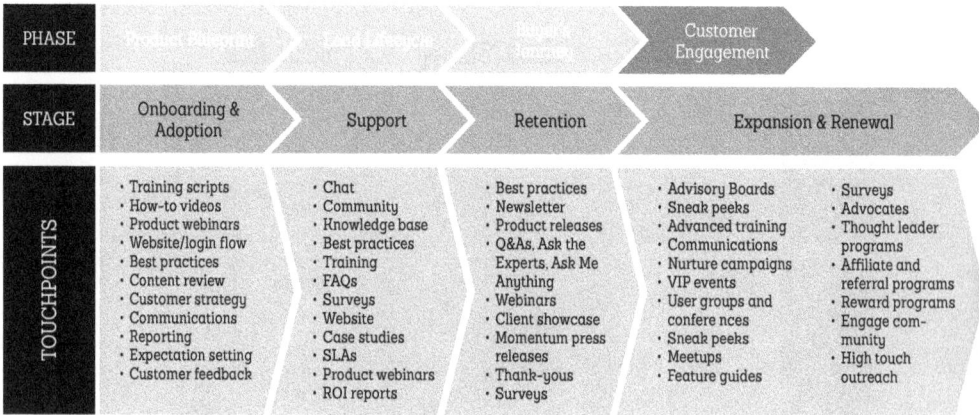

## MARKETING MAP OF INFLUENCE – MARKETING INFLUENTIAL TOUCHPOINTS

But what the heck do you do once you have identified these areas you touch and influence? You start to build your very own Map of Influence. (I call it the Marketing Map of Influence, but you can call it Mary's Map of Influence, or Jessica's Map of Influence, or Insert-Your-Name-Here Map of Influence. Or just embrace the acronym MOI, French for "me." Meaning you. And your influence.)

We've already defined influence as developing enough trust with peers, managers, and leaders that they not only believe in what you can do but actually *look* to you for answers. We've looked at the general phases of the customer journey and who owns them—product blueprint (product), lead lifecycle (marketing), buyer's journey (sales), and customer engagement (customer success). And we've defined touchpoints as places throughout the customer journey where marketing is already involved or should be involved.

Now we put it together. Venn diagram time! Whoo hoo.

Wait, what the . . .

Customer Journey Venn Diagram

Kidding, not kidding. It really looks more like this:

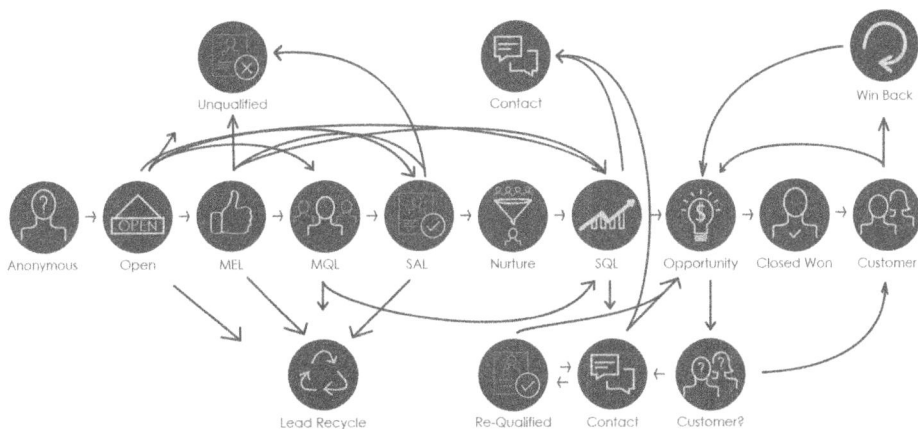

Customer Journey

Still a fairly swirly twirly hot mess. I like it. But this type of graphic is hard to work from. I want you to come away from this section with a clear understanding of all the opportunities you have along the customer journey to influence via touchpoints, so . . . let's flatten it out a bit and use that as our foundation.

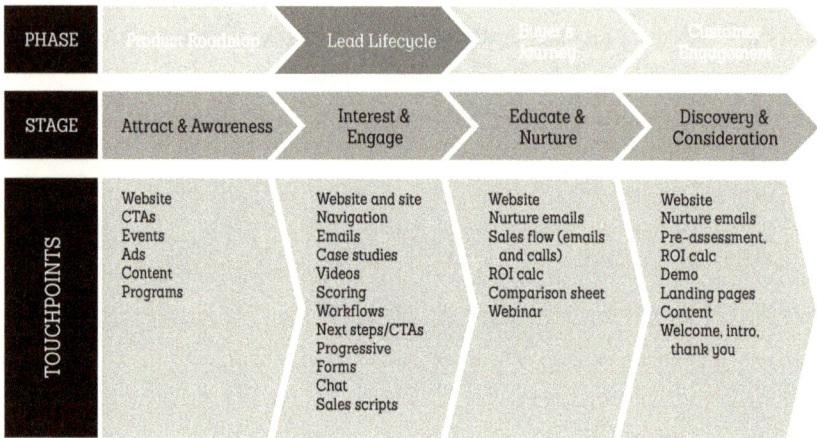

| PHASE | Product Roadmap | Lead Lifecycle | Buyer's Journey | Customer Engagement |
|---|---|---|---|---|
| STAGE | Attract & Awareness | Interest & Engage | Educate & Nurture | Discovery & Consideration |
| TOUCHPOINTS | Website CTAs Events Ads Content Programs | Website and site Navigation Emails Case studies Videos Scoring Workflows Next steps/CTAs Progressive Forms Chat Sales scripts | Website Nurture emails Sales flow (emails and calls) ROI calc Comparison sheet Webinar | Website Nurture emails Pre-assessment ROI calc Demo Landing pages Content Welcome, intro, thank you |

Example: Customer Journey with Touchpoints

There. This shows how we're going to break things down. Over the next few chapters, we'll look at the touchpoints for every stage of each phase of the customer journey—and, admittedly, it's going to be a lot. But we'll take it slow and keep it all aligned with our handy chart.

Before we drop into that, though, I want to first touch on how you can begin to identify touchpoints in each phase of the customer journey, even within each stage of that phase, and start to build out your Map of Influence. First you will want to review your company go-to-market strategy if you have one. Next, align this strategy with your customer journey phases and stages. For example, if you have a low-touch, high-transaction sales cycle but your strategy is to focus on long-term customer satisfaction, loyalty, and advocacy, you will likely have a more expansive phase for your customer engagement. No clue what I'm talking about? No worries. We've got four chapters' worth of examples centered on phases of the customer journey. We'll begin with the lead lifecycle, then move to the buyer's journey, then customer engagement, and finally loop back to product blueprint. (I'll explain why we do product last in a bit, but I'm guessing some of you are relieved.)

Next, as you read about a phase, start to identify stages within the phase. For example, for the lead lifecycle phase you might identify: attract & awareness >> interest & engage >> educate & nurture >> discovery & consideration >> evaluation. I list out standard stages to consider, but you and your company might have different ones.

Now comes the fun part. Think about different touchpoints in each stage and write them down. I'll be going over many possible touchpoints, but again, I want you to think of more. Sift through and expand on what I discuss so you have a list tailored to you and your company.

Finally, look at your list of touchpoints and think about what areas would be most impactful. What levers can you pull to shorten the sales cycle or increase conversion? Note the most impactful touchpoints.

You will go through these steps for each phase of the customer journey. By the time you get to Chapter 8, you'll be building your Map of Influence using the touchpoints you identified while reading Chapters 4 through 7. This will let you see areas where you're already involved and where you should be involved. And while you'll continue refining your map over time, you can start using it immediately as a guideline to help you influence and sway and create more value.

A couple quick notes: We're going to be thinking through each stage of each phase, noting all the ways we can influence at various points. Some of these things will overlap and feel messy; that's okay. It's inevitable. But I'll try to make things a bit simpler by categorizing touchpoints into a few buckets—the stages of different phases.

Think about each stage from the standpoint of channels you use or could use, programs and campaigns you can focus on, content you should create and leverage, and the tools that could aid you when developing plans from a more strategic, go-to-market point of view.

We're essentially going to have a massive brainstorming session together for a few chapters. To get the most out of it, grab a pen. Let my suggestions, questions, and thought process spark your own.

When identifying touchpoints, don't think about whether they're possible, whether you actually have the information or resources to properly engage there. Just identify them for now. Going through this exercise will help you become part of the conversation. Imagine your manager is going into a go-to-market strategy planning meeting and you happen to have a report ready that shows a rise in customer complaints about a feature that isn't working. "OMG, you are amazing! Thank you! I can use this to help define the features we should be focusing on. What would I do without you? What would the company do without you?"

You get the point.

Let's get started.

# CHAPTER 4

# Swayer: Lead Lifecycle

Now the fun starts! The phases of the customer journey, as we have discussed, include product blueprint >> lead lifecycle >> buyer's journey >> customer engagement. And we're going to go through each of them, one by one, touching on every stage within the phase and touching on a number of touchpoints within each stage.

Let's start with what you already own as a marketing professional—demand-gen, advertising, website, content, PR/AR, social media, and so on. Although implementing these programs comes after the product blueprint phase in the customer journey, I want to start here for the purposes of identifying touchpoints and building your Map of Influence. It's much easier to influence this phase, as you're already part of it and own it in its entirety. Identifying touchpoints, putting everything into practice, and building influence will be much easier if you start within your own realm first. Remember, building influence is going to take some time (as much as I wish it could happen overnight with a swish of a magic wand).

So we start here, on familiar ground that we know we own. But let's look with fresher eyes. Think about how you can affect your programs, campaign, and content from a *go-to-market strategy* perspective and how, through these things, you can influence the company even more than you already are. How is what you are doing in this phase helping the bottom line, the overall company growth and performance? Are you enabling sales to sell more, better, faster? Can you create content and programs that you can repurpose and reuse throughout the entire customer journey, from adoption to expansion and retention? Are you adding to the overall company revenue? Because let's face it, if you had one slide you could show your CEO, it should simply show the overall revenue number that marketing touched in some way.

I'm going to focus on some specific areas where marketing professionals can reinforce our position in our *own* domain. Areas where there are obvious opportunities to gain more traction, increase conversion, measure the results, and show impact. These will be different for each person and in every organization, but hopefully the examples that follow will help you look at programs from a different perspective, one that basically asks, how are they impacting revenue? And how can we make it even better?

As you think about which touchpoints exist for you and your company, also think about the metrics you can and want to measure. And think about it against your goals. How many leads are you bringing in, what quality are they, and how much do they cost? How long will it take (preferably broken out by program and channel) to convert them to the next level, then the next, until they are a closed-won deal? What rate do they convert at as they go through the different stages? What is the net-profit value over their entire lifetime (customer lifetime value, or CLTV)? (You should ask this even if you have a very transactional B2C business.) And hopefully you can determine your ROI. I like to look at ROI by program (like webinars and content) as well as by channel (like social media, email, website, partners). Finally, if you have any data from past programs you can point to for either running a program or not, this information is always helpful. If you don't have any, look for industry benchmarks and use those instead.

At this point I am assuming you would have reviewed your current go-to-market strategy, if you have one, and aligned it with your customer journey phases and stages. Your phases and stages may look different from the ones I give in this book. For example, if you only sell online and have a very transactional selling process, you might not have a need for an extensive buyer's journey. And even when the stages I break out are aligned with what you identify in your company, you may have different terms in your systems. "Attract" may be called a "Lead," "Engage" might be a "Marketing-Engaged Lead," "Consideration" might be an "MQL," and so on. Just be aware of that, and the examples in this book should still help you.

So now let's walk through an example of crystalizing the stages, and identifying touchpoints, of our first phase, the lead lifecycle phase.

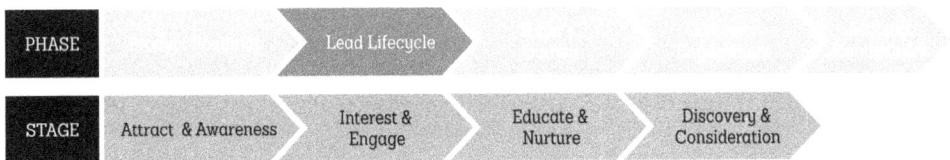

| PHASE | Lead Lifecycle | | | |
|-------|----------------|---|---|---|
| STAGE | Attract & Awareness | Interest & Engage | Educate & Nurture | Discovery & Consideration |

Lead Lifecycle Phases and Stages

## STAGES OF THE LEAD LIFECYCLE PHASE

This section should be pretty easy to digest. It's basically your marketing funnel. Let's say your stages look something like this: attract & awareness >> interest & engage >> educate & nurture >> discovery & consideration.

Now think about all the different programs you have that fit into these different stages, from thought leader programs to webinars to PR/AR to content strategy to promotions. What are your themes for the year, for the quarter, for the month? Do you have any partner programs you are working on? Essentially, look at your marketing plan for the year or quarter and see what tactics are in development to deliver on your programs.

## IDENTIFY TOUCHPOINTS IN THE LEAD LIFECYCLE

From the perspective of an overall go-to-market strategy and company goals, begin identifying touchpoints you already know and own, but now think about them strategically. Let's say the go-to-strategy is to double revenue this year and then double it again next year, with a three-year plan to go public. In order to accomplish this, the company will enhance the product features to be more attractive to F500 companies, as the average deal size is three times that of smaller companies. And let's say that marketing plans to focus on increasing account-based marketing (ABM). After all, you already know who the F500 are. So that's your go-to-market strategy.

Now think, how do all of your programs, campaigns, initiatives, activities, websites, and content align with this strategy? Think about it from the perspective of the overall marketing funnel. Think about your overall programs, the channels you market in or to, specific initiatives you are working on, and the tasks associated with getting everything to market. What are the top-of-funnel campaigns you are working on—digital advertising, social media channels, events? What programs are you running to attract prospects and leads, and what are you doing to build awareness? And how are all of these helping achieve the go-to-market strategy? How are these programs, channels, and content helping you reach the company goal of doubling revenue year over year? How are the campaigns, advertising, and website helping move the F500 audience from lead to customer?

Next, what do you do on a day-to-day basis? Post on social media? Write and publish a blog post? Produce a webinar? These are additional touchpoints you can focus on if they are relevant, are impactful, and provide you with an opportunity to influence. What levers can you pull? Or, given a certain scenario, what levers would you be able to pull to make an immediate impact? What areas of expertise do you and the rest of your team have? Does someone on the team have expertise in running ABM programs or working with vendors? Let's check out some examples based on the specific stages of the lead lifecycle phase of the customer journey.

## Attract & Awareness Touchpoints

In the attract and awareness stage of the lead lifecycle phase, the goal is to create awareness for your products, solutions, and company through exposure. It's to help your audience find you, understand what you offer, and perceive the value your solution brings. Basically, it's the top of the funnel, where you are focused on lead- and demand-generation programs to bring in prospects.

With your overall go-to-market strategy top of mind, try to identify touchpoints you can focus on, improve on, and optimize. Think about the channels you leverage now—maybe you need new and improved ones to align better with your go-to-market strategy. What levers can you pull that will make a more strategic impact? Are there programs you can optimize? Think big. And think small. And write it all down. Here are some places to start.

In terms of channels and programs, you can look at events (both in-person and virtual), your website, digital ad campaigns, and webinars. Have you thought through your calls to action (CTAs)? Do you have CTAs on all of your web pages and landing pages? From a content standpoint, maybe consider how you can develop or modify your messaging. What other content needs to be created, or modified, for more strategic impact? From a tools standpoint, can you build templates to encourage consistency, or leverage your marketing automation tool for personalization of website content and email programs? Can you implement, or optimize, a chat program that helps build a frictionless journey for your website audience? Do you have a clear workflow for bringing in leads and moving them through the funnel? The examples of touchpoints given for this stage of the lead lifecycle phase—website, ads, talking points, webinars, CTAs, and so on—are likely applicable regardless of your company size, industry, and products.

Now that you have seen some examples of touchpoints and maybe added some of your own—in your head, in a document, or even on a Post-it Note—how can you influence some of these touchpoints? Remember, the goal here is to think strategically. It's not just about how you can drive awareness and capture top-of-the-funnel leads. It's about how you can be more effective, be more efficient, and optimize current programs to ensure you are impacting the go-to-market strategy. Here are some things you can do to better align with your company's go-to-market strategy.

Since marketing owns branding, messaging, and most forms of communication—and knows the content intimately—you can develop a *talking points* cheat sheet for others in the organization to leverage. This can be either a physical or online document that covers everything from the company mission and product information with key features and functionality to value propositions and answers to objections. Providing clear and concise talking points everyone can speak from ensures consistency and continuity, which helps the prospect learn and understand more quickly, which usually accelerates the purchase process. See what just happened? By taking information you already have and repurposing it, you shortened the sales cycle. Sales and the executive leaders are going to love you for that. Just make sure that once you have developed the cheat sheets, you educate everyone in the organization on how to use them, and the value the talking points (and you) bring to the process.

Now let's look at *templates* as a touchpoint. Think about what you can templatize, from the standpoint of making both your job as a marketing professional and your internal audiences' job easier. You want to develop templates that everyone can use. For example, if you have an ABM program that is being managed and implemented by a third-party vendor, such as Demandbase, you want to help them develop cohesive and consistent campaigns. The template might be around messaging and value propositions, or it could focus on campaign look and feel. It could be a completed ad campaign template with assets the third party can repurpose. By developing a template, you have a consistent document you, others in the marketing organization, and third-party vendors can use. So it doesn't matter where prospects see or hear about you; everything they see and hear is the same. This builds trust for them and can shorten their decision-making process, thus decreasing the sales cycle. And who wouldn't want that?

Another idea is developing templates for other departments to use. For example, I want my product managers and engineers to be the ones providing content for upcoming releases, as they know the details better than anyone. So I have a template for them to put that information together. Anything I can do to help them create cohesive and consistent documents is a win-win. The template for the product team is more of a questionnaire, but it makes it easy to get the right information for programs, content, and the website. This template has five questions they need to address: (1) Who is the target audience for the solution? (2) What problem is the solution solving and how does the solution enhance the customer experience? (3) What are the value propositions for this feature, function, or solution? (4) How does this differentiate from other solutions? and (5) Where can we find the technical requirements that were used to build the solution?

These are questions product managers and engineers should already know the answers to. But sometimes, to help put things in context for whoever is filling out the information, I'll provide a value proposition checklist and information on our upcoming themes and programs, so they have a sense of what marketing programs are coming out in the same time frame. The easier you can make it for people to provide you the content you need, the better—and the easier it will be for you to gain influence.

Another touchpoint marketing professionals can leverage is *personalization*. The more personalized the customer journey is for your prospects, the faster you can build trust with them and guide them through the funnel. You'll need to dig deep into what this looks like for the different segments, roles, or industries you need to address. But once you do that, you can do fun things like implement an automated system that dynamically displays pertinent content to a specific audience on your website. Kind of Big Brothery, but at least your audience is only seeing content they're more likely to care about. The more you can make the customer journey self-service, the faster sales will close, with a potentially higher ticket price as well. And you will be able to clearly show the influence you had on sales, conversion, and revenue.

Add all this to your Map of Influence; it should look something like what is depicted below. We'll get into how to prioritize in a future chapter.

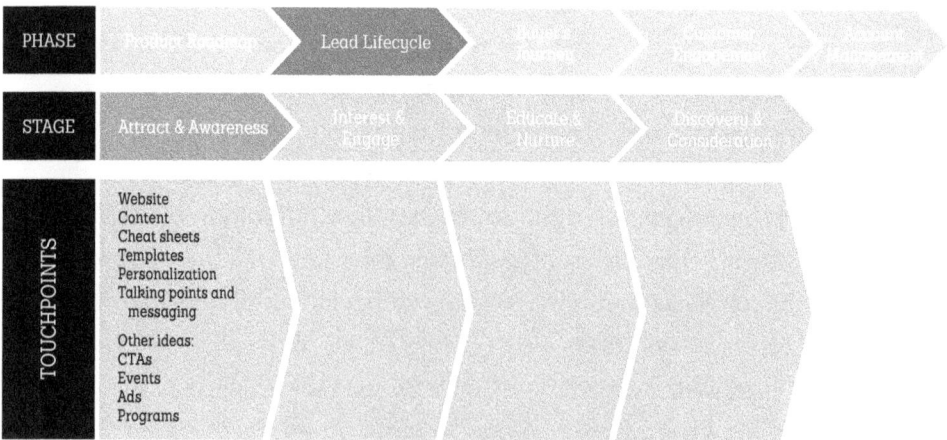

| PHASE | Product Readiness | Lead Lifecycle | Buyer Journey | Customer Engagement | Partner Enablement |
|---|---|---|---|---|---|
| STAGE | Attract & Awareness | Interest & Engage | Educate & Nurture | Discovery & Consideration | |
| TOUCHPOINTS | Website Content Cheat sheets Templates Personalization Talking points and messaging Other ideas: CTAs Events Ads Programs | | | | |

Attract & Awareness Touchpoints

## Interest & Engagement Touchpoints

This part of the lead lifecycle is where prospects are interested in your company and products, and are actively engaged to learn more. As long as you continue to provide useful information that will move these people through to the next phase, seamlessly and without friction, they are likely to give you more and more information—on themselves, their company, timelines, budgets, and so on.

When identifying touchpoints in the interest and engagement stage, a good place to start is with your channels, especially your website, as it plays a key role in developing interest and engaging with your prospects. What does your website bounce rate look like? And where are referrals coming from? When was the last time you optimized your site—or heck, even looked at Google Analytics? When thinking about your programs, what are some touchpoints here that could help with the go-to-market strategy and goals? Maybe your email programs, or your chat program? Can you identify touchpoints in your content where simple tweaks could provide a significant boost in revenue? Think about customer case studies and testimonials, and videos that could be used on your website, in email campaigns and social media and sales outreach. Speaking of sales, think about providing sales scripts. From a tools perspective, are the workflows set up properly to make sure leads are getting to the sales team? Does your marketing automation tool accommodate progressive forms, so you're not continually asking prospects for the same information they have already provided you?

Now let's look at some examples, how to implement them, and the impact and influence they can lead to.

Your *website* is your number-one platform for disseminating best practices, engaging prospects, moving them through the funnel, and converting leads to customers. You control this channel, and even with simple, free programs like Google Analytics and Tag Manager, you can measure the performance of your site and its pages. By looking at this data, you will better understand which pages are performing well (or poorly) and can adjust accordingly.

Another website-related touchpoint is your *bounce rate*. You can have a huge influence on the number and quality of the leads by fixing your website bounce rate. Fixing your bounce rate is pretty easy and can lead to a 10 percent plus increase in conversion. Boom—just like that! If your bounce rate is high, it usually means people are finding you, but you're not providing them the answers they were expecting. What a waste. Pro tip: Make sure your ads and content directing people to your site actually reflect what your company provides. And make sure your site and landing pages reflect this as well. It goes back to being consistent and providing useful information.

Another touchpoint with your website is the *content* itself and how it is delivered. I once worked for a company that created a visual effects tool for which the end users were graphic artists for games and films. But the website was so static it was laughable. No videos, no cool graphics. Just a bunch of downloadable PDFs and long-form content. Yippee! Just what this audience of crazy visual effects artists was looking for. More content isn't necessarily the answer. The answer is purposeful content that is pertinent to and digestible for your audience.

Since this is a major area of focus for marketing, I don't want to get into too many examples here. You know your programs and campaigns better than I do. But again, the idea here is to look at your programs and campaigns with a different eye. Think about how all the programs you have planned can be improved and optimized to align more with the go-to-market strategy and overall revenue targets. What can you do to improve open rates on emails? Can you do more videos or use other, more interactive mediums to engage with prospects in a way that might help shorten the sales cycle? Are your next steps and CTAs working to move prospects through the phases and stages more quickly? You can probably think of several things off the top of your head that could use some focus—and maybe some that you could divest your time and resources of as well.

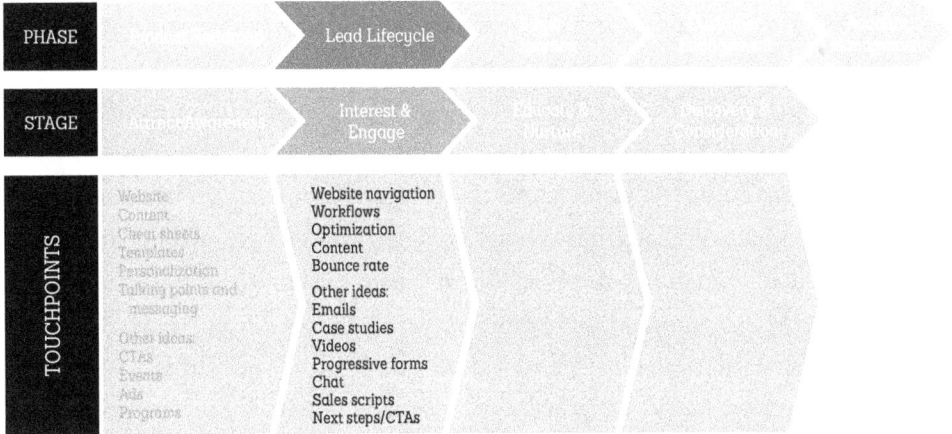

Interest & Engagement Touchpoints

## Educate & Nurture Touchpoints

Having a plan in place to continually educate and nurture your leads should be part of your overall marketing strategy. A good nurture strategy incorporates programs with automated paths that further educate your prospects along their journey. These nurture paths should be well thought out, never afterthoughts. For them to be as effective as possible, you need to think about the different targets and audiences, their roles and needs, and build a frictionless path for them to self-educate and move through the funnel. You have put in a lot of money and effort to get these leads in the first place. So spend the time figuring out how to best nurture them, and then implement that plan. Having a solid nurture program will help move leads from MQL to SQL faster, shortening the sales cycle. But don't forget to think in terms of your own go-to-market strategy and company goals. Here are some areas to consider.

When thinking about this stage, focus on the specific programs first, then on how the channels, content, and tools fit in. For example, what kind of nurture programs do you have, and are they established for your sales teams as well? And what other sales-enablement programs do you have or can create? Maybe you have a thought leadership program that focuses on customer use cases and best practices, or maybe you have an ROI calculator to share. Whatever programs you are planning for, think about the different channels they are on or could be part of. Your website is a big one, and as part of that, so is the chat functionality. Social media is often overlooked in this stage, due to the assumption that channel is for top-of-the-funnel leads. But it can be used strategically to educate prospects as well. In terms of content, you should have a lot of options; content is core to helping customers understand your products and solutions. From a tools standpoint, your MarTech stack will come into play, especially as it relates to the workflows and making sure you are continuing to nurture these leads.

How about looking at some examples?

Yep, your *website*. It is going to come up a lot in this chapter as a potential touchpoint to optimize. As with social media, sometimes marketing professionals don't think about how they can leverage their website for anything beyond top of the funnel. But, as most of your quality leads will come from your website, it is important to develop a flow there that naturally guides prospects through the self-educating process. It's your first opportunity to nurture prospects that come to your site, regardless of how they got there. You should always be thinking about what the next CTA for a specific person is and develop different paths, or workflows, based on an individual's role and where they are in the customer journey.

There are plenty of articles out there that talk about how to develop *workflows* and paths for your prospects, so I won't get into details here. What I will say, though, is you should think about your workflows like a decision tree. Where did the prospect come into the customer journey, and where do you want them to go next (in a way that lets them think they are really making that decision)? Does this workflow provide a path all the way through to closed won? For example, if you have an ABM program, you can easily send these very targeted leads to specific content that would be applicable to them. You might send them an email about a new report that talks about ROI costs, with a link to a landing page and the report itself. Then, if they click on the report to download it, you can have a pop-up that leads them to an ROI calculator. And so on. Understand what they are going to want to see next, and provide that to them before they have to go find it themselves.

I could build out paths all day, but you get the point. Too often I see marketers develop content and web pages for a specific audience (awesome idea) that then has no call to action (CTA) on that page, so the forward momentum just stops (not so awesome an idea). What do you want your prospect to do next; what do you want them to learn? You need to make moving to the next step frictionless and a no-brainer. Oh, and by the way, this flow can now be used to develop your email nurture campaign as well. This is like a twofer!

Another touchpoint marketing professionals can influence in this stage is *chat*. Chat is such an amazing, powerful, yet often overlooked tool. It can be used as a marketing tool on your company website, as a sales tool embedded in the product or trial process, and as a tool for your customer success team. You can set up specific flows within the chat tool depending on the segmentation, then automate the process of educating and nurturing a lead, making it a super low-touch and faster sale. Brilliant! Or, if you want the prospect to go from view-ing a specific page to looking at pricing packages, why not just ask them in chat? "Hey, want to see how much this will set you back? I bet it's not as bad as you're thinking." How easy was that? You've moved prospects through multiple phases and stages of the customer journey, quickly and noninvasively, without any interaction from the sales team.

There are so many things to look at and ways to optimize in this stage, from developing ROI reports and calculators to really focusing on your nurture email streams and making sure you develop them by segment. As in the other stages, there are plenty of opportunities here to fine-tune campaigns and content to ensure they're as effective as possible and focused on the overall company goals.

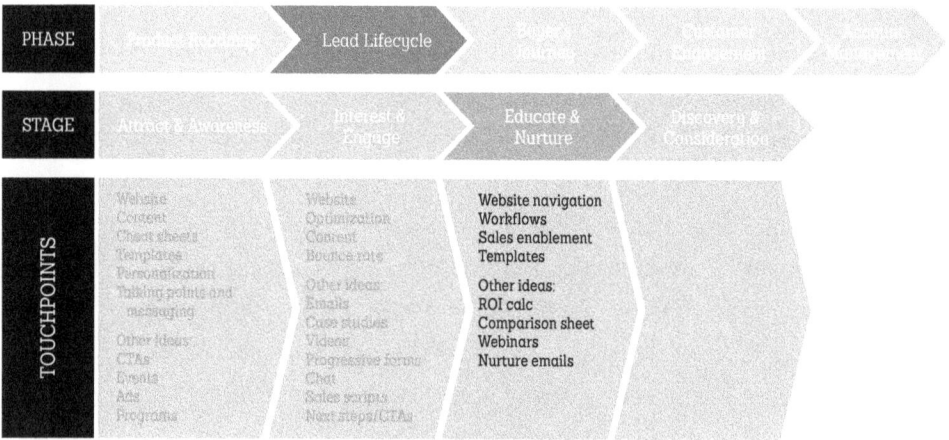

Educate & Nurture Touchpoints

## Discovery & Consideration Touchpoints

Are we having fun yet? Are you looking at things with your new go-to-market glasses on? Let's keep going.

Discovery and consideration is the stage of the customer journey where prospects start to deep-dive into your offering—getting to know the value it brings, the features and functionality, industry best practices, and how to use it. This is where the prospect might consider doing a demo, trial, proof of concept, or assessment of some sort. Prospects are going to want to see the product in action and have a sense of the true value it brings, especially as it relates to them directly, as every company feels they are unique. With that in mind, what are some touchpoints you can identify and optimize for maximum impact?

From a channel standpoint, besides the beaten dead horse (aka your website), external channels such as industry publications, thought leaders' blogs and podcasts, and other media outlets come into play here. Basically, this is a great time to leverage external non-biased outlets to promote your amazing products. Programs here might include thought leader programs that include your customers in webinars, as well as any customer advocacy programs. This is the stage where your prospects are trying to convince themselves and others in their organization that your product is the right one, so help them out here. Make it easy for them to find case studies, ROI calculators, assessments, and other tools and content that help them realize the tremendous benefit of your solution.

Let's look at a well-defined *thought leader program* as an example. A thought leader program incorporates rich content from industry luminaries, customer advocates, company experts, and executives into your programs. It might include a webinar, blog, or podcast series that highlights case studies and different industry leaders, or you might have special channels within your community to share tips and tricks. If you don't have a thought leader program in place yet, now is a good time to develop one. These programs provide your best customers, advocates, and champions a platform to share best practices, ROI, and results and showcase what they are doing for their company. And they bring in more qualified leads and shorten the sales cycle. I love my sales teams, but a customer or industry expert endorsing my product is almost always going to result in a quicker sale. By leveraging these folks via a thought leader program, you can influence purchasing and accelerate sales.

Another great way to build your influence is with *customer reviews and testimonials*. When was the last time you actively sought reviews? It's not hard to do and can significantly help your prospects decide which solution to go with—yours or the competition's. If you do NPS surveys, you can look at your promoters and simply reach out and ask if they would do a review. Or set some funds aside and give away gift cards to people who do public reviews.

Customers talking about how great your offering is and the value it brings to them is truly priceless. Imagine if you did a quick outreach and got even just five new testimonials. I guarantee you the sales team will love having these. Sales can add a testimonial to their emails, talk about them on calls with prospects, include a slide filled with one quote after another in their sales deck, and more. You can also leverage them in social media posts. Also check to see if anyone who has done a review would be willing to do a full case study.

Think about all the areas you can optimize and influence, all the touchpoints at your fingertips that will lead to better-qualified leads, result in a shorter sales cycle, and produce more revenue, faster.

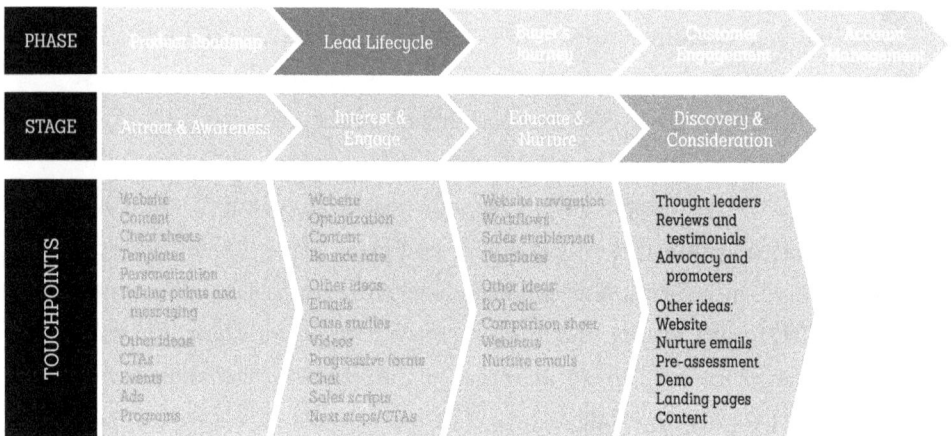

| PHASE | Product Roadmap | Lead Lifecycle | Buyer's Journey | Customer Engagement | Account Management |
|---|---|---|---|---|---|
| STAGE | Attract & Awareness | Interest & Engage | Educate & Nurture | Discovery & Consideration | |
| TOUCHPOINTS | Website Content Cheat sheets Templates Personalization Talking points and messaging Other ideas CTAs Events Ads Programs | Website Optimization Content Bounce rate Other ideas: Emails Case studies Videos Progressive forms Chat Sales scripts Next steps/CTAs | Website navigation Workflows Sales enablement Templates Other ideas: ROI calc Comparison sheet Webinars Nurture emails | Thought leaders Reviews and testimonials Advocacy and promoters Other ideas: Website Nurture emails Pre-assessment Demo Landing pages Content | |

Discovery & Consideration Touchpoints

# BUILD IT, AND THEY WILL COME

So you have now reviewed your company's go-to-market strategy and aligned it with your customer journey, and you've taken time (or soon will!) to list all the touchpoints you and your team have in the lead lifecycle phase. Once you prioritize which ones you could potentially focus on and plot them out, this becomes the first piece of your Map of Influence! Ta-da. Now let's go look at the rest of the phases.

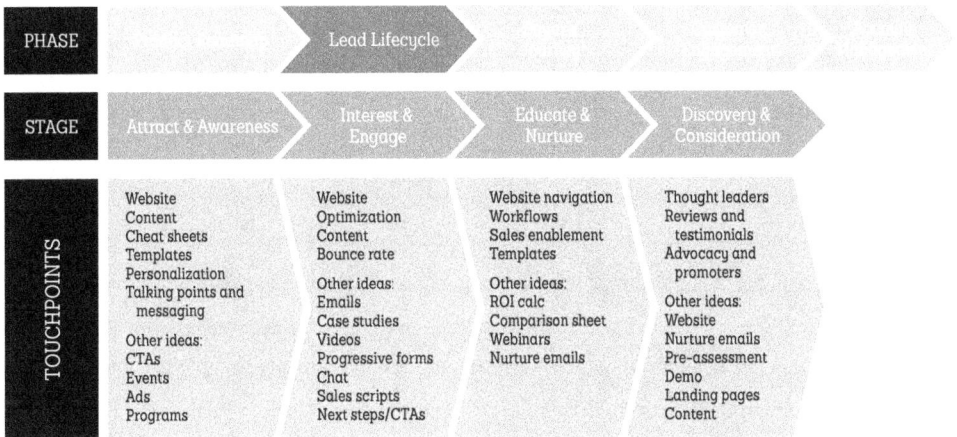

| PHASE | Lead Lifecycle | | | |
|---|---|---|---|---|
| STAGE | Attract & Awareness | Interest & Engage | Educate & Nurture | Discovery & Consideration |
| TOUCHPOINTS | Website<br>Content<br>Cheat sheets<br>Templates<br>Personalization<br>Talking points and messaging<br><br>Other ideas:<br>CTAs<br>Events<br>Ads<br>Programs | Website<br>Optimization<br>Content<br>Bounce rate<br><br>Other ideas:<br>Emails<br>Case studies<br>Videos<br>Progressive forms<br>Chat<br>Sales scripts<br>Next steps/CTAs | Website navigation<br>Workflows<br>Sales enablement<br>Templates<br><br>Other ideas:<br>ROI calc<br>Comparison sheet<br>Webinars<br>Nurture emails | Thought leaders<br>Reviews and testimonials<br>Advocacy and promoters<br><br>Other ideas:<br>Website<br>Nurture emails<br>Pre-assessment<br>Demo<br>Landing pages<br>Content |

Map of Influence: Lead Lifecycle Phase

# A Word on Content

Which comes first, the program or the content? Well, that really does depend. One of the essential components of your overall marketing strategy and the attract and awareness stage is your content strategy. This should go without saying, but you should not be creating content just for the heck of it—each piece needs to fit into your overall strategy, and each piece should have a marketing plan attached to it, just like any other marketing program. I have seen so much good content go to waste because there wasn't a comprehensive program in place to disseminate it. It gets created, then you post it once on social media, add it to your website, and essentially forget about it. On the other end of the spectrum, I have seen really shitty content get tons of traction, because there is a concerted campaign around disseminating it.

Your content strategy should be developed around your overall marketing strategy and upcoming programs, and mapped to your themes. Content should be created to support your programs. For example, if you are launching a new feature, you can create a data sheet and case study to illustrate how great it is. Sometimes a program itself will support new content—like turning a webinar conversation into a guide, an e-book, or multiple blog posts. In some cases, you may need to create a one-off or ad hoc piece of content, but you still need to think about how to make the most of it.

In an upcoming chapter, we'll look at how you can create smart, reusable content that can be repurposed for different audiences and programs.

# CHAPTER 5

# Swaying: Buyer's Journey

While sales owns the buyer's journey, there are so many opportunities for marketing professionals to help and have influence in this phase. I've never understood why there is friction between sales and marketing. Marketing is here to help bring in quality leads, shorten the sales cycle, and make it frictionless for prospects to buy. All of this increases revenue—oh, and makes the lives of salespeople a heck of a lot easier. They should welcome us. And we should welcome them! In order to achieve happy prospects, happy sales, and a happy company, marketing needs to include sales in our planning conversations and absorb their insight. They talk to prospects and customers every day. They pay close attention to the competition and know how your company needs to differentiate. They hear the objections frequently. They know which value propositions are resonating with prospects and which features are meeting the needs of customers. Sales is a wealth of information.

I wasn't always so enlightened. During my first few months at Oracle, I launched a solution I had taken over from someone else. The week before the launch, I was so excited. I was about to train the entire direct sales team of about a thousand folks on what the solution was, how to sell it, and what the coinciding marketing programs would include (i.e., press release, website update, case study, ads, etc.). Some of the training would be done via conference calls, while some would be done in person at the Sales Center at Oracle headquarters in Redwood City. My office was in the building directly across the street, so five minutes before the first live training was about to start, I grabbed my amazing presentation, data sheets, and battle cards and headed (I might have skipped) across the street. I am lion, hear me roar!

My presentation seemed to be well received—no one fell asleep, and I was getting some head nods. After I finished, I went around to introduce myself, as I hadn't personally met many of them yet. One of the sales guys was sitting in front of his monitor, likely looking at his to-do list. I was all skippy-smiley marketing person as I approached and handed him a copy of the data sheet and battle card for his reference. Without even looking at me, he took the paper and threw it directly into the garbage can—not even the recycling bin! My first reaction was "What a jerk!" But instead of saying that out loud, I simply asked why he did that. He finally looked up at me and said, "Because you never asked me about the solution. What we are hearing are the customer pain points. What do they really need? Can we actually sell it? For how much? And you never bothered to ask me how you could help me." Whoa. I got it. Good point.

I lost some serious cred there. Instead of increasing trust, and therefore my influence, I screwed up. I apologized for making assumptions without conferring with any salespeople, then asked him for his help. For the next week, we met at lunch, and I essentially interrogated him on every aspect of the solution, features, pricing, competition, customer needs, and so on. Turns out, the solution was well positioned, but with his help, I made some modifications to the sales tools and content that made it a much better, easier sell.

That experience taught me a valuable lesson. Always make sure those impacted by the launch of new or enhanced products are involved in defining the marketing strategy and plan to take products to market. To this day, I try to bring sales into the process as early as possible to make sure that their voices are heard and that I am giving them the data, context, and platform they need to develop the best possible solution for our customers.

Now let's consider specific areas along the buyer's journey where marketing can influence the sales team and the sale of products and solutions.

## STAGES OF THE BUYER'S JOURNEY PHASE

Reflecting back on your go-to-market strategy and your company's customer journey, you should be able to identify the stages in the buyer's journey. If you don't have a sense of them, look at the workflows in your CRM; it will likely have something there. Or use my example below, as your flow will likely be similar.

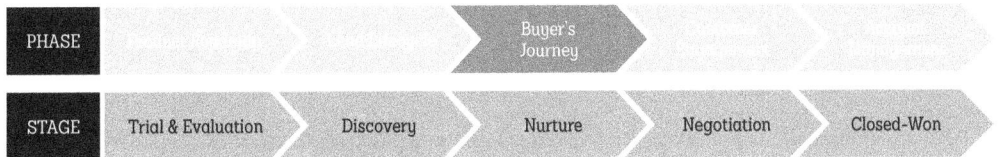

| PHASE | Buyer's Journey | | | | |
|---|---|---|---|---|---|
| STAGE | Trial & Evaluation | Discovery | Nurture | Negotiation | Closed-Won |

Buyer's Journey Phases and Stages

So for the first stage of the buyer's journey, your company might offer some kind of trial, which could have a time limit. Or you might have something as simple as a video to demonstrate the effectiveness of your product. Regardless, you likely have some way of showing how your product operates. From there, the journey continues to discovery, where the sales team further qualifies the prospect, their likelihood to buy, and what the potential revenue will be (pipeline). From there, sales will likely have an opportunity to nurture the relationship with the prospect. And finally, hopefully, there is an opportunity to negotiate the terms of the sale itself and close out the prospect, turning them into a paying customer.

# IDENTIFYING TOUCHPOINTS IN THE BUYER'S JOURNEY

If those are the stages (trial and evaluation >> discovery >> nurture >> negotiate >> closed-won), let's now identify different ways marketing can impact each of them. We as marketing professionals know we're affecting the buyer's journey, but let's strive to be clear about how we are and how we might. With your go-to-market strategy and sales hat on, let's identify some touchpoints for these specific stages.

## Trial & Evaluation Touchpoints

Trials and evaluations, sometimes referred to as pilots or proof of concepts, are a critical component to a lot of go-to-market strategies. Varying in length, anywhere from fourteen days to six months, they offer prospective customers an opportunity to see a product in action. Sometimes they provide full access to all features and functions, and sometimes only certain functionality is available. Sometimes it's more of a demo, or there is a sandbox provided. The prospects in a trial might belong to either marketing or sales—it depends when and how trials are offered. But regardless of who "owns" the folks in trial, helping them through the process will make it an easier, stronger sale, so it behooves everyone to have a solid workflow and strong communication throughout.

Look at ways you can help prospects move through a trial seamlessly, and make sure expectations are properly set, especially if the trial includes features not available at some levels. From a channel standpoint, are there things you can do within the product to help prospects understand the value of your solution? Even though these folks are well into the customer journey, can you leverage social media channels more? Maybe share how-to videos or reviews and testimonials? A huge channel you should introduce your prospects to, especially if they are in trial, is your knowledge base and community platform, if you have one. Give them a place to get answers without needing to interact with sales (or anyone, really). Think about your marketing programs, and see if there is a way to tweak or extend what you already have going. For example, if you have ad campaigns, why not use ones that have testimonials and re-target those in trial? This keeps you top of mind and reminds them of the value your product brings. And from a tools standpoint, as mentioned earlier, maybe you have a sandbox or other way of helping the evaluator play around in the product, using pertinent data.

Several times in my career, I've worked for companies whose solutions were extremely sophisticated; sometimes the trial involved moving the prospect's entire system to our product. In multiple cases it included switching off their existing solution too, just to see if it would work for them.

Imagine if you wanted to try a new emailing system, and you had to first shut down your Gmail account (no more me@gmail.com), move all of your contacts to the new system, try it for fourteen days, and then, if you didn't like it, switch everything back. Oh, and you can forget about getting me@gmail.com back, as well as your emails. They are long gone. You get the point. Sometimes as part of the trial process, we are actually asking folks to shoulder a huge undertaking that costs them resources and money—oh, and likely our product can't be easily tested in fourteen days. As a marketing professional, you need to develop content that will set proper expectations with prospects for the trial experience and beyond.

Marketing can also have influence in defining the overall *trial experience*. Can you make it immersive? How can you encourage prospects to bring colleagues along for the ride? Can you work with product to personalize the experience somehow? How can you get prospects to the aha moment sooner, so they are ready to buy?

In looking at specific touchpoints marketing can influence, you can help produce stellar *how-to videos*, in addition to other onboarding documents, that prospects can then reference during their trial. Another touchpoint is the in-app experience for the prospects evaluating your product. Work with the product team to determine areas of friction in a product, then offer a resource at that friction point, like a pop-up how-to video. It's kind of like when you're working out and you're not sure how to do a bicep curl (or maybe you're too tired to do it right), and your fitness instructor comes over to help you through it. How can you as a marketing professional get evaluators through that point of friction (or frustration and exhaustion)? Think about how you can move the prospect through the trial quickly and effortlessly and get them to that aha moment. Once a prospect is there, the sale is easy.

Another way marketing can help evaluators get to their aha moment more quickly is through *content*, such as tips and tricks for running a successful trial, or best practices and case studies. One thing that helps move the needle quickly from evaluation to purchase is providing some kind of report on their results, their expected results, or the results of other successful customers using your product. For example, if you have a product that automates something and will save the end user X amount of time, send the evaluator a report showing how much time they saved during the trial period, and extrapolate that out for an entire year. "Oh, looky here, you saved one hour per transaction during your trial. If you were to do five hundred transactions this year, you could save five hundred hours of time by automating with our amazing product. This is similar to what other industry leaders, like Company Z, are seeing once they implement our solution. Check out Company Zed's case study here!"

Remember, you aren't looking to acquire customers. Customers are looking to acquire you. They have done their research online, and what moves them to a decision faster than anything is if their trusted colleagues (or untrustworthy competitors) are recommending your solution. So strive to actively obtain and produce testimonials.

To have the most impactful testimonials, ensure the correct person within your customer account is doing the testimonial for you. In other words, if your target persona is the CFO, having a testimonial from the IT person won't mean a thing. Then make sure you are posting the testimonials where the right audience will see them. In the case of a marketing system, for example, a good review or testimonial from another marketing professional will move someone from marketing through a trial faster, so maybe have it pop up within the trial, send it as part of an email, or incorporate it into the how-to videos. Remember you have different people to convince in different stages of the customer journey. For example, when your prospect is getting closer to making a decision and signing the contract, a review from a CEO would be more helpful.

Pro tip: Create testimonials in the format that will most resonate with your prospects, and share them through mediums where they will see the testimonial. You could do a simple quote that goes in an email, but if your target isn't looking at emails, it's not going to do much good there. On the other hand, if your persona is all over TikTok (not judging), then you should place your testimonials there somehow.

What else can you think of right now that would allow marketing to help with the trial experience? Maybe you could make sure your website has a good navigation flow for people to start a trial—that is, make it really clear how to Try (start a trial) versus Buy (actually buy your product). What other content could you make available to the sales team to help them guide prospects through the trial? Or maybe you are thinking of how you can impact the workflow of the lead itself. How do trial leads get followed up on—by whom and when? Remember what I said earlier: 50 percent of the leads that marketing sends over to sales go untouched. This includes leads from prospects signing up for trials. Makes you wonder, doesn't it? Why is this happening? Are we bringing the right leads and targets into trials? Think: What can you do in this stage to help?

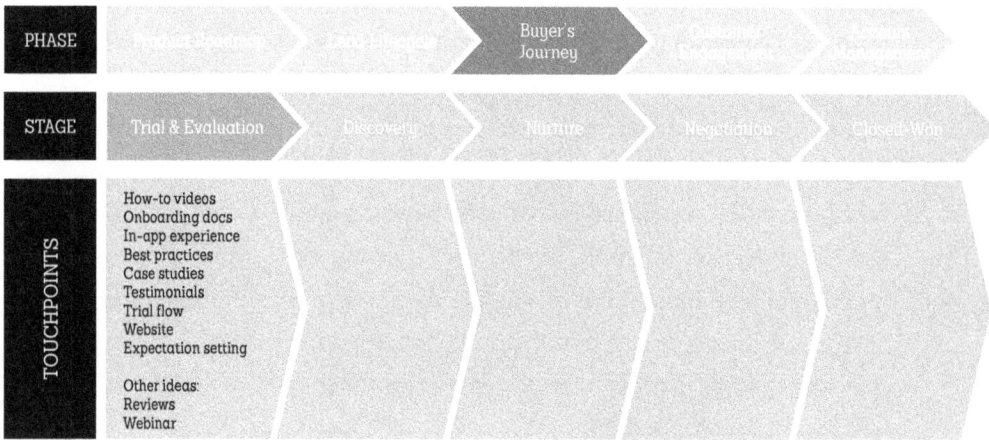

| PHASE | Product Roadmap | Lead Efficiency | Buyer's Journey | Customer Onboarding | Account Management |
|---|---|---|---|---|---|
| STAGE | Trial & Evaluation | Discovery | Nurture | Negotiation | Closed-Won |
| TOUCHPOINTS | How-to videos<br>Onboarding docs<br>In-app experience<br>Best practices<br>Case studies<br>Testimonials<br>Trial flow<br>Website<br>Expectation setting<br><br>Other ideas:<br>Reviews<br>Webinar | | | | |

Trial & Evaluation Touchpoints

## Discovery Touchpoints

The discovery phase, sometimes referred to as BANT, is where sales dives deep into the prospect's budget, authority, needs, and timeline. Depending on the sales cycle for your product or solution, this phase can go on for a while—possibly up to a year or more—with sales trying to schedule meetings, nurturing with follow-up calls and emails, developing a relationship with the main contact, and turning that contact into a champion within their organization. Sales is also looking to make sure that everyone in the buying-decision process is included in the conversations.

It's important that marketing professionals educate themselves on what the salespeople focus on as part of their sales process. Are they talking about the values of the product, or are they more focused on features? Do the salespeople have talking points on objections they may be hearing from prospects? Do they have different conversations depending on the role of the prospect they are communicating with? One of the first things I do when I start a new role, and have others do when they start on my team, is listen in on sales calls. This can give you so much insight into what prospects are looking for. I also read the emails sales sends out to prospects and receives, to see if there are areas we can improve—or if there are some great emails we can turn into templates for other people to use.

Discovery provides marketing with some interesting opportunities to identify and influence touchpoints. From a channel standpoint, chat can be used to help sales capture more in-depth information from their prospects. And this chat can be implemented in both the website and the product. Email is another channel that sits in both marketing and sales. Usually marketing will send nurture emails from the marketing automation tool, but sales can (and will) send emails from either the CRM or the email platform.

As far as programs are concerned, webinars, videos, and other forms of how-to often come from marketing. And in terms of content, marketing can help with sales scripts, sample emails, and interesting content and programs for sales to share. Finally, tools are an important part of the workflow, where lead scoring and distribution are critical.

Let's look at some examples. This kind of goes without saying, but make sure you are targeting your preferred, and agreed-upon, audience. Then it's critical for marketing to nurture the leads, and only send qualified leads when they are ready for the sales team. Otherwise, it's going to be hard for everyone: You, because it will take a long time to nurture them enough to share with sales. Sales, because they will spend extra cycles trying to move the prospect to a closed-won deal. And then you again, because you're going to have to hear, once again, how much the leads suck.

But there are many ways you can influence here. First, take a close look at your *lead scoring* and adjust as needed. I try to do this quarterly with simple updates or when I receive information that warrants an update. For example, if you have scored webinar registrant no-shows as bad leads, but sales has been able to reach out and convert many of them, then maybe you should consider increasing the lead score, even though the lead didn't attend the live webinar.

I once had salespeople complain that the same guy popped up in the priority list every day, no matter how many times the marketing tools tried to change his score to bump him back down to unqualified. This was because he loved our content, so he came back daily to see what else we had to offer, but he admitted he was never going to be a customer. While I appreciated that he liked the content we created, he was not a good, qualified lead, and I didn't want sales wasting their time following up (again and again). The guy could have been a competitor for all I knew. A good solution is to keep folks like this in the marketing nurture programs until they specifically reach out asking to speak to a salesperson. This is easy to do by scoring them with a negative score or creating a "Never Going to Buy" category. Then these leads stay in the marketing queue but aren't surfacing for sales over and over. If and when this person is ever ready, they will let you know, trust me, and not by simply downloading another e-book or registering for a webinar.

Another way—and one of my favorites—marketing professionals can have influence in the discovery stage is to help set the *prioritization* for the sales team: which leads or prospects to follow up on and in what order. (Note: This is usually not necessary for a named accounts sales team, but it can still help.) To do this, I work with sales to develop a seek list or priority list (most CRMs have some type of list priority capability). Create a list that updates in real time and adjusts the priority based on scoring and behavior. That way, sales knows who to reach out to first (hopefully the low-hanging fruit—folks with the highest propensity to buy now).

Imagine you are a salesperson, and you come in at 6 a.m. to hit the ground running with your queue of four hundred contacts. Who do you call first? Sure, focus on those on the East Coast, but then what? Zero in alphabetically by last name or company name? People named Sally? Or maybe, just maybe, you could focus on those that are further along the funnel and have a higher propensity to buy? Through scoring both demographically (role, title, location, etc.) and behaviorally (signed up for a trial, watched a testimonial video, attended three webinars, indicated they need a solution like what we offer in the next three months, etc.), you can help determine the day-to-day priorities for the sales team. You can also set up your CRM so that the sales lead owners get an alert if their lead takes some kind of action, like starting a trial, increasing their time on the website, or reviewing multiple how-to videos or case studies.

By first scoring leads appropriately, marketing professionals can ensure sales is getting quality leads. Then, by creating a priority list, marketing can take away some of the sales team's angst and allow them to focus on the best leads according to rank.

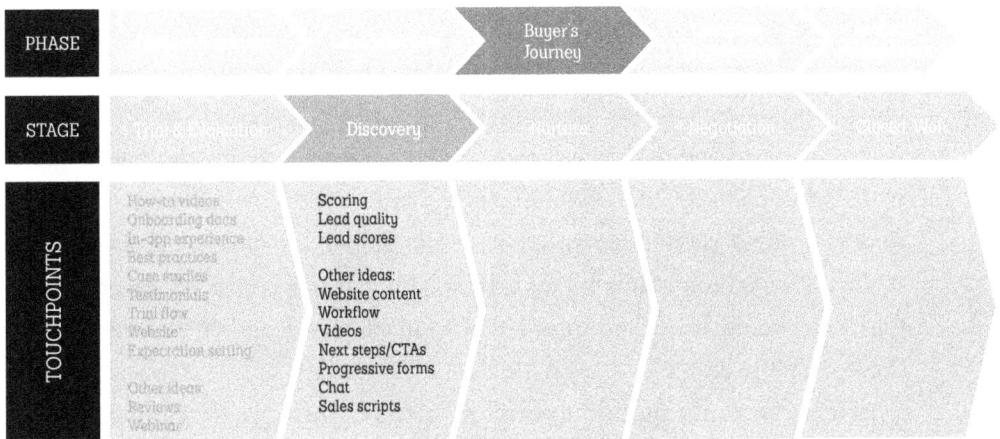

| PHASE | | Buyer's Journey | | | |
|---|---|---|---|---|---|
| STAGE | Trial & Evaluation | Discovery | Nurture | Negotiation | Closed-Won |
| TOUCHPOINTS | How-to videos<br>Onboarding docs<br>In-app experience<br>Best practices<br>Case studies<br>Testimonials<br>Trial flow<br>Website<br>Expectation setting<br><br>Other ideas:<br>Reviews<br>Webinar | Scoring<br>Lead quality<br>Lead scores<br><br>Other ideas:<br>Website content<br>Workflow<br>Videos<br>Next steps/CTAs<br>Progressive forms<br>Chat<br>Sales scripts | | | |

Discovery Touchpoints

## Nurture Touchpoints

What do I mean when I talk about nurturing? Well, it depends. Sometimes it makes sense for the sales team to "keep" and nurture a lead in order to continue developing a relationship with the prospect, while other times those prospects should get recycled back to marketing, for marketing to nurture. The principles and rules of engagement vary by company, but the end goal is to make sure the most appropriate nurture path is offered to the prospect. For example, you might have an amazingly qualified lead, and they are definitely going to purchase your product . . . next year. Your options are to have sales continue to nurture and build that relationship, send it back to marketing until such time as the prospect is ready to buy, or some combination (e.g., marketing emails are limited to sending out webinar invites only, and all other communication comes from sales). But here we're going to talk about if the sales team decides to keep and nurture a lead. In this stage of the buyer's journey, there are many things marketing can do to help.

There are a lot of potential channels and programs in this phase that marketing can and should be working with sales to influence. There are opportunities for external articles in industry publications, as well as endorsements. There are ways marketing professionals can help with the sales channel itself, like developing automated nurture drip email campaigns. Social media can play a role in the nurture stage as well, if this is a channel your target looks at. When it comes to content, there is no end to the need for it in this stage. Marketing can help by creating industry analysis—state of the industry or how to prepare for the coming year—reports, comparison sheets, and product dashboards. Or marketing might develop an ROI calculator or assessment tool that would help the target understand potential outcomes from their perspective.

Here are some specific examples. Just as you would create an email *nurture campaign* for leads that are owned by marketing, create one to help the sales team nurture the prospects they are working with. Have you ever seen those emails: "Hey, it's me again. Haven't heard from you, so I have included the exact same crap in this email that I did the previous thirteen times (thirteenth time is the charm, right!?). I'm super sad and frankly surprised you still haven't responded. Insert sad panda emoji here." A better way (well, any way would be better than that example) for sales to follow up with leads they own would be with a series of emails that progressively tells the story of your solution and provides useful (and varied) content.

Guess what? Marketing can help create a campaign like this that is automated in the CRM, so emails can easily be made to look as if they're personal emails from the sales rep. I usually create a series of about five—and literally call them email 1 through 5—that helps move the prospect through the buyer's journey more quickly. Email 1 might refresh the prospect on what our solution does, with a CTA to check out a quick demo video. Email 2 might be an industry report talking about why successful companies have made the shift to a solution like yours (or, even better, explicitly mentions your solution in a good light). The CTA would be to download the report. Email 3 might talk about the value propositions and features, with a CTA to check out an on-demand product webinar. Email 4 should be a customer case study or industry best practices piece. The CTA here would be to check out a trial. And email 5 could have some tools, like an ROI calculator that hopefully leads to a call with sales or even a purchase online. By doing something like this, you (or, I should say, the salesperson these emails are coming from) have continued to educate the prospect along the buyer's journey, moving them from one stage to the next.

I also like to create "ad hoc" emails that talk about upcoming events, like a webinar or an upcoming industry report, and add them to the CRM. This gives the salesperson an easy and noninvasive way of reaching out. "I know you are still working on budget and haven't made any decisions yet. I just wanted to reach out and let you know we have a killer report/guide/webinar on the state of your industry that I thought might be helpful. Cheers . . ." Did I mention that all of this can be automated? I'm pretty sure I did.

And then nothing says I love you more than giving the sales team some type of *interactive tool* they can use to show the value of the product or solution to prospects. Depending on your industry, product, target, and so on, the tools could vary. Two tools that have worked for me are ROI calculators (this should be on your website already and part of the marketing nurture path as well) and assessments. These remind the prospect of the value of your product and validate the prospect's decision to choose your product or solution. This is usually the point in the buyer's journey where they are starting to feel the weight of the responsibility for making a decision and spending potentially millions of dollars. Validation helps convert folks quickly. So let 'em have it.

These things can be simple. The assessment can be a four-question survey, with an outcome that "coincidentally" points to their needing exactly what you have to offer. For example, in the case of a marketing person evaluating a webinar platform your company offers, you might ask if they need the platform to integrate with their CRM, knowing full well the answer will be yes, of course! "Well, how do you like that? We just happen to have a native integration with all of the key CRMs." Okay, maybe you don't need to make it that obvious, but you get the point.

There are so many other touchpoints here that could help sales nurture a solid relationship with the prospect: competitive analysis, battle cards, feature comparisons, tips and tricks, best practices, case studies. Talk to sales about what they need to get the prospect to the next step. It might even be swag, so put some budget aside for something like this.

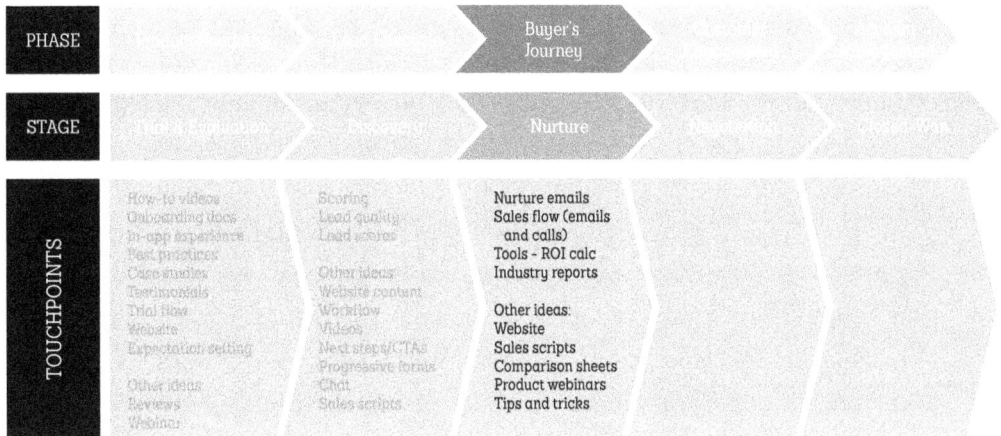

| PHASE | | | Buyer's Journey | | |
|---|---|---|---|---|---|
| STAGE | Trial & Evaluation | Discovery | Nurture | Negotiation | Close/Win |
| TOUCHPOINTS | How-to videos<br>Onboarding docs<br>In-app experience<br>Best practices<br>Case studies<br>Testimonials<br>Trial flow<br>Website<br>Expectation setting<br><br>Other ideas:<br>Reviews<br>Webinar | Scoring<br>Lead quality<br>Lead scores<br><br>Other ideas:<br>Website content<br>Workflow<br>Videos<br>Next steps/CTAs<br>Progressive forms<br>Chat<br>Sales scripts | Nurture emails<br>Sales flow (emails and calls)<br>Tools - ROI calc<br>Industry reports<br><br>Other ideas:<br>Website<br>Sales scripts<br>Comparison sheets<br>Product webinars<br>Tips and tricks | | |

Nurture Touchpoints

## Negotiation Touchpoints

You may think the negotiation phase is solely for sales to deal with, and God knows you don't want to get involved in the actual negotiation between potential customers and sales. But marketing professionals can influence this phase in other ways. For starters, having clear and concise pricing information on your website helps significantly, as does making sure the terms and conditions are always up to date. (And while you are at it, make sure the terms and conditions include clauses that allow you to display customer logos and names on your website and in press releases once the customer instance is up and running.) You know where this is going . . . let's go find some touchpoints.

The main channels for this stage are the website (and the functionality on the site to actually make a purchase) and the sales team itself. In terms of programs, while it is late in the sales process, marketing can still identify some touchpoints where they can help close deals. Namely, marketing can develop promotions that move the needle for prospects, and marketing can contribute to the pricing strategy. In terms of content, marketing should be looking at consistency, even looking at language in quotes and proposals. In terms of tools, the CRM will be the most significant, along with the sales operations team that processes completed contracts. While there are not as many opportunities here to help, areas where marketing can have impact are significant.

Let's look at *proposals and quotes* as a touchpoint. When sales starts to develop the actual proposal, quote, and contracts, marketing should make sure everyone in the company is using consistent language, look, and feel. I cannot tell you how many times I've seen bizarre, noncompliant, made-up proposals from salespeople, filled with typos and out-of-date information. Um, yeah, we got rid of that feature five years ago. Oh, and we're now on version 12.3, not 7.4.

So how can you as a marketing professional have influence here? Marketing can develop templates for sales to use with tools like PandaDoc or DocuSign. Not only will sales be grateful they don't have to start from scratch (or copy that really old contract), the templates will have the added benefit of consistency. Whoo hoo. Your legal team will thank you as well. And done right, using marketing- and legal-approved templates should make the contracts easier for prospects to review and therefore shorten the time needed to get the contract through their legal system. Yay! Shortened sales cycle. See what you did there, just by creating a nice template for contracts?

What other touchpoints are there? What else can marketing give to a potential new customer in the negotiation stage that might help close the deal? Can you offer them *incentives*, such as a joint press release, a speaking opportunity, or maybe a thought leader webinar showcasing them? Sometimes the enticement can be for the primary contact (like a $50 Visa gift card), and sometimes it will benefit their company (like a speaking slot at an industry event). Regardless, think about things marketing can offer, even if you need to budget it in. And then pass those things to Saleswoman Pamela: "If you sign the contract today, I can get you a keynote speaking slot at this year's conference, or booth space."

A VP of marketing friend of mine helped her sales team close a multi-million-dollar client when she created an entire program showcasing them and their dominance in the market. The program included case studies, webinars, a press release, speaking opportunities, and more. It was a year-long program that essentially turned the client into a thought leader in their industry. And bonus, my friend got a ton of marketing material and programs from it. Talk about a win-win-win.

There are so many more ways marketing can influence the negotiation stage of the buyer's journey. Making sure sales has the ROI calculator handy when objections come up from the prospect (or more likely the prospect's CFO). Leveraging the website to ensure the buying process and flow is easy. Working with product and sales to determine the pricing strategy and potential feature bundling. And— simple but transformative—committing to work closely with the sales operations team to ensure an effortless process on everyone's part to close a deal.

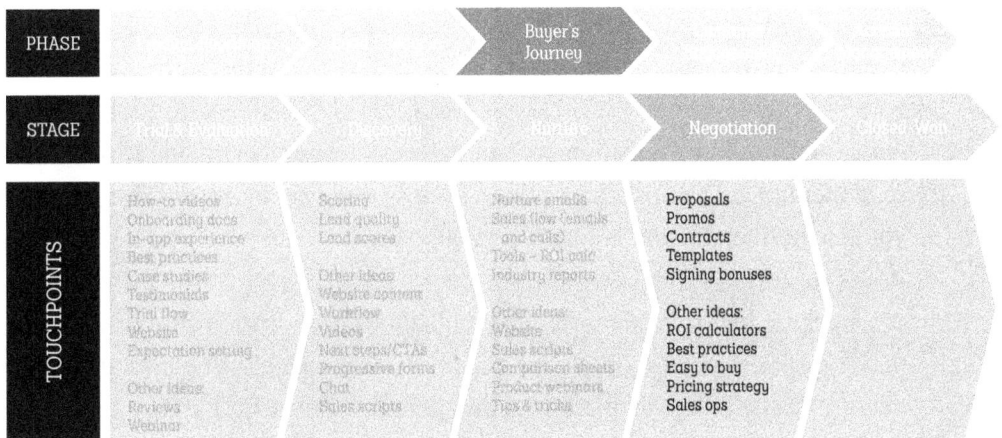

| PHASE | | | | Buyer's Journey | |
|---|---|---|---|---|---|
| STAGE | Trial & Evaluation | Discovery | Nurture | Negotiation | Closed-Won |
| TOUCHPOINTS | How-to videos Onboarding docs In-app experience Best practices Case studies Testimonials Trial flow Website Expectation setting Other ideas: Reviews Webinar | Scoring Lead quality Lead scores Other ideas: Website content Workflow Videos Next steps/CTAs Progressive forms Chat Sales scripts | Nurture emails Sales (low) (emails and calls) Tools – ROI calc Industry reports Other ideas: Website Sales scripts Comparison sheets Product webinars Tips & tricks | Proposals Promos Contracts Templates Signing bonuses Other ideas: ROI calculators Best practices Easy to buy Pricing strategy Sales ops | |

Negotiation Touchpoints

## Closed-Won Touchpoints

Hopefully you have gotten to closed-won deals. Yay, revenue. There are areas here where marketing can help with this last leg of the buyer's journey. The idea in this stage is to make it as simple as possible for prospects to buy, then make sure there is a harmonious transition for the buyers (and, let's face it, for the customer success team as well). Still not sure how you and marketing can help? I've got you covered.

Again, think about the programs you might be able to build, influence, or own. These programs might include welcome kits or packages (remember when people would send you a box of T-shirts, hats, and mugs?). Or maybe your company has a monthly webinar onboarding series (that probably falls on you to produce anyway). And don't forget the Getting Started documents you had to make look pretty. As far as channels, especially for these programs, there are several here that marketing can leverage—for example, email, website, and your community knowledge base. In terms of content, there may be a how-to video series and FAQs in addition to data sheets, tech specs, and more (these likely fall on your plate too somehow, even if it's "just a five-minute project to pretty up the doc").

Let's dissect these a little more. Do you have a *welcome kit* ready to go? This can be anything, from a simple welcome email from your CEO to a basket of swag sent to everyone involved with the purchase. Back when paper was a thing, I used to create laminated cards listing important company contacts and their phone numbers, and we'd send them to customers for easy access. Now there are better options, you know, like an email address or a chat box on your site. But hey, it was the nineties. You get the gist.

I hear a lot from potential clients (believe it or not): "Can you make it easier for me to buy your product?" Seriously! But as absurd as it is, it's true: Businesses don't always make this easy. Exhibit A: Up until recently, in order to buy extra licenses of Salesforce, you had to sign a paper and fax it back over to them. Come on, Salesforce!

The last time I had to buy more licenses from them, I didn't even have a fax machine. I've made final purchasing decisions solely based on how easy it was to purchase from one company versus another. So think about what you can do on your own website to make the sale seamless and frictionless for the purchaser.

Note: Sometimes marketing doesn't own the website where a prospect is purchasing, but you can still influence the process. Think about how many fields are required to be filled out for a purchase. Can some of this information be captured as part of the onboarding process instead? Or maybe you already have some of it in your CRM? Or here's a good one: I worked with a company once where prospects couldn't make a purchase without being in a trial first, and then they could purchase it within the product—and it wasn't even intuitive where they should go within the product to make that purchase. But even if they knew where to go, why would you make someone who is ready to buy go through a trial? Well, you shouldn't. See if you can change things like this.

Also, think through the client's next steps after they make their purchase. What should they expect? Will there be a *kickoff* call or a handoff from the sales team to the customer success team? Where can the new client go for more information? It's like ordering a pizza for takeout but then not receiving any further info on whether the order was received, when said pizza will be ready for pickup, the accuracy of the order, what the cost was, and so on. Marketing can positively influence the customer experience by helping develop a strategy to inform customers of next steps, as well as helping define service level agreements (SLAs) and crafting any correspondence that is needed. This is a great time to remind the new client of the value of your solution and help validate their purchase, especially if they might have sticker shock with a big-ticket item. This is one of the first interactions new customers have with you and your company, so put the best foot forward. Even if the information will be coming from sales or customer success, marketing can and should help develop it.

Another way marketing can influence closed-won deals is through developing a plan and content to take the customer through *next steps*. If there are things the customer needs to prepare, help format this document with the customer success team. This ensures consistent messaging, makes sure expectations are set properly, and provides continuity with look and feel. I recently bought a new house, and while the builder of the community reached out immediately to welcome us, I didn't hear from my agent for weeks! I literally wasn't sure of next steps. Should I write a check now? Was this really a done deal? Was my agent going to do the walk-through for me? What the hell is a walk-through? Was his job done now that he had his commission? If I ran the realtor's marketing team, things would be a little different, let me tell you!

There are so many other touchpoints and ways marketing professionals can help in this stage of the buyer's journey. Can you develop an email welcome series or kits that get mailed out? Maybe you can repurpose how-to videos or an on-demand product webinar that dives deep into features. Think about what would help create an amazing experience for the customer, and see if you can influence that experience.

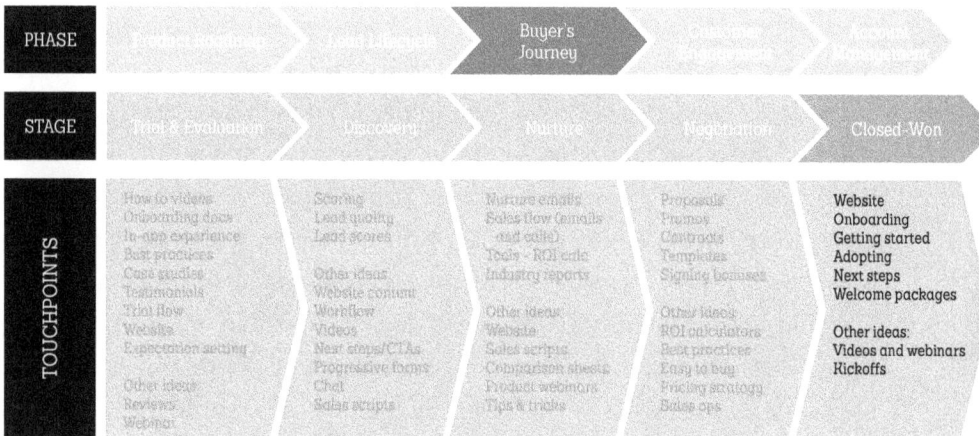

| PHASE | Product Roadmap | Trial Lifecycle | Buyer's Journey | Outcome Engagement | Account Management |
|---|---|---|---|---|---|
| STAGE | Trial & Evaluation | Discovery | Nurture | Negotiation | Closed-Won |
| TOUCHPOINTS | How to videos<br>Onboarding docs<br>In-app experience<br>Best practices<br>Case studies<br>Testimonials<br>Trial flow<br>Website<br>Expectation setting<br><br>Other ideas:<br>Reviews<br>Webinar | Scoring<br>Lead quality<br>Lead scores<br><br>Other ideas:<br>Website content<br>Workflow<br>Videos<br>Next steps/CTAs<br>Progressive forms<br>Chat<br>Sales scripts | Nurture emails<br>Sales flow (emails and calls)<br>Tools - ROI calc<br>Industry reports<br><br>Other ideas:<br>Website<br>Sales scripts<br>Comparison sheets<br>Product webinars<br>Tips & tricks | Proposals<br>Promos<br>Contracts<br>Templates<br>Signing bonuses<br><br>Other ideas:<br>ROI calculators<br>Best practices<br>Easy to buy<br>Pricing strategy<br>Sales ops | Website<br>Onboarding<br>Getting started<br>Adopting<br>Next steps<br>Welcome packages<br><br>Other ideas:<br>Videos and webinars<br>Kickoffs |

Closed-Won Touchpoints

Let's face it, most marketing professionals are not salespeople. I know I am not. And I don't want to be. But that doesn't mean you can't help the sales team as prospects weave their way through the buyer's cycle. You're probably influencing this phase already. Maybe you weren't thinking about areas of influence as touchpoints, and maybe you didn't know how to identify them. Or maybe you didn't consider how they fit into the overall go-to-market strategy or your overall marketing strategy and plan. Maybe some of these touchpoints are things you already do on a daily basis. But now I'd like you to look at them from a different perspective.

When prospects are in trial, you can provide sales with content and collateral that will help them sell better, and help prospects decide to buy faster. When that prospect moves to the discovery stage, you can better qualify leads through lead scoring and developing functional workflows that move leads through the funnel properly. For longer sales cycle products and solutions, when the cycle might take over six months, you can provide sales with tools and content to continue nurturing and educating prospects. And even as prospects enter the actual negotiation and purchase phase, you can help by developing scripts and templates. You can influence pricing and the feature bundles that are created and shared on the website. Once prospects have converted into clients, you can help ensure a smooth transition with welcome kits, "getting started" content, and so much more.

Again, you may already be doing a lot of these things. You now just need to be more intentional and see where you can have *more* influence. Make sure you educate your sales team on your marketing programs (both in the lead lifecycle phase as well as the buyer's journey phase), explain why you are doing them, and set expectations for when resulting leads will mature enough to move from phase to phase and stage to stage. For example, you as a marketing professional know that leads from events take longer to nurture and grow than leads from people filling out forms on your website. So when you talk to sales, help them understand this; it will help explain the content you are building and also the priority contact list you might be developing for sales.

Marketing should help define the workflow of leads, as well as create programs and content that ensure prospects have what they need to continue moving through the stages of the buyer's journey.

# CHAPTER 6

# Swayed: Customer Engagement

The job of customer success is to implement the product and onboard customers. Once the customer has been familiarized with the product, customer success works closely with that customer to make sure end users adopt and use the product the way it was intended. Some folks from the team will provide technical support, while others will focus on keeping and growing customers (i.e., increasing usage, increasing revenue, and decreasing churn). This is all done through successful customer onboarding, ongoing training, engagement (updating the client on new feature releases, for example), retention, and a focus on customer satisfaction (i.e., giving the customer what they need and expect or, even better, overdelivering). The customer success team is usually the first point of contact when issues arise, and so they work closely with engineering to define and prioritize bug fixes. And to ensure the voice of the customer is heard when defining product features, customer success should also work closely with product on the roadmap to help prioritize and build better solutions. They already work closely with marketing on customer communications regarding releases, issues, and best practices. And, when it comes time, they help us identify prospective advocates for testimonials, case studies, and thought leader programs. They act as the voice of the customer, and as such they should own customer communication in conjunction with marketing to disseminate information on new functionality, features, and tools. The community manager, if there is one, usually resides in the customer success team and owns the knowledge base, forums, and community, although sometimes this position falls in marketing.

As with the other phases of the customer journey, there are many touchpoints here that marketing can influence.

## STAGES OF THE CUSTOMER ENGAGEMENT PHASE

Since this book is focused on B2B, the likely first stages in this phase will be installing or implementing the solution and then getting customers to use it. Once the customer is using the solution, you then need to provide them with support. Depending on the size and structure of your support team, and the complexity of the product itself, you might have specific tactics to retain customers and reduce churn. This usually falls on the customer success team, but everyone can help here, from ensuring expectations are properly set to developing ease of use in the product itself. You may also have an account manager who is focused on expanding the size of the deal and renewals. It's never too early to start thinking about how the renewal will work—specifically who within the customer account will need to be involved—and start building that relationship. The final part of this stage is obtaining referrals, reviews, and other feedback that support the company's success.

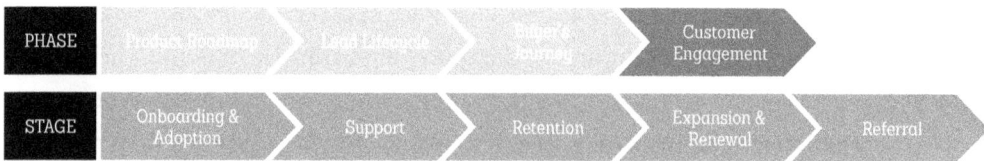

| PHASE | Product Roadmap | Lead Lifecycle | Buyer's Journey | Customer Engagement | |
|---|---|---|---|---|---|
| STAGE | Onboarding & Adoption | Support | Retention | Expansion & Renewal | Referral |

Customer Engagement Phases and Stages

# IDENTIFYING TOUCHPOINTS IN THE CUSTOMER ENGAGEMENT PHASE

Hopefully you already have some great ideas on how you can influence ongoing customer success. This phase is a great opportunity for marketing professionals to connect more directly with customers and thus better understand and represent the voice of the customer. Not only can marketing provide a lot for this audience by way of up-to-date content, but marketers can gain a lot too by building long-lasting relationships with customers.

## Onboarding & Adoption Touchpoints

Onboarding and adoption is the stage where the product has been installed and the customer is actively engaged in using your product. For SaaS companies, we often measure monthly active users as one metric of success. While it is customer success's role to get customers up and running, marketing can help with content and documentation along the way to ensure a smooth onboarding experience. The more customers are using the product, the more likely they are to renew or purchase additional licenses or upgrades.

When it comes to channels, there are several areas for marketing to tackle. The website is now potentially the customer login site, so how can you make it easier (and not mess up your bounce rate)? The community or knowledge base will become pivotal for getting customers to adopt and use the product. Marketing can help develop and produce programs such as product webinars. And this is the perfect audience to develop and share content around best practices. (These don't have to be new pieces of content. They can be repurposed from other programs and campaigns. See the next section on repeatability to learn more.)

Let's look at some specific examples of touchpoints and how you can have more influence. Take *how-to videos*, for example. Whether in developing and producing the actual videos or simply reviewing scripts for customer success, marketing can properly set expectations and ensure consistent messaging. At Autodesk, we saw that customers were "getting stuck" in one feature of the product. While we did have plenty of comprehensive how-to videos and training, customers didn't appear to be leveraging them to get over the hurdle. When we dug a little deeper, we realized they didn't have time to watch a sixty-minute training video; they just wanted the piece they needed to continue using the solution at that point in time. We broke the longer video into easy-to-digest one- to two-minute snippets, which we tied directly to the product through Intercom. And if they got stuck in a particular section of the workflow, the option to look at the video would pop up.

There are plenty of opportunities like this. I know you already have a lot on your plate, but it behooves everyone to ensure customers use your solution. If the solution is not adopted to the intended extent (not enough end users utilizing the solution or using it to its fullest capabilities), it can impact CAC, CLTV, and churn. Also, if the end users aren't using all the features, functionality, and modules, they're not experiencing the product to its fullest. Marketing professionals should do anything they can to get clients adopting and using the product, as this will only increase ROI and revenue. It's important.

So where else can marketing professionals help and influence here? Well, believe it or not, sometimes the issues customers face have a simple solution marketing can help with. I once consulted for a company that told me selling the product wasn't the problem; getting customers to adopt and use the product was. This company had a 50 percent adoption rate, which meant half the folks that paid for the solution were not using it. It led to unhappy customers and a high rate of churn, and therefore a lower CLTV, more headaches for the success team, bad reviews, missed revenue targets, and more.

Turns out there were two main issues, the first of which was a bit laughable: It wasn't clear where to go to log in to the product.

Apparently, customers needed to go to a different application to log in, but instead they were showing up on the main website, couldn't figure out where to go, and would then just say, "F&%$ it!" Would it have killed this company to add a "Log In" button on the main website? More likely it would have killed the business if they hadn't added the button. Which they did. That was the easy fix.

The next issue was more complicated. The audience they were selling the solution to was different from the target that would actually be using the solution. Basically, it would be like your manager going off and buying a tool for you to use and then forcing you to use it, even though you might not feel you needed the tool, or you would have preferred a different one. My answer to this was to provide a welcome kit that could be shared with new users when they received their initial login information. It explained what the product did and how it would make the end user's life so much easier. It briefly listed the benefits of using the tool and included links to training videos. I then advised the company to create product webinars and office hours, specifically to help end users realize the full potential of the product.

We as marketers can help with a lot at this stage. From initial and ongoing training to webinars to product updates and content—it's good for marketing to be involved in the development of all these documents and tools. Not only does it help with adoption; it helps ensure consistency in how customers implement and use your product.

Hopefully, you can weave some of this into plans you already have in place, so as to not add too much work. Or you can take what is developed and leverage it elsewhere. For example, can you take the information from the product webinars and turn those into how-to videos and guides? If you are doing product webinars, can you open them up to noncustomers as part of your nurture plan? Whenever possible, don't work more; just work smart.

As with all the other phases and stages, the number of touchpoints marketing can influence here are extensive. To think these through, ask: How can we help set expectations on the website and through the welcome kits? Can we help with the training content? How can we better engage and capture customer feedback? What can we do to help the customer success team, the customer, and our company?

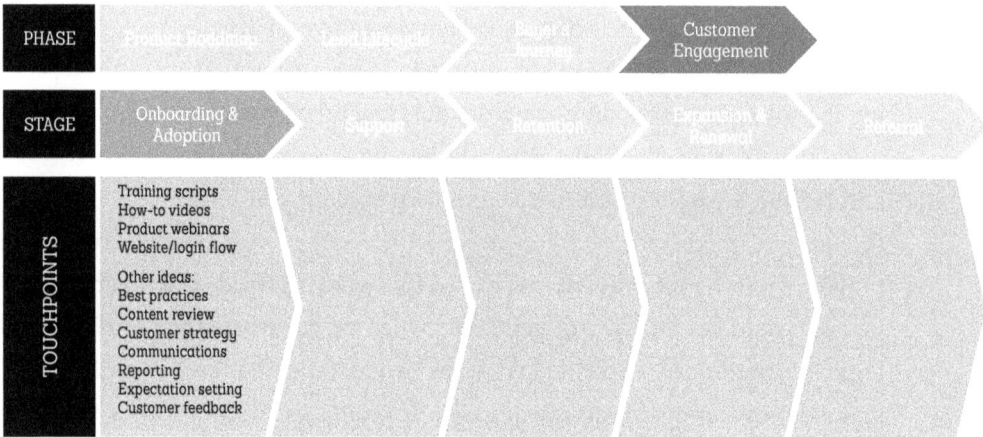

| PHASE | Product Readiness | Lead Lifecycle | Buyer's Journey | Customer Engagement |
|---|---|---|---|---|
| STAGE | Onboarding & Adoption | Support | Retention | Expansion & Renewal | Referral |
| TOUCHPOINTS | Training scripts<br>How-to videos<br>Product webinars<br>Website/login flow<br><br>Other ideas:<br>Best practices<br>Content review<br>Customer strategy<br>Communications<br>Reporting<br>Expectation setting<br>Customer feedback | | | | |

Onboarding & Adoption Touchpoints

## Support Touchpoints

For obvious reasons, marketing doesn't own the actual support of our customers, but marketing likely owns the vehicles and mediums through which customers engage with us for support. Because of this, it benefits everyone for marketing to work directly with customer success to ensure workflows are functioning properly and customers have easy access to the tools and information they need to be successful.

There are surprisingly many opportunities for marketing to influence the actual support and success of your customers. From a channel perspective, chat provides a means for customers to communicate with support. And marketing is likely providing a lot of content for the community in the form of tips and tricks, best practices, and use cases. Also, from a content perspective, marketing is usually involved in developing the FAQs and reports, even if it's from a branding or look-and-feel viewpoint.

Let's work through some of these specific touchpoint examples. As we discussed before, *chat* can be leveraged on the website and in the product. Regardless of where chat is located, it needs to be set up for ease of use while also ensuring information, problems, issues, and resolutions are being tracked and recorded. In addition, chat provides opportunities to disseminate content consistently. Marketing can develop the flow for the chat tool, like Drift or Intercom, and develop documentation to "automate" support. For example, if three questions keep coming up repeatedly for customer support, can you help create a FAQ or guide, then add those questions and answers to the chat tool, automating the Q&A process? If support spends 20 percent of their time helping people reset their password, can you create a script in the chat bot that helps people reset it without having to go to a support person, thus leveraging the customer support team's expertise for more critical things? I guarantee you, your support team will *love* you for this!

Think about how marketing can influence the *community* and knowledge bases, which are great places for customers to self-educate, interact with other users and experts, and get answers. They're also great places for marketing to showcase best practices through tips and tricks, case studies, aggregated "industry" reports, and testimonials. Even if the marketing organization doesn't own the community platform, there is still an opportunity to create content that will keep customers happy and engaged. The community site is also a great place to find happy (and unhappy) customers. Try doing a survey on your community site, and by all means stalk the community site for thought leaders, quotes, potential case studies, advocates, and more.

Another great touchpoint is *webinars*. Can you help produce and promote product webinars? Or even build out product tours to help with the actual onboarding? Ask your customer support team what else they need to be more successful. Hopefully you can build these webinars to be used in multiple ways for multiple audiences.

By now you are probably sick of me saying it, but there are so many touchpoints here for you to help your customer support team and your customers.

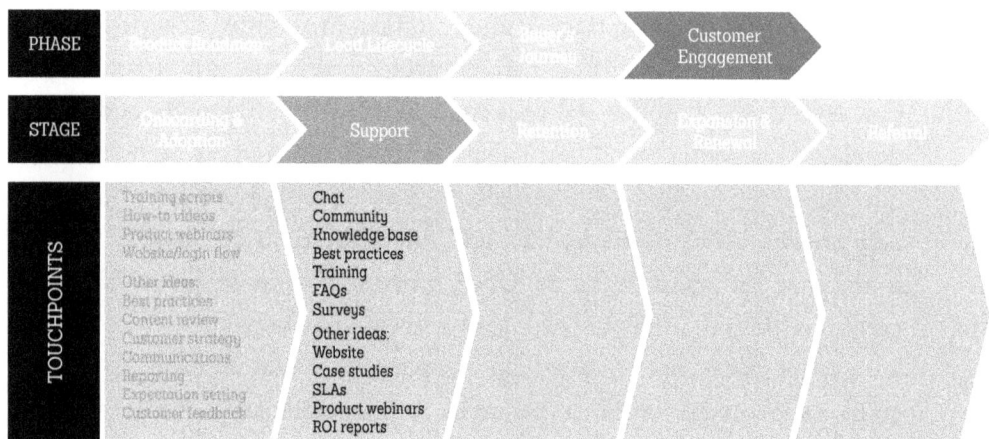

| PHASE | Product Roadmap | Lead Lifecycle | Buyer's Journey | Customer Engagement |
| --- | --- | --- | --- | --- |
| STAGE | Onboarding & Adoption | Support | Retention | Expansion & Renewal | Referral |
| TOUCHPOINTS | Training scripts<br>How-to videos<br>Product webinars<br>Website/login flow<br>Other ideas:<br>Best practices<br>Content review<br>Customer strategy<br>Communications<br>Reporting<br>Expectation setting<br>Customer feedback | Chat<br>Community<br>Knowledge base<br>Best practices<br>Training<br>FAQs<br>Surveys<br>Other ideas:<br>Website<br>Case studies<br>SLAs<br>Product webinars<br>ROI reports | | | |

Support Touchpoints

## Retention Touchpoints

Customer success is usually held accountable for retention, but sales, product, and marketing all need to share ownership. This stage of the customer journey provides marketing a great opportunity to learn more about customers and provide them with a platform to showcase their successes. From best practices and tips and tricks to Q&A and "Ask Me Anything" webinars, marketing is already very much involved in this phase. So let's just do it more, and better. The goal is to keep customers happy and continually learning how to better use your solution.

In addition to some of the touchpoints previously listed, there are plenty of other areas for marketing to influence. The community and product itself are key channels to consider. As far as programs are concerned, product releases are a great opportunity to have more impact. Get involved early in the process and consider how to market the product directly to your current customer base. There's nothing worse than a customer finding out about a new feature or functionality from someone other than you. So how can you ensure they know? Through newsletters, emails, in-app notifications, and product release webinars. These are the same webinars you would likely use to entice *new* customers, so you're not duplicating efforts.

Again, the main goal here is to keep your customers up to date on how great your product is and help retain them. As a touchpoint, working with your product managers to share best practices helps the end user be more effective in how they use your product. Plus, it gives marketing the opportunity to highlight champion users and companies, who are generally happy to showcase their expertise. You can share best practices in the community, through FAQs, in written and video case studies, in monthly newsletters, and more. Better yet, get your customers talking about best practices. In doing this, you can elevate them as thought leaders in the industry, giving them a competitive advantage. This all leads to happy customers who want to stick with you for the long haul. This kind of loyalty helps with not only retention but also expansion and renewal.

Another great touchpoint where marketing can significantly help is *Q&A sessions*. One reason I love these types of sessions is that they can be done in a variety of formats and channels. You could do it on Facebook or LinkedIn Live. You could have "office hours" in Slack, if that's where your end users hang out. Or you could do a special Ask Me Anything or Ask the Expert event where your CTO joins the chat in your community. Or have one of your most knowledgeable customers pop in to talk about some of the cool things they've been able to do with your product. Not only will these help the customer be more successful; it will build loyalty. Then you can take these questions and answers and repurpose them as FAQs, blog posts, or social media content.

Another critical way marketing can help in this stage of the customer journey is by developing a *communication strategy*, and possibly implementing it, for customers. Take this conversation I overheard one day while at Webgility. The customer had asked for a specific feature, and the response from the customer support rep was "Oh yeah, we added that to the product last year. Let me help you find it . . ." *Dang,* I thought. *We listen to customers, build a feature they've been asking for, and then fail to let them know this great feature exists.* I'm not picking on Webgility, because I have seen this over and over again, at large and small companies. Since marketing owns communications, people assume marketing owns disseminating information to customers. But that's not always true. Whatever the current reality is at your company, make sure there is a strategy (monthly newsletters, product releases with webinars, quarterly roadmap updates) and a true owner of the function.

Think about other ways you can help customers engage with the product and your company. Can you help determine what should be in a dashboard or send out nightly reports? Can you share help articles with customers to make them more efficient? Are you communicating with them on new features and functions, and how to use them, making your product even more beneficial? Ask customers, why did you choose us? And then make sure you are fulfilling that need.

Unfortunately, not many companies invest resources in customer retention. Which is too bad, because you've already spent the time and money to capture these folks as customers; you don't want to lose them. Having a customer success team isn't always enough. If you're lucky and work for a company that has a community manager or customer marketing manager, yay for you. If retention is an issue for your company, you might want to push for the hiring of one of these roles. But if you do, you might want to consider calling it something else, something an executive would better understand, like plain ole marketing manager. According to industry expert Ann Handley, if executives don't understand marketing in general, when you ask for very specific, niche resources, "they just shut down."

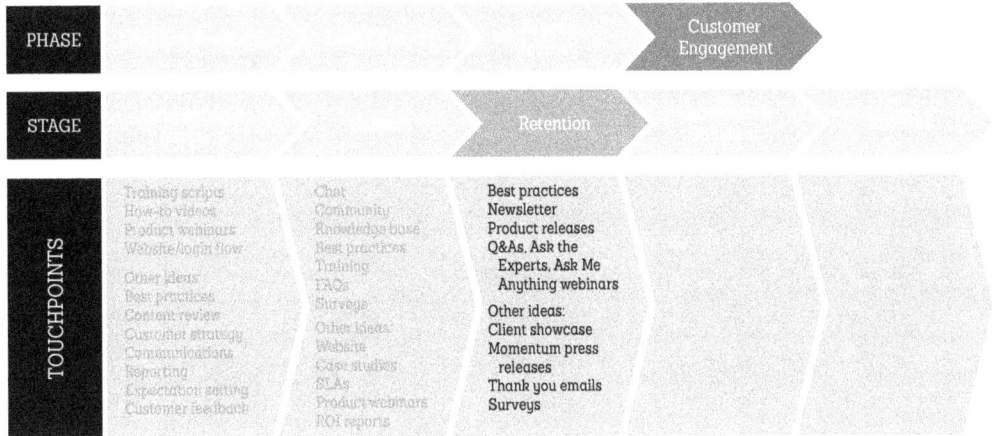

| PHASE | | | | Customer Engagement | |
|---|---|---|---|---|---|
| STAGE | | | Retention | | |
| TOUCHPOINTS | Training scripts How-to videos Product webinars Website/login flow Other ideas: Best practices Content review Customer strategy Communications Reporting Expectation setting Customer feedback | Chat Community Knowledge base Best practices Training FAQs Surveys Other ideas: Website Case studies SLAs Product webinars ROI reports | Best practices Newsletter Product releases Q&As, Ask the Experts, Ask Me Anything webinars Other ideas: Client showcase Momentum press releases Thank you emails Surveys | | |

Retention Touchpoints

## Expansion & Renewal Touchpoints

When we get to the expansion stage of the customer journey, there is incredible potential for marketing to influence. What I mean by *expansion* is that customers have added on to the original contract. Maybe the client added more users or bought another pack of seat licenses. Maybe the contract was expanded to include another department or a subsidiary. Or maybe the customer opted for a higher tier or level of support or was upsold new components. It's always hard to justify hiring a customer marketing manager, as I have mentioned, but for B2B companies this is a no-brainer and has real benefits when you're looking at how to expand a current contract. Regardless, marketing professionals should develop a nurture program for customers to ensure expansion (and retention) of those accounts. I've talked about nurturing prospects in various stages of the customer journey with both marketing and sales, but it's also important to nurture the customer so they understand the current and future value of your solution. This will help expand the overall contract and ensure they renew when it's time (or better yet, even before it's time, because they love you that much).

As with other components of the customer engagement phase, there are lot of areas where marketing is probably already involved. The key is for you to identify touchpoints where you or your fellow marketing professionals can impact the overall company strategy. It's one thing for you to tweet about a feature that was just released. It is quite another to develop, run, and own the Advisory Board, for example. From a program standpoint, maybe you already help with user groups and meetups by researching venues. But how can you take it up a notch so that the user group or meetup will be more effective, especially in expanding the current contract with the customer? Marketing should be communicating product status and product update release information (with a consistent cadence); sharing best practices and use cases; helping the customer understand their ROI via emailed reports; showcasing customers in your programs through case studies, press releases, and webinars; always making sure the websites are up to date, useful, and comprehensive . . . I could go on and on, but hopefully you get the point. There's a lot we do here, and all of it will help with renewal when the time comes. Here are some ideas on touchpoints you might consider.

As mentioned, there are a lot of things marketing professionals can do here (communications, more training, product webinars, etc.), but I'm going to focus on a few programs and a content strategy I think are helpful. Ones that will really make customers feel the love. And feel heard.

The first is *special events*. Nothing says "I love you" to a customer more than inviting them to a special VIP event (okay, maybe having a product that actually works says "I love you" even more, but after that comes VIP treatment).

Give them a few drinks, a nice meal, and a cool wine opener, then ask them for input. I like to call this an Advisory Board. In addition to likely owning the logistics of this type of event, marketing professionals can develop it into something customers look forward to. Marketing can also help in expectation setting, especially around new feature asks. "Dear customers, we love you, but we aren't going to add an espresso machine into our new blade servers. But way to think outside of the box. And here is a gift card to Starbucks. XOXO."

In addition to helping develop the event itself and setting expectations, marketing can also capture information discussed in the event, share out notes and updates, and work with product to ensure these ideas are being considered and prioritized properly—what should loop back into the go-to-market strategy, and what should be tabled for the time being. I once worked for a company that, twice a year for at least three years, had a meetup with customers, sort of pretended to listen to them, didn't take them seriously, changed nothing in the product, didn't report back to the customer, and then repeated the process all over again every six months. Pro tip: If your product team is not going to use the information gathered from trusted customers to improve the product, I don't recommend doing Advisory Boards. Nothing says "I don't love you; I might actually hate you" more than that.

Other events you might consider setting up include a user group, an annual conference, and regional meetups. It's likely marketing will end up producing these events, and yes, that is more work, especially if you don't have a customer marketing manager handy. But happy customers are loyal customers, which leads to retention, expansion, and renewals.

You might also consider doing some kind of special customer *training*. It's one thing to do product webinars, guides, and how-to videos, but specifically designing these for your customers, and sharing them at an invite-only event, can not only train them on advanced features but also make them feel special. You could even release features to them before the general public—a little sneak peek at what is coming soon. Pro tip: Sneak peeks also act as a way to test new features before they go live to the general population.

Marketing can also become more involved in the actual relationship with the customer. Relationship building is key, and while technically the account manager and customer success rep "own" this, marketing professionals should think about the relationship from the standpoint of the company. Here's the ol' "put yourself in their shoes" scenario. You have a one-year contract for a contact-appending service through a company. It's super expensive, but you need it. Once it's deployed, you never hear from anyone again at the company, even when you reach out for help. Now, eleven months into your twelve-month contract, you suddenly get a package of warm cookies and cold milk with a contract for another twelve months (true story). While the cookies were a nice touch, not hearing from anyone for eleven months was annoying. I actually did *not* renew with them and went with a competitor that had been courting me for six months, checking back in every month. Building relationships with customers, especially as a B2B company with one-year or multi-year contracts, is critical.

Marketing professionals can work with account executives or customer success managers to develop a twelve-month plan (assuming you have a one-year contract) that continues to build on the relationship. Send them cookies in month one, not month eleven. Look at the customer nurture programs and think about how you can help the account executives implement them better. And track as much data as you can along the way to show your relevance.

What else, what else? Can you do a customer engagement program? Have a special VIP dinner in conjunction with an upcoming industry event? Maybe include certain customers or users in an in-person or virtual roadmap and vision discussion? Understand how your customers might expand (more users versus existing users paying for new features), and then develop programs with that in mind, especially as it relates to the go-to-market strategy. A company can bring in revenue by acquiring new customers and by keeping current customers. Make sure this is part of the overall equation and strategy.

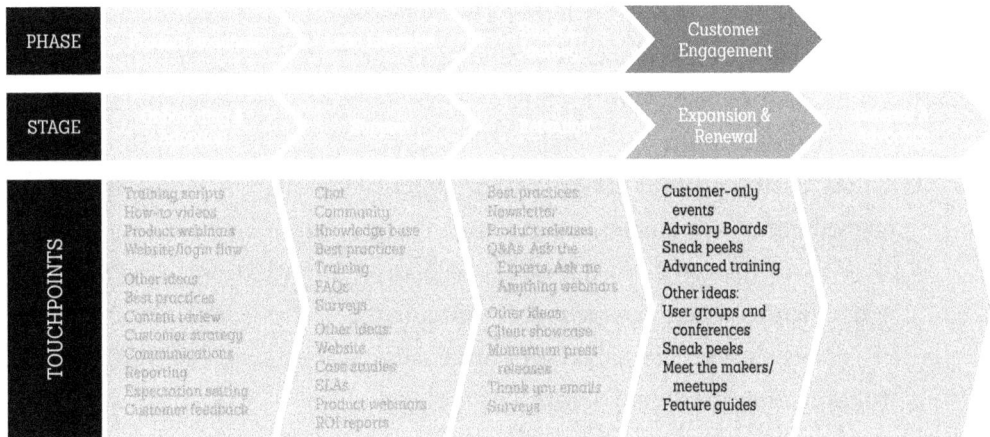

Expansion & Renewal

## Referral & Advocacy Touchpoints

Another area marketing professionals should heavily influence is referral and advocacy.

The customer success team needs to understand overall customer performance and recognize areas of friction and opportunity for the product. The account management team needs to build a good relationship with customers and have a good sense of not only customer satisfaction but adoption and usage. This is done through surveys, including Net Promoter and customer satisfaction scores, ticket completion, and so on. Working hand in hand with customer success and the account management teams, marketing can ensure the surveys are administered and identify potential advocates within the customer account.

Here are some touchpoints you might want to consider. Then I'll dive deep into some examples.

One of the easiest ways to engage with customers, while gaining a tremendous amount of information that everyone in the company can leverage, is through *surveys*. Remember our friend Fred Reichheld? Well, this is his baby. The NPS essentially measures the loyalty of your customers. You've all done an NPS survey, whether you knew it or not. "On a scale of 1 to 10, how likely are you to recommend product blah blah?" This survey provides a snapshot of how customers feel about your product, which can in turn help renewal rates, expansion, churn, and more. That is, if you actually look at them. I can't tell you how many times I have seen NPS reports with no action taken. At minimum, the promoters from an NPS survey are perfect targets for advocacy, case studies, and other programs that marketing owns.

It goes without saying, but I'll say it anyway. Take the promoters and turn them into thought leaders and advocates. Ask them to do reviews and case studies. Set up some kind of referral program for them that benefits them both as individuals (send them a gift card) and as a representative of their company (bump them up to a higher support tier or provide a discount when they renew). You want to recognize these people and then reward them for their loyalty and ongoing love.

| PHASE | | | | Customer Engagement | |
| STAGE | | | | | Referral & Advocacy |

| TOUCHPOINTS | Training scripts How-to videos Product webinars Website/log-in flow Other ideas: Best practices Content review Customer strategy Communications Reporting Expectation setting Customer feedback | Chat Community Knowledge base Best practices Training FAQs Surveys Other ideas: Website Case studies SLAs Product webinars ROI reports | Best practices Newsletter Product releases Q&As: Ask the Experts, Ask Me Anything webinars Other ideas: Client showcase Momentum press releases Thank you emails Surveys | Customer-only events Advisory Boards Sneak peeks Advanced training Other ideas: User groups and conferences Sneak peeks Meet the makers meetups Feature guides | Surveys Advocates Thought leader programs Other ideas: Affiliate and referral programs Reward programs Engage community High touch outreach |

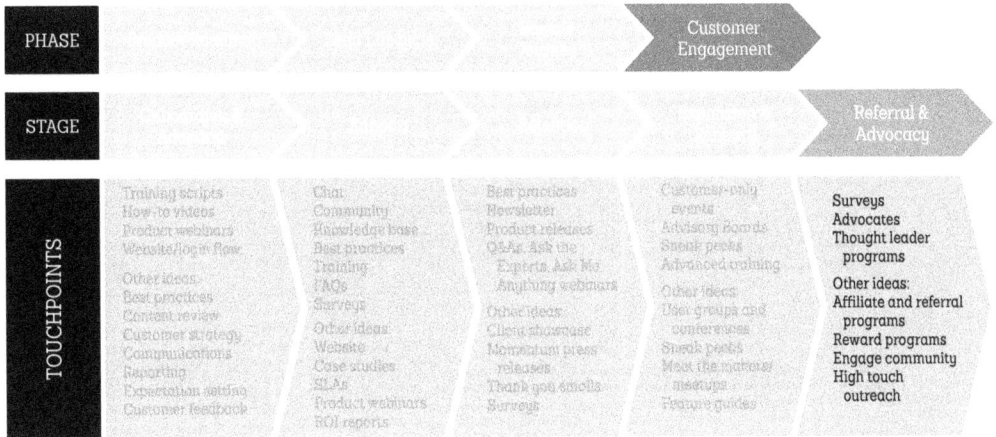

Referral & Advocacy Touchpoints

I know this sounds like a lot. You already have a ton on your plate, and now I'm telling you to step it up even more. And we haven't even gotten to the product blueprint phase of the customer journey. But don't quit on me. In later chapters, I'll show you how you can do more faster, boost your efficiency, and gain trust and influence throughout the company.

# CHAPTER 7

# Swayable: Product Blueprint

As we have seen, there are so many touchpoints within the customer journey that marketing could and should participate in. The last phase we'll look at—the product blueprint phase—is one of the most important areas of collaboration. While the product is inherent in all other phases of the customer journey, this phase specifically looks at the product strategy, definition, development, and release. As marketers, we want to think about the friction points customers might experience, where users get stuck in the product, and what features are being utilized or underutilized.

Understanding the product blueprint is critical for marketing, as it helps us understand how our customers are using the product, what areas marketing needs to focus on, and how to incorporate these learnings in the development of the go-to-market strategy. It also helps marketers build out the right programs and the right content— for sales, customer success, and marketing.

## STAGES OF THE PRODUCT BLUEPRINT PHASE

There are a lot of layers in the product blueprint phase of the customer journey, especially if you consider (as I do) that product strategy, as an outcome of the overall go-to-market strategy, should be owned by marketing. To make it easy, I have built out a flow in this phase with the stages I usually identify for the type of company and product I work with: strategy >> definition >> development >> product releases.

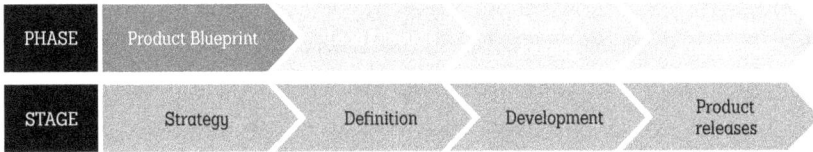

| PHASE | Product Blueprint | | | |
|---|---|---|---|---|
| STAGE | Strategy | Definition | Development | Product releases |

Product Blueprint Phase

# PRODUCT STRATEGY AND DEFINITION

## Overall Strategy Touchpoints

The product team is responsible for developing the overall product vision and strategy based on the company's business strategy and go-to-market strategy. Note that I say product is driven by the go-to-market strategy, not the other way around. The product team does need to set the direction for what the end state of the product will be, though. Marketing can help define the product by providing customer feedback gathered from surveys, tickets, and conversations (yes, you should have this information at the ready). And marketing can also help here by focusing the product team and the product itself on the overall company performance goals. You know—strategy.

The website, the customer support platform, and your community will be the biggest channels you can look at to have influence in this stage. These channels are where information from customers comes in and goes out. Product requests, bugs, and tickets all come through one or more of these. And often the tools to collect this information are located on the website—like chat, for example. If you think about how you develop your brand and awareness, these are all marketing programs you should start to build back in this phase, long before it hits the lead lifecycle phase. From a content standpoint, there is likely product documentation, including product "brochures," that talks about features, value propositions, and differentiators. Hmm, that looks like something marketing could help with. Now let's look at specific examples of touchpoints related to product strategy.

Ah, *feature requests*. What a great touchpoint for marketing to focus on. Product often gets long lists of feature requests, including must-haves, need-to-haves, we-will-leave-you-if-we-don't-haves. You name it. Some of these feature requests come directly from customers, while others come from your own sales and customer success teams as a result of their conversations with prospects and customers. What's critical to understand is that features help close deals and keep current customers happy. Therefore, marketing should use metrics to help product understand if a feature or function will improve conversion rates. For example, if the data shows that there were ten closed-lost deals valued at $10 million, with the reason for their not closing being the product didn't do XYZ, then maybe that feature request should be taken more seriously. Conversely, the data might indicate what features aren't a high priority right now and should come in a later release.

Always think of touchpoints from the standpoint of company goals and what metrics are needed to ensure you are on track. What is the potential CLTV, what is the CAC, and how do these play into the overall strategy? You should always know these numbers (along with conversion and ROI numbers). If you know what it costs to acquire the customer and you know what they are worth over their entire life as a customer, you can help better define the product and strategy. Let's say you want to increase CLTV. This can be done by increasing the overall value of the product to ensure a longer life with the customer and a higher price garnered for the solution. You can help identify areas where value can be added based on customer feedback.

Now let's say you want to reduce CAC. Consider what can be done in the overall trial experience to reduce time to close and, at the same time, lead prospects to a higher price point purchase. Can the time for the evaluator to get to the aha moment be accelerated, so the deal closes faster? Can marketing develop such amazing content, systems, and processes that you can move some targets from a high-touch to a low- or no-touch sale? Wouldn't that be a coup? Unfortunately, you won't get commission for the sales, but it's still a big win for you and marketing.

There are countless other ways marketing professionals can influence the product strategy. Maybe you can help product and the engineers really understand the revenue targets so they're taken into consideration when defining the roadmap. Marketing can also ensure there is *brand alignment* between the product itself and the corporate brand. Have you ever signed up for an online service from a company's website and been taken to the product site or application that looks nothing like the site you just came from? In the back of your head you're thinking, *Oh crap, what did I really just buy, and who has my credit card info?* Work with your product team to make sure the branding, messaging, and look and feel are consistent across all your sites, platforms, and product.

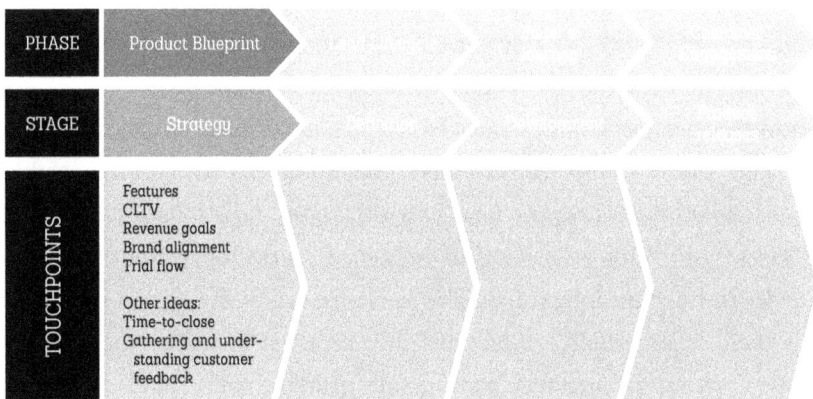

| PHASE | Product Blueprint |
|---|---|
| STAGE | Strategy |
| TOUCHPOINTS | Features<br>CLTV<br>Revenue goals<br>Brand alignment<br>Trial flow<br><br>Other ideas:<br>Time-to-close<br>Gathering and under-<br>standing customer<br>feedback |

Product Strategy Touchpoints

## Product Definition Touchpoints

The strategy and ideation stage of building out the product blueprint looks closely at how to solve a problem. The definition stage looks at how to create the solution. This might seem like more of a product/engineering-only area, but there are actually several ways marketing professionals can influence the direction the solution takes.

Customer feedback plays heavily into product definition. Any channel where you can capture this information would be a good place to find some touchpoint nuggets. These channels can include obvious ones—for example, your customer support platform, like Jira. Or they may be less obvious, like your social media channel, where your customers are commenting about your product and support. From a program standpoint, you have some options here as they relate to branding. And of course there is the ol' NPS survey and the information that can be gleaned from that. When it comes to content, some touchpoints to think about center around messaging and particularly value propositions.

As it is when looking at the overall corporate mission, it's important to think about *brand and messaging* when defining the solution here. If your messaging is on how you can save your customers time, that should be part of the solution the product team is building. In general, customers aren't looking for a specific product; rather, they are looking for a product that elicits a specific result. Therefore, helping product understand the overall messaging (i.e., the value you claim, how this product differentiates from the competition, etc.) is critical.

Let's look at *prioritization* as a touchpoint. Now, you may think, *Can something intangible like "prioritization" be a touchpoint?* I say, "Heck yeah." It's your Map of Influence, so do what you need to in order to be more influential. This is always a fun discussion internally as well as externally—what are the must-haves versus the nice-to-haves? What feature will push a sale over the fence, and what lack of feature will cause a prospect or customer to walk away? When I worked at Oracle, we discussed all the many features that could have been developed at the requests of prospects and customers. These were huge corporations essentially asking for bespoke solutions. We've all experienced that: "But my company is special, so the solution needs to be unique." But really, are these companies that special or different? Since you and your company already have your target audience selected, I'm guessing these companies either aren't significantly different or aren't actually your target. What Larry would say is give them everything they *need*, not everything they *want*. Such a simple way of looking at it. Assuming you work with a good product (and if you don't, here's your chance to help change that), customers are looking to your company for best practices and the value your solution brings.

As a marketing professional, you can help guide the company discussion of which features to develop and prioritize, by referring to industry best practices and thought leader content you've been creating, as well as data that helps determine how to define the product. For example, if sales says a deal was lost due to lack of feature Y, and support tickets validate this, it's a good indication of a must-have. Even if you don't have access to the data, you can still influence the process by asking a simple question of everyone involved: "Is this something customers absolutely need or something they want? Is it a must-have or a nice-to-have?"

Expanding the conversation with product and engineering is a great way to expand your influence. Not only do we as marketing professionals need to help them understand the significance of the messaging, we need to help them understand it in context. I believe a lot of friction in organizations could be solved simply by sharing things in *context*. Does it ever feel as if you are talking to a five-year-old while at work? "But why, why do we have to take a nap now?" Okay, maybe more like: "Why do we have to figure out a way to reduce onboarding time by two days?" Your response of "Because I said so" doesn't work any better here than it does at home. You need to help the product team and engineers understand *why* reducing onboarding time by two days is significant. Maybe your differentiator is a faster implementation time. Or maybe that expectation was set early on. This goes back to your go-to-market strategy and why you need to influence it.

I was once in a meeting where the CTO essentially said one of the features I was asking for was not significant enough to reprioritize at that time (in other words, to delay other features). When I showed him the impact doing this feature now would have on increasing revenue in twelve months, he was shocked. Right then and there, he immediately shifted the team's schedule. With a three-minute conversation, sharing context, we likely increased the company revenue significantly. Heck yeah. More of that, please! This is worth emphasizing: To help the product team see things from your perspective, always show them the significance of your input and requests in context (preferably as it relates to revenue).

Other touchpoints in this stage might include gathering and *understanding customer feedback* or implementing a mechanism to capture this information. You can also look at brand alignment (i.e., make sure what is being built fits within the company strategy and mission). Ask how you can leverage NPS here as well, and also what role you can play when it comes to Advisory Boards.

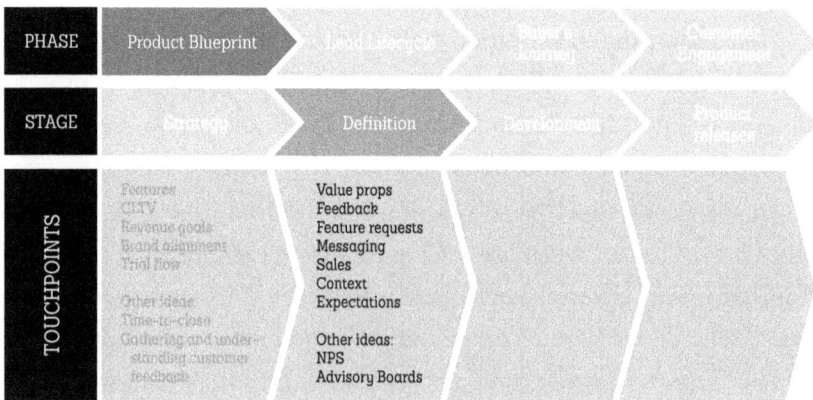

Product Definition Touchpoints

## Product Roadmap and Development Touchpoints

The product roadmap guides product and engineering in terms of priorities and timeline and helps sales and marketing prepare for launches and associated programs, documentation, and training. While there are opportunities to review and iterate on the roadmap, it should provide a solid view of what's coming over the next twelve to twenty-four months from a product, feature, and functionality standpoint.

Once the roadmap is in place, the product team can begin developing the necessary requirements and technical specifications engineering needs to start building. As all this unfolds, it's important for these organizations to understand how it all fits into the go-to-market strategy, as there are several different routes development could take. That's where you come in. There aren't too many options in this phase for you to have more impact, but key ones are pricing, product launches as a campaign, and all the content that goes along with it. In addition, the website is a key channel here for updating folks on what's coming, as well as providing the latest and greatest on your product.

Let's take a closer look at some touchpoints you might leverage in this stage to help build influence. Thinking about target *audience* and persona information is key when developing a feature—and simply reminding product and engineering of this can be key in influencing how a product is developed and delivered (which should improve customer satisfaction). I was once an alpha tester for a large, well-known marketing automation tool. I was so excited. I would finally have a tool I could easily use and manipulate as a marketing leader, one that would help me make better decisions, automate my processes, and show my impact. "Built for marketers," they told me. "Out of the box, easy to set up," they told me. "Drag and drop functionality," "so easy a monkey could do it," and a whole bunch of other marketing BS. I'm pretty sure I heard angels singing.

Turns out their early prototype would have worked swell for me if I was a programming genius. You literally needed to know how to code to use it, which I told them. My feedback went back to their product and sales team, who kept telling me I was wrong (which was the polite way of saying I was an idiot). After a few tense go-rounds with their CEO and the product team, I finally had a conversation with one of their engineers. I walked him through how I would want to use the product and what my expectations would be for how I, as a marketer, would "drag and drop" this feature or that. I told him how I thought certain functions should work from the user's perspective. He admitted that while the functions were built for marketing professionals to use, they had built it assuming someone else within the customer organization would implement, operate, and maintain it. You know, like an engineer or programmer. Not so "out of the box" then, eh? So off the team of product managers and engineers went to rebuild it. They came back six months later with a tool I could manipulate on my own. I'm glad they ultimately listened to feedback, but taking their eye off their target persona during product development ended up delaying their initial release by half a year.

Marketing can help alleviate situations like this when they have trust built up and can influence the product team—just by reminding everyone of the personas, the target audience, and the audience's expectations.

Another touchpoint marketing can engage with is using *customer data* to validate the product team's choices. When looking at customer data, a company is measuring many things—including, critically, which features their customers are using, and why or why not. Sure, this could fall under customer success's purview, but marketing should have a good understanding of this as well. Are your customers not using a feature because they don't need it, don't know it exists, or don't know how to use it? These questions should be considered when product is building out the specs to enhance that feature or prioritize the development of other features.

I was once in a product meeting where they were talking about rebuilding a specific feature since no one was using it as intended. Had to ask. "Um, clarifying question to the team. Do we need to train customers on how to use it as it was intended, or should we consider rebuilding it to our customers' needs? How are they actually using it and why? Maybe that is really the question. Are they looking for a different feature altogether? And would it make sense for us to explore that? Okay, sitting down now."

Also, when it comes to *pricing*, do we know how our customers' behaviors are affected by price? Do we know which plans people are selecting? And do we know why they choose a particular plan? Is it because it's cost effective although it's missing features, or are they selecting it for the features first? Inevitably, pricing will come up in this stage, when determining which features and functions to prioritize, what to go to market with, how features are bundled together, and what the company can charge for the solution and packages.

In all of this, there are two things marketing should bring into the roadmap and development conversation. The first is the perceived value of the solution by both end users and those doing the purchasing, if different from the user. What are they getting for the price they are paying? What are they willing to pay? The second is bundled pricing. Are the features bundled correctly to help people discern what they are getting in which packages or tiers? Do bundles have what they are looking for? And what are they willing to pay for it? As marketing owns the messaging, the website in general, and the pricing page on the website, we play a pivotal role here.

One company I worked for had phone support as part of their lower-tier package (instead of email or even chat support). In addition to that, there really wasn't enough differentiation between the lower-tier package and the next one up, so most people just went with the lowest package. The company goal was to get more people signed up for the mid-level package. So I moved phone support to the middle tier, and instantly more people started selecting that tier. By simply moving that one feature to another package, we increased revenue by 20 percent the next three months alone. Boom. Marketing = Revenue Center. But wait, that's not all. We continued to look at what was in each tier and what customers used in terms of features (and the profit margin on those features). We shifted more things around, then increased the price for both the mid-tier and highest-tier package, each by around 40 percent. We could do this because marketing understood the value of each of the features, knew which ones customers couldn't live without, and knew what they were willing to pay. We also spent a significant amount of effort to establish the value people were getting for each and every feature, as well as the package itself. Doing this contributed to a 50 percent increase in revenue for that year.

Okay, some of you are probably freaking out right about now. I'm not asking you to immediately jump into conversations like this. But you do need to make sure you understand the product you are marketing and how users use it or want to use it, so that you can provide some input along the way. Know your product. Know your customers. Have a rudimentary understanding of their price sensitivity. This way you can help drive the direction of the product in a meaningful way, and hopefully increase conversions.

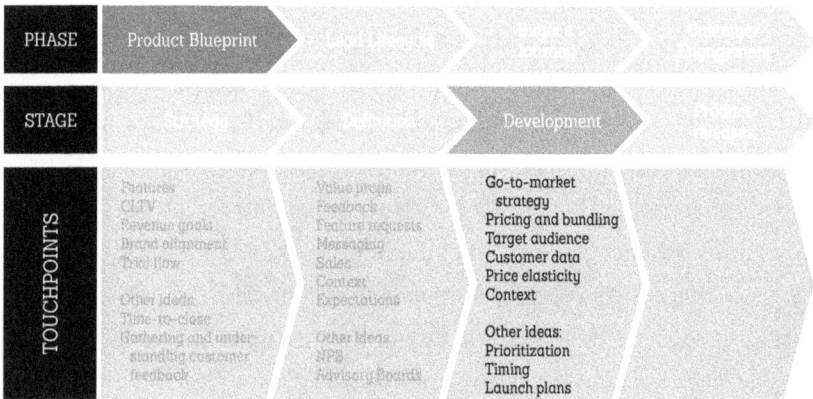

| PHASE | Product Blueprint | Local Blueprint | | |
|---|---|---|---|---|
| STAGE | Strategy | Definition | Development | Review |
| TOUCHPOINTS | Features CLTV Revenue goals Brand alignment Tool flow / Other ideas: Time-to-close Gathering and understanding customer feedback | Value props Feedback Feature requests Messaging Sales Context Expectations / Other ideas: NPS Advisory Boards | Go-to-market strategy Pricing and bundling Target audience Customer data Price elasticity Context / Other ideas: Prioritization Timing Launch plans | |

Product Development Touchpoints

## Releases and Communications Touchpoints

Even before the feature or product is ready to launch, there should be a lot of coordination between product, engineering, customer success, sales, and marketing about how details will be communicated. The cycle will vary by company in terms of releases. You may have an agile product-management process, where releases are happening daily with larger releases quarterly; you may have monthly releases; or you may have some combination. Regardless, you need to have a plan for getting this information out.

When looking for touchpoints in this stage, think about all the channels you use to disseminate information, like emails, social media, and your website. Then think of all the programs you have running or need to set up to ensure information regarding product features and improvements is seen and heard, not just by your customers but by your target audience at large. This could be as part of a PR plan, corporate newsletters, website content, and more. And make sure you develop tools and collateral to enable sales to be successful.

So how can marketing have even more sway in this stage, other than by simply owning the *launch strategy* itself? Thanks for asking. When product and engineering look at development schedules for products and features, it's important they be aware of any critical events or deadlines marketing has. Hopefully, you've already shared your calendar of events with them, but walking them through it in context (there's that word again!) is always helpful. For example, if you have a major industry event coming up and you want to get in front of your audience with a game-changing feature, then the roadmap may need to be adjusted to ensure the feature is out in time. This is another example of the go-to-market strategy leading the product strategy.

In addition to sharing important upcoming dates, events, or programs, marketing should also share themes and messaging being planned for the next twelve months, grouped by month and quarter if possible. The more alignment here, the more marketing professionals can effectively drive the overall launch and subsequent programs, which should lead to a higher closed rate and revenue.

When it comes to product *release communications*, they come in a variety of formats, most of which marketing already owns (media alerts and press releases, emails, website updates, newsletters, community announcements, social media, etc.). The key here is for marketing professionals to help guide the message. Is this new feature a game changer, or is it a must-have that's finally being incorporated into the product? If the latter, this is a great opportunity to reach out directly to customers rather than have a more public launch.

Leveraging the customer community and knowledge base to disseminate important updates is critical. Sometimes marketing owns the distribution channel, but sometimes customer success owns it, or pieces of it. Regardless, marketers can influence the message itself and its distribution by providing guidelines for how to write a good article, how to engage with constituents, and how and where to promote content within the community.

Another way marketing can influence product launches is with actual *programs*. Depending on the overall launch strategy, it might make sense to do an actual product webinar. These are usually done when there are significant features to walk through, or if the features are complex and need further explanation. These product webinars can be produced just for customers, or they can be directed at prospects and the overall industry. Marketing can help define what would work best and help with promotion and segmentation if necessary. We might recommend different formats, such as a podcast versus a blog post or Facebook Live versus a true webinar. Whatever the medium, we'll likely own, produce, and promote the event and maybe even elevate the discussion by bringing in customers to talk about their success with the new feature.

There are so many other areas where marketing can get involved, share context, shape critical events, and work with other teams. Each company has a different process and structure, so don't limit yourself to what I've put here, and don't try to squeeze a square peg into a round hole. You need to think about your own company and all the ways you can influence the product blueprint and product teams in this stage.

| PHASE | Product Blueprint | | | |
| --- | --- | --- | --- | --- |
| STAGE | | | | Product releases |
| TOUCHPOINTS | Features CLTV Revenue goals Brand alignment Trial flow Other ideas: Time-to-close Gathering and understanding customer feedback | Value props Feedback Feature requests Messaging Sales Content Expectations Other ideas: NPS Advisory Boards | Go-to-market strategy Pricing and bundling Target audience Customer data Price elasticity Context Other ideas: Prioritization Timing Launch plans | Content Editorial calendar Themes Social media PR/AR Webinars Other ideas: Website Newsletter |

Product Release Touchpoints

The general cycle for a company is product ideation, product build, sales, support, and then finally marketing. What I am recommending companies do instead is go from a product-led company to one driven by the go-to-market and business strategy. For some product teams, and companies in general, this is a dramatic shift in mindset and process, but it's a necessary transformation if the company really wants to scale and grow. All of this can and should be led by marketing—*you*—and now you have the beginnings of what you need to do this.

# CHAPTER 8

# Putting It All Together: Map of Influence

N o doubt, that was a lot to take in. But you now have a better understanding of why you need to be more involved throughout the go-to-market strategy planning. You can see how it aligns with the overall customer journey. You have a framework to identify touchpoints along the way where you can be influential, or more influential, with a focus on the go-to-market strategy. You've gathered the material to build your own Map of Influence. Yippee! And I shared a lot of examples on how you can plan for, have influence on, and execute impactful programs throughout all phases of the customer journey as they align to the go-to-market strategy. And when you say it like that, it makes such clear sense why we should all be working collaboratively and cohesively across organizations to achieve overall company goals. (Also makes sense why I think marketing should own the whole enchilada!)

You are probably saying, "Yes, yes. I get it. But how do I actually put the Map of Influence into practice? How do I create synergies across the go-to-market strategy leveraging my Map of Influence?" Well, now that you have identified everything you can and do touch, you need to prioritize them. Then you need to slowly incorporate these enhanced touchpoints, based on the go-to-market strategy, into your daily routine.

## PRIORITIZING YOUR MAP OF INFLUENCE

In order to successfully implement your Map of Influence, you need to think strategically. There are probably over a hundred areas, pieces, fragments, slices, snippets—touchpoints—you can influence. I shared examples of these in the previous chapters, and I hope you've added heaps of your own ideas. Everything you've contemplated adding to your Map of Influence is critical, otherwise I doubt you would have thought to put it on the list in the first place. That said, you can't do them all—or maybe you can, because admittedly you are a kickass marketing Wonder Woman. But either way, you have to start somewhere, which means you need to find a way to prioritize all these amazing options.

Start by looking at the channels and programs you already own and the touchpoints, components, programs, and content that will be the most impactful. When I say most impactful, I'm talking about things that will touch the customer (in a good way), areas where you or others on your team have expertise, and touchpoints that will shorten the sales cycle, bring in more qualified leads, or garner a higher price tag. If you want, you can think about the touchpoints as levers. Which levers can you push or pull, and which will lead to the greatest impact and revenue?

### Shit You Own

I think it goes without saying, but I'm going to say it just in case: Anything you individually own, you should prioritize first. This will obviously depend on your job, your role, and the company. Next, think about the programs, content, and tactics your team, coworkers, and marketing organization own. This is a great opportunity to bring the rest of the marketing team along for the ride. Share your little secret with them: the Map of Influence. It will enable you to implement your plans faster and more effectively, and it will help increase the influence of your entire organization.

When you are considering the touchpoints and strategy, recognize that you may need to shift resources in order to execute your plan. But that's okay, because at the end of the day, your strategy and plan should be much more effective now.

## Levers

A lever is something you can "pull" or "push"—in other words, put into place—that you know will help grow the company. These are predictable programs you know will lead to predictable outcomes. I like to call this the "If I had a million dollars" scenario. If your boss, CEO, or investors came to you, probably in a hurried manner, and said, "If I gave you an extra million dollars, where would you invest it? Today! Right now! What would the return be, and when?" What would you say? Believe it or not, I get this question a lot. (Disclaimer—amounts may vary. In fact, they're likely closer to the twenty-thousand-dollar range.) And said boss/CEO/investor usually stands right there waiting for me to answer. "Well? I'm waiting!" Luckily, I have no shortage of ideas of what I would do, all based on the go-to-market strategy. And because I have my Map of Influence all laid out, I can answer right then and there. Or at least propose a few ideas to start the discussion.

Sometimes the million-dollar question is asked with goals in mind. For example, the company may be short on revenue for the quarter, which ends in six weeks. So you need to think about which of these programs, touchpoints, and levers you can predictably pull to help revenue in the short term. If this is the case, you should prioritize the program that will give you the best return in the shortest amount of time. Look at your Map of Influence and pick programs that have had a high conversion rate, or maybe focus on high-end low-hanging fruit targets and also referrals. On the other hand, if short-term revenue isn't the goal but long-term multiyear contracts are, maybe focus on ABM programs. Note, you will likely have to select more than one touchpoint to implement.

I'll cover more scenarios later in the book, but the "If I had . . ." is a good place to start. Ask yourself this when building out any program. Which levers would you pull and what would you do differently if you had $50K or $250K or a million dollars or whatever? Heck, I'd be happy with an additional $10K at times. So where would you invest that? Which of the touchpoints can you feasibly work with to make that additional $10K impactful in the time frame you've been given?

Luckily, most of the levers you can pull quickly and easily are within your own organization, within programs you control and can influence readily within your own team.

## Channels

When prioritizing your touchpoints and potential areas of influence, think of the different channels you have access to and can leverage. Again, start with ones you already own, like social media. This one is actually pretty easy. What touchpoints involve simply taking what you are already doing in certain channels (like Instagram and Facebook) and posting on other channels, social and otherwise (like LinkedIn, your blog, the community)? But don't go at it willy-nilly. Build these ideas into your program; don't let it all be an afterthought. Leveraging your social media channels is something I would consider low-hanging fruit. Even if the return is not exponential, it's super easy to implement.

Also think about how you can use your website smarter. Can you optimize it more? Can you implement a better flow from lead to trial to purchase? You, or the marketing organization, own this channel, so remember you can leverage it across the customer journey. Think about overarching things you can do, such as a redesign or change to the navigation. Or smaller, more incremental things, such as adding how-to videos to your resources page. Pro tip: If you'll need some development or engineering time to make changes to your site, include that in your process, plans, and budget. And again, remember the goal is to determine what to prioritize here.

Partners are a great channel to think of when determining what touchpoints and levers to prioritize. One company I worked at had a tremendous affiliate program in place. So when I found myself constrained with budget and other resources needed to meet my goals for the quarter, I turned my affiliates into an extension of our company—a new sales channel. I developed some bonuses and changed the compensation structure, trained them, enabled them with some tools, and sent them on their way to sell on our behalf. That way, I could focus on top-of-the-funnel lead-gen programs, while this squad of salespeople went out and sold. Worked like a charm.

I understand this might not be an option for you, but still think about your partners and how you can leverage them to fulfill one or more of your touchpoints. Although technically it's not you doing the work, it still shows innovation and builds trust and influence both internally and with your partner network.

## Expertise

When you are prioritizing, look for areas of expertise you already have. Are you an amazing writer? Then focus first on tasks where your writing skills will shine, and that won't take you as long to create, develop, or implement. Are you a numbers geek? Then prioritize tasks where you can leverage this skill, such as building an ROI calculator or better internal and external reports.

You can even use this as an opportunity to stretch yourself, by looking at areas where you would like to expand your knowledge. If you want to become a customer marketing manager, maybe work on the community site. Or, if you want to learn how to do video editing, focus on how-to videos, if that's on your list of potential touchpoints. Granted, it may take you a little longer to get these up and running, but it shows initiative, meets the goal of implementing an influential touchpoint, and allows you to learn a new skill. How fun would that be?

As you sift through your touchpoints and think about where to focus, always remember who you are trying to influence. Your colleagues, your manager, other teams in your organization, the executive leaders? I'll cover in depth the who, why, and how to influence later on in the book, but keeping this in mind now will help you prioritize as well.

## READY, SET, GO

So, in theory, you've now listed your touchpoints in order of priority. Because there are parts that will affect others, I would share your Map of Influence with folks on your team and others in the company whom you trust and who can help you reach your goals. For example, go to your manager and tell them you've been thinking about how you can be more strategic and effective in your role. Then share a few examples of the touchpoints and your plans around implementing them. They may be able to guide you and get you resources you didn't have access to, or maybe they can introduce you to someone (or a whole team) whose involvement will bolster your plans' success.

Now pick one or two touchpoints, preferably in the order you prioritized (long-term goals, short-term goals, impact, attainability, etc.), and put them into practice. If possible, start with ones you can do without significant new resources, and can show results for, quickly. For example, if you feel you can move people through the trial faster by having how-to videos professionally produced, start there. I can't imagine you would get pushback from folks. "Hey, I have a theory that if these looked, um, more professional, we could convert people faster. Oh, and don't worry about the budget. I shifted some funds to do this. Are you game, Ms. Customer Success Manager?" I'm guessing this is something they've been asking for help with for years, so yes, they are game. Not only will they think you are amazing for helping them do their job better and freeing up their time; you have started to build trust and influence with them. And maybe they will help with a little quid pro quo when the time comes.

In any case, make sure you set expectations with people. Let them know what you anticipate showing from a successful implementation, and give them best- and worst-case scenarios. For example, if you expect to see an increase in conversion by 3 percent within the first quarter, let people know. Then make sure you are measuring the right things to show, one way or the other, what the outcomes are. Set milestones too. If you are setting milestones and adjusting when needed, you hopefully won't ever get to the worst-case scenario.

Always refer to your Map of Influence. Heck, have it framed, and hang it on your cube wall for all to gawk at in awe of you. As you have the time and resources, continue through your list of possible touchpoints to influence, in order of priority. Focus on the ones with the highest return, and quick hits. We'll talk about how to measure in a later chapter.

I want to emphasize that more is not necessarily better. We're aiming for quality and impactful results. If you hit it out of the park with your first three touchpoints implemented, you probably don't need to get to touchpoint twenty-five. Instead, you might want to double down on the others. Therefore, measuring and understanding the results is critical. If you know something is working, great; you can now go back and, hopefully, get more funds to focus on programs that are performing well. Or you may realize early on that it's not working the way you intended, and then you can pivot.

Now apply, rinse, and repeat. Apply, rinse, and repeat.

And speaking of repeat, the whole next chapter focuses on just that. What a great segue.

# CHAPTER 9

# RPM: Turning It Up a Notch (or Two)

Hopefully you have a sense of the many different touchpoints along the customer journey that are aligned with the go-to-market strategy. And hopefully you've put some of those together into a brilliant Map of Influence you can start to use. That's all a big part of this G for G.R.I.T. thing. So what's next?

Now I'd like to take you into the world of RPM.

I've been using the acronym RPM (Repeatable, Predictable, and Measurable) for about ten years now. It was my way of "packaging" what I thought was an effective and fast way of reaching overall goals and revenue targets. Because, as you know, it's not just about leads or MQLs; it's about quality leads, how quickly they convert to revenue, and what CAC, CLTV, and ROI all look like. And OMG, that's a lot of acronyms! RPM helps you get to market faster, more efficiently, and more cost effectively, with predictability in the outcome of your programs. How is that possible, you ask? We'll get there, but let me set the stage first.

I was in a board meeting once where the discussion was around closed-wins for the quarter. Someone brought up an example of a customer that went from filling out a form on the website to signing up for a huge deal in one week, without ever talking to sales. Amazing, considering our normal sales cycle was six months. "Yes, give me more of those!" said one board member. "Um, what?" I asked, perplexed. He responded, "Why can't all of our closed deals be like this? Why can't you bring in more leads like this? Why are we putting money into marketing if leads just magically pop out of our @$$ through a plume of unicorn poop and pixie dust and buy our product? We want more of that! Go do more programs like that!" Got it: unicorn poop and pixie dust. All right, so I might be embellishing here, but you get the point. The perception was that the lead had magically appeared out of thin air. Poof! At least that's what it looked like on paper to the board. And don't get me wrong. I really wish this were the case.

But of course, there are always two sides (or more) to the story— and many, many marketing touchpoints of influence behind it. Luckily, I had gone into that meeting with a full understanding of the long customer journey all the closed deals had gone through that quarter and was prepared to discuss what that path looked like. Turns out, the lead (I'll call him Bob) really came from a customer referral. Marketing had implemented a program to try and get our customers to refer our solution to trusted colleagues. We sent out a description of our target audience and persona, along with a simple email we'd developed that customers could copy, paste, and share with a code for 10 percent off for their colleague if they signed up. In exchange for the referral, our customer would get a discount during the next renewal phase (a pretty hefty discount of 15 percent). One of our customers (I'll call her Amy) actually referred Bob. Amy told Bob (with a little help from our email) about the pains she was experiencing, which systems she had evaluated, and why she'd ultimately decided on our solution. Bob then had his operations guy sign up for a trial. In the meantime, several other folks, with different roles within that company, went to our website and downloaded material, attended webinars, and educated themselves on the solution and offerings. They apparently had an internal meeting where they all told Bob they loved it, wanted to use it, and recommended he purchase our solution. Which he did. In less than a week.

What looked like an easy win on the surface had many components to it, all of which marketing had thoughtfully and strategically planned. The first thing we'd done was recognize that a specific customer journey—a referral—led to big, fast wins. We also had a good sense of which customers had followings as industry experts and would be good advocates of our solution. We didn't offer this referral program to everyone, after all. Next, we knew we could build some stickiness and even more loyalty by offering a percentage off the next renewal phase for those doing the referring. (This discount was for tens of thousands of dollars, so we had to run some numbers to make sure it wouldn't negatively impact our revenue.) By creating repeatable programs (i.e., programs that could be repurposed, reskinned, and extended), we were able to develop paths for the critical roles involved in the decision-making process at Bob's company (operations, finance managers, C-suite, etc.) to get to their own aha moments quickly. Because we knew our target company and the different personas within those companies, we were able to build a frictionless journey for Bob and his team.

Knowing your targets and personas, knowing their behavior (i.e., what they will want to do or see next), and knowing which levers to pull help you build predictability. If you know that the next natural step after someone reads an article is for them to want to understand how your solution has helped others, having a CTA inviting the reader to look at a case study makes sense. And if you know they will then want to see it in action for themselves, directing them to a trial or self-guided demo seems like the next obvious thing. The consumer might think they are driving their own behaviors and actions—and in effect they are—but you are leveraging past experience of similar prospects to predict the overall journey and make the path as frictionless as possible. This predictability enables you to be smart with your programs and campaigns, and where your budget goes.

From there you need to measure the success of that customer journey. Did they convert when and where you thought they would? Did they navigate the way you thought? Was there a specific turning point that pushed them over the wall to purchase? Based on this, can you reevaluate the overall journey and remove even more friction, to shorten the cycle and predict pipeline and revenue? Also consider who you are sharing metrics and results with, and how you do it.

The next few chapters will look at RPM and how you can build out your programs as effectively as possible. You should come away with a good understanding of how you can shift efforts just a bit to accomplish a lot more, through building repeatable, reusable programs and content and utilizing the most effective channels. Then we will look at predictability, going back to your Map of Influence to identify levers you can pull for the outcome you're seeking. Finally, we will look at how to measure, what to measure, who you are measuring for, and how to present the outcomes and results for maximum effectiveness. You should then have data in your "back pocket" so you can report out the numbers intelligently and convincingly and articulate how you got there.

At the end of the day, did we shorten the sales cycle for Bob? Heck yeah! We didn't shorten it to a week, but it was reduced by about 50 percent. Yep, instead of taking six months, it "only" took three months (not including the time it took marketing to set up the referral program in the first place). Setting up the referral program included nurturing our customers and putting programs in place that rewarded them for referrals, in addition to creating a seamless journey for all the referrers. It's great if you can make all this so seamless it appears leads closed in a week, without assistance from the sales team. But it's critical those in leadership positions understand this is actually a well-thought-out, intentional program that had the desired effects.

So grab your magic wand, your unicorn, and your pixie dust, and let's dig in.

# CHAPTER 10

# Repeatable: Over and Over Again

Who wouldn't want to create one amazing piece of content and use it over and over and over again? Or tweak a program ever so slightly to expertly leverage existing content for a new channel? Or how about slapping a new cover on an old white paper, calling it an e-book, and voilà! Instant new leads. With so much already on the plate of a marketing professional, why not use more effectively what we've already spent time and money creating? Ironically, we tend to produce way more content and programs than we really need. We have to get smarter about what we produce and how we use it—and reuse it. Let's face it. We are being asked to do a lot more with less and less: less budget, less resources, fewer people, you name it. We've got to make it all work.

Story time! Gather 'round!

Once upon a time in a marketing organization, I was thrilled to learn we had "tons" of content. Yay. Sounds good. I asked the person who managed the content to tell me more about it, as he'd recently done a content audit. What types of content did we have? How, and where, was it being used? And by who? When a new piece was created, how was it distributed? Were there campaigns around the pieces of content, or did they fit into other programs? Did we know which pieces were performing well? Which pieces helped improve conversion rates? Did sales get trained on what we had, where to find it, and when and how to use it? All good questions.

Turns out we had over three thousand pieces of "marketing" content. Wow, three thousand? Seems like a lot. Maybe even too much? I asked how effective all that content was, and the reply was "Well, only about 5 percent is ever even found." Thank goodness I wasn't drinking coffee at the time, or I might have spit it out. I have the crazy ability to process and analyze data almost instantly, but it didn't take a human calculator to figure out that this was not sustainable.

Just to be clear, of the three thousand pieces of content that had been created, only 150 could even be found (5 percent). Then content guy sheepishly added that only 10 percent of what people could actually find had been looked at in the past six months. "Um, maybe even longer, like a year," he added. Thus, fifteen pieces of content were being used out of three thousand. That is 0.5 percent! And that is *not* a typo. Imagine if each piece of content took an average of eight hours to write, design, format, edit, and launch. That's twenty-four thousand hours! If you want to extrapolate even more, that's eleven and a half years of one person's time, just spent writing stuff no one reads, and over $1 million in salary alone. That's a lot of hours, money, and effort going into creating content that no one can find, let alone read. Oops. We can do better!

In digging a little deeper, I found out that a lot of this content had been pushed out only one time via a social media channel. Never to be heard from again. Poor little piece of content. Then I found some cool e-books and guides that had never been shared, posted, distributed, or used *at all*.

Think about how much of your time has been wasted on similar content and programs. Maybe someone asked you to create it—"Hey, you know what would be great? If you could make a fill-in-the-blank that discusses blah, blah, blah." Or maybe it was a reactive piece to respond to something happening in the market, but not necessarily well-thought-out or positioned for success. And when you have these ad hoc bits and pieces, it can be hard to fit them into your already running programs without some kind of disruption.

Now imagine creating *one* really stellar piece of content a year as a foundation, calling that your pillar piece, and leveraging that piece over a hundred times—in multiple programs and channels, and for all your target audiences and segmentations. Creating it with a bit of flexibility for when times call for a quick adjustment? And maybe even personalizing it a bit? Mind blown! By strategically thinking about who the content is for and mapping it directly to the customer journey—what they need, how they will use it, when they need it, and the format—you can develop better content and less of it, which can be repurposed and reused.

You can meet several goals here. The first is that you generate better outcomes with less effort, time, and money. Second, repurposing and reusing should lead to better results through consistency of messaging, especially when you are segmenting or implementing personalization. This is significant if you have multiple contacts in different roles within a target company. You want each of them to understand your offering from their own perspective and role, but at some point, they will get together internally to get on the same page. So consistency in messaging is critical. Third, having fewer, more concise pieces of content that can be repurposed and reused enables you to be more agile when following the needs of your audience or whatever craziness is going on in the world. Finally, by having only one or two pillar pieces of content to produce, you can focus your efforts and resources on developing the best possible pieces and strategy to disseminate them.

Let's look at an example. Say you have commissioned an industry research paper. You pay $75K for it and really need it to perform.

You work closely with the research firm to ensure the paper is useful to your target audience and the different levels and roles of decision makers; has a long shelf life, meaning it will still be pertinent in a year; and is more of a listicle piece so you can chunk it up to reuse and repurpose, something like the top ten best practices for your industry. Now you take that paper and add personalization to the title page if you are running an ABM campaign. You might also reorder the list depending on which audience you are sharing it with. For example, if one of the best practices is more significant to a marketing person reading the paper, shift the list around so they see this best practice first. Or chunk it up so they *only* see tips relevant to them. We'll talk about extensibility soon; just know that you can build out over a hundred touchpoints around this one piece. You can have monthly themes laid out for the foreseeable future based on the ten best practices. If you do this right, with this one piece, you can have a year's worth of webinars, blog posts, articles, social media posts, and more.

And as a bonus, having a pillar piece of content you continue to leverage should lead to faster decision-making on the prospect's part. You've engaged them with the content they were looking for, which educated them on your solution. You had a thoughtful process with CTAs to guide them through the customer journey. They came away knowing all the critical information and with an understanding of the value of the solution. You've set expectations for what the customer will get, why they need it, and their next steps. You essentially have provided a frictionless process for a prospect to educate themselves, truncating the buyer's journey and reducing the amount of effort needed from sales. All using one piece of reusable content.

How does all this help you gain more influence and trust? It's pretty simple (ish). Done correctly—and with intent, which we'll get to in just a bit—having better, more consistent content, built to reduce friction and increase a prospect's ability to educate themselves, shortens the sales cycle, improves conversion rates, and usually leads to increased deal size, which equals more revenue. Oh yeah, and all for a fraction of the cost and time. The key is to determine which programs to focus on, what (repeatable) content is needed to support this, and how the heck to measure it all. We'll get to that.

## TOO GOOD TO BE TRUE?

This next section is going to add some work to your plate and may take a bit of time. But putting in the effort upfront to think strategically about your content will pay off significantly throughout the year, and I can promise it won't take twenty-four thousand hours and eleven-plus years to create! It will entail getting a better sense of the customer journey, which involves talking to sales and your customers. You should consider doing a content audit, defining what is needed and mapping it to the customer journey. Then evaluate what you can repurpose, noting what new pieces need to be created, and finally develop a plan to get it out in the world.

### Understanding the Customer and Their Journey

You spent a significant amount of time in the last section of the book on the go-to-market strategy, thinking about the different touchpoints in the customer journey and how you can influence them. Now we're going to go through the phases of that journey again, but we're going to think about it from the prospect's or customer's point of view, starting from the product, going through the lead lifecycle and buyer's journey, and all the way to customer engagement.

It's key here to look at the customer journey not only from the perspective of the individual persona you are targeting but from the perspective of all the players in the buying process for that account. Who else in the organization do you need to engage with? What are their roles within the company and as part of the decision-making process?

When do they come into, or out of, the flow? What are their pains? They are likely different depending on their role.

Let's look at an example. Say you are selling a marketing automation tool. Your main target persona is likely the lead-gen marketing manager, who will be the end user and your likely champion. The marketing manager's pain is not being able to automate their programs and see their results—in other words, be effective and show the organization's impact. But there is also the IT person, who is going to have to implement and integrate your solution. Lots of pain there. The sales and marketing operations person will be interested in how to set up the system for success. And don't forget the CFO who will have to approve the large annual bill. All these personas' needs and pains are critical to address, and at the right time.

Once you have identified the *who* and their pain, determine *where* they come into and out of the customer journey. And then determine *what* they need to move on to the next step. Let's take the IT person from the example just mentioned. They will likely come into the customer journey during the evaluation phase, when there are multiple solutions to review. They'll want to make sure that integration is easy, preferably out of the box. Then they'll likely come back during the trial phase to help set things up and see if everything is behaving as expected. They'll likely have an opinion on which solution to buy. But the IT person's biggest role will come once the solution is purchased and they need to implement it. Even knowing something as simple as this can help you determine what kind of content to develop, in what format, and where and when to make it available.

The pain the IT person experiences is making sure this project doesn't take up too much of their time in the short and long run, as well as making sure whatever is implemented doesn't completely jack up the current tech stack. That said, IT does want to help folks in their company become more independent and less reliant on IT for help, so they want to automate as much as possible. The IT department will likely be responsive to or looking for quick how-to videos and written documentation on implementation. And they will be looking for a list of integrations with your products and solutions.

Go through this from the perspective of everyone involved in the customer side of the process. Then you'll know the audience, their pains, where they come into and out of the journey, and what they are looking for and in what format. This is super simplified, but hopefully it illustrates what you should be thinking about. Don't have this information handy? Then hop on a call with customers and ask them. Ask them what they need to educate themselves, and ask what they need to decide. You can add these to your Map of Influence if that's helpful (as shown below).

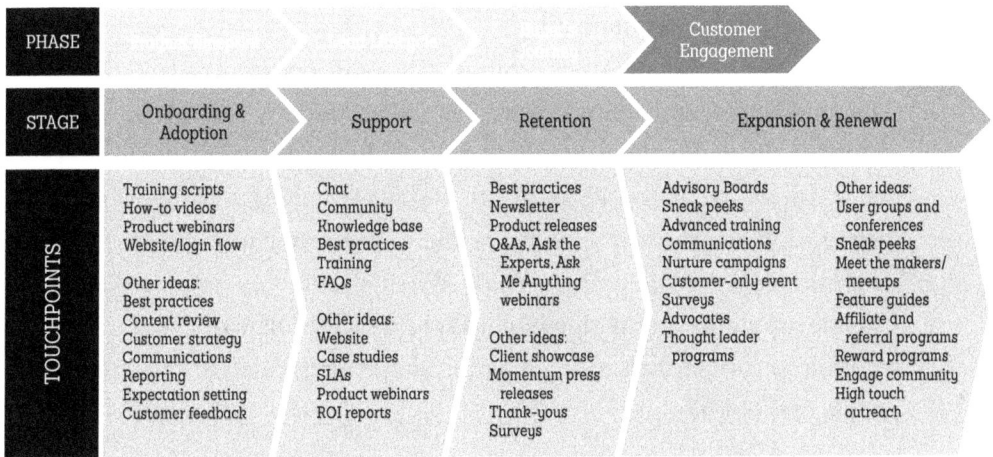

| PHASE | | | | Customer Engagement | |
|---|---|---|---|---|---|
| STAGE | Onboarding & Adoption | Support | Retention | Expansion & Renewal | |
| TOUCHPOINTS | Training scripts<br>How-to videos<br>Product webinars<br>Website/login flow<br><br>Other ideas:<br>Best practices<br>Content review<br>Customer strategy<br>Communications<br>Reporting<br>Expectation setting<br>Customer feedback | Chat<br>Community<br>Knowledge base<br>Best practices<br>Training<br>FAQs<br><br>Other ideas:<br>Website<br>Case studies<br>SLAs<br>Product webinars<br>ROI reports | Best practices<br>Newsletter<br>Product releases<br>Q&As, Ask the<br>  Experts, Ask<br>  Me Anything<br>  webinars<br><br>Other ideas:<br>Client showcase<br>Momentum press<br>  releases<br>Thank-yous<br>Surveys | Advisory Boards<br>Sneak peeks<br>Advanced training<br>Communications<br>Nurture campaigns<br>Customer-only event<br>Surveys<br>Advocates<br>Thought leader<br>  programs | Other ideas:<br>User groups and<br>  conferences<br>Sneak peeks<br>Meet the makers/<br>  meetups<br>Feature guides<br>Affiliate and<br>  referral programs<br>Reward programs<br>Engage community<br>High touch<br>  outreach |

Next, talk to sales. Share what you've been thinking about from a customer journey and persona perspective. Then ask them which two or three pieces of content they use the most and why. Ask them what else they need to be successful. They will likely say case studies and customer testimonials, as well as some way to show ROI.

Armed with all this information, go do an audit of your content. It doesn't have to be long and arduous. For example, if you have three thousand pieces of content, just look at the top 5 percent. I use a simple Excel spreadsheet (check the Resources section in the back of the book for a sample template) that lists the name of the content, where it is located internally and externally, and the content type (blog post, tool, slide presentation, etc.). Then I have a column for the action to take. Sort what you have in terms of Keep, Modify (update/repackage), or Dump (usually for obsolete features or testimonials from folks who are no longer active customers). Finally, identify and list gaps where you don't have content and can't find anything to repurpose. You are trying to see if you can reuse anything that has already been created. Don't limit yourself to traditional printed documents: Think about your blog posts, webinars, podcasts, articles, speaking and sales presentations, case studies, and video testimonials.

Now think about how the pieces you plan on keeping, modifying, and creating fit into your customer journey and Map of Influence. If you're thinking about the marketing automation system example, what would work for initially engaging a marketing manager? How could you nurture the IT person while the marketing manager is off doing a trial? When should you engage the CFO/check-signer and with what? Maybe an ROI calculator or case study? You should start seeing a pattern here in terms of the content people are looking for.

## HOW TO BUILD FOR REPEATABILITY AND EXTENSIBILITY

Here is a typical scenario. Companies often must choose between a headcount in marketing and budget for marketing programs. Raise your hand if you have seen this. It's a bit of a catch-22. But here's the thing: Once you know what your customers need to make a decision, and what sales needs, you can focus on that content. So you might be able to get away with less resources.

## Repeatable

Start thinking strategically about how to build content that can be repurposed for a variety of personas, programs, and channels. Don't reinvent the wheel if you don't have to. Repurpose as much as you can. In other words, take something that was working and adapt it for a different use or audience. Think of it as recycling the programs and content that have worked well before. And don't forget to think about how this works with your one or two pillar pieces.

Here are some examples of how to do this.

- With a new audience—This one is simple. Just start sharing content with them.

- With new marketing channels—Try your pillar piece in a different channel. See if it works better on Facebook versus LinkedIn. See if people are downloading it more from your website or via an email campaign. Is it converting better or worse than in other channels?

- With a new campaign—Think about how you can repurpose something for a new campaign. One easy way is to use existing content as part of an ABM campaign. Can you personalize a guide by adding a cover page that says "Made for special company ABC"? Or make it a follow-up to a webinar. And don't forget to share it with partners when applicable. Boom! Instant exponential reach with little effort.

- With new types of content or mediums—Take multiple blog posts and turn them into an e-guide. Or transcribe your podcast and turn it into a "tips and tricks" blog post. Can you turn a webinar into an infographic or article? I bet you can.

- In new markets—Thinking of expanding into new markets or regions? Leverage your content, especially your main pillar piece, to test these areas. Does your messaging resonate?

Are people interested in the piece, do they continue along the journey, or do they stop? Do you need to customize or localize anything?

- By creating quick hits—Need more prospects in the pipeline or need to ensure they close by end of quarter? That was kind of rhetorical. Leverage good-performing content and programs for quick hits. Add the content to your nurture campaign or as a pop-up in the trial experience to move people to the aha moment more quickly. Or think about how to use content as part of a promo. "Sign up for the webinar today. First one hundred people will receive this e-guide and 10 percent off."

- By modularizing—Turning something into bite-sized pieces can exponentially increase your reach and extensibility. Can you take an hour-long product webinar and turn it into ten three-minute instructional videos? Or on Instagram, can you promote a collection of useful tools and content via swipe file?

- By aggregating—Consider compiling multiple pieces into a "new" document. For example, take multiple case studies and work them into something like an e-guide or momentum piece on a specific industry.

Think about what you have now and how you can repurpose it, but also think about these options when you build new content. In other words, build new content with the intention of repurposing it.

But wait, that's not all. You can also reskin your content and programs for different audiences and channels. Essentially, you can put a different face on it. Okay, this is starting to sound like a horror movie. Let's call it repackaging. What you want to do is build content that can easily shift from one audience to another with minimal tweaks. Or, even better, you want to leverage your technology and build dynamic content that will automatically shift to fit the role or audience.

Let me give you an example. Take a simple case study. You likely have a section on results. How about changing the results ever so slightly to accommodate different audiences? For your marketing manager, it might say "increased leads by 15 percent." For the sales persona, it might say "increased pipeline by 10 percent." And for the executives signing the check, it might say "the solution paid for itself in three months." Same customer. Same testimonial. Same results and outcomes. Just presented differently for different audiences.

To be clear, you shouldn't do this for *everything*. Just significant pieces that are part of very prescriptive campaigns and programs, for specific audiences. If a company executive is not your target audience, don't spend the time or effort to repackage your case study for them. Don't focus on it. But if you can do it in an automated way, through tools, it couldn't hurt. If you do have a tool in place that allows for this to be automated, or even personalized, then definitely set that up.

Repackaging is great if you have a new audience and want to test messaging. It also works well, as in the preceding example, if you have multiple roles within one organization you need to market to. It also helps build consistency across those roles. The solution and messaging essentially stay the same, but the different results resonate with each role and help them understand the value as it pertains to them.

You can also repackage by using personalization, as in some of the examples offered. Many tools and solutions out there exist to help with this. Vidyard and Bonjoro are great examples of how to do this with video. You can then use these videos in email campaigns and on your website, and your sales team can use them as well. Imagine that—creating one kickass video and then personalizing it to the specific person you are targeting. It's pretty powerful, effective, and efficient.

As a guideline I have an 80/20 rule, meaning that at a minimum, 80 percent of what you create remains intact, while up to 20 percent can be personalized or repackaged. You can think about doing this not just for individuals but also for markets, regions, and industries. If you take that amazing pillar piece you are going to create and swap in industry-specific images and value propositions, you now have a significant piece of content for a new market, with minimal effort.

Finally, consider reusing or recycling as part of the process. This is where doing a content audit really comes in handy. Basically, you want to take a program or piece of content that was initially successful and run it again with minimal changes. Here are some ways to approach it.

- Quick hit—Recycle when you need that quick hit, something to get out to market fast.

- Supplement—See how what you already have can supplement a program you're running; then slot it into your plan for the quarter. For example, maybe you have an article from a few months back. Can you repurpose it as a "handout" for an upcoming event where the author of the article is speaking?

- Combo—I love this one. I call them my Resource Kits. Pull a bunch of content together for a specific audience, create a landing page, and then promote it via emails, social media, and nurture campaigns. Say you are targeting marketing managers. Pull together an on-demand webinar, a blog post, an infographic, and a video case study. Ta-da! You've got yourself an instant lead-gen program using old(er) content!

- Facelift—Getting back to horror movies, take an old e-book out of the vault (or, as I like to call it, the Archives), dust it off, change the title, update the graphic and dates, and send it back out into the world. Or heck, just simply take an old, yet still relevant, white paper and call it an e-guide.

- Repost—Take an article that has done well and is once again relevant, and share it out. And it's okay to note its history. "We wrote this last year but, in light of current blah blah, thought we would share it out again."

- Recycled ads—That's right. If they worked wonders before, why not use them again? You may have to update some verbiage or design, but if these are the ads you used to promote content you are reusing now, they should be pretty much good to go.

There are so many ways to leverage existing content and use it in different ways, in different forms, in different channels, and for different audiences. Repurposing content and website optimization are my two go-tos when I start a new job, since they are low-hanging fruit. Remember to think about how you can incorporate new pieces well past their "use by" date. It's much easier to get funding to create an industry report, for example, if you can show how it will be used now and well into the future.

## Extensibility

I worked for a company once that was shifting from D2C to B2B—and not to just any ol' B2B but the Fortune 500. The biggies. It was an entirely different audience, with different needs. And I had no content that would convince this new target audience of chief human resource officers (CHROs) of F500 companies to purchase our solution. Also, as this was a new offering, we hadn't been doing it long enough for me to have any ROI information to prove to CHROs that our solution was amazing. So what I did instead was develop a thought leader program. We brought in an industry luminary to talk about what was happening in the industry and things companies needed to evaluate and address within their own organization. Mind you, the luminary never had to mention our company. It was implied we had a solution for the industry needs just by having an industry luminary talk about it.

Then I took that webinar and developed an industry guide for our main target persons. From there, we created ten blog posts that we scheduled to go out every few days. We had an entire social media campaign around the guide and blog posts, with multiple tweets and posts per piece of content. Then we "chunked" up the webinar into snippets that we used on social media ads, on our website, and in embedded videos in our email campaigns. Think about all of these examples in the repackaging and reuse sections. There is so much opportunity to extend the life of your content and programs.

As an example, start with a webinar that you have produced, marketed, and run. In addition to turning the webinar into an on-demand event, you can turn it into an e-guide. That e-guide might have ten different components to it. Each of these can be developed into a blog post. From there you can extend it further by leveraging social media, creating a campaign for each of the blog posts, that might have five social media posts per blog. You can also take the webinar and "chunk" it up into ten bite-sized, shorter videos. Then you can create social media posts for each of these, giving you twenty more opportunities for outreach, in addition to using them on the website and in emails.

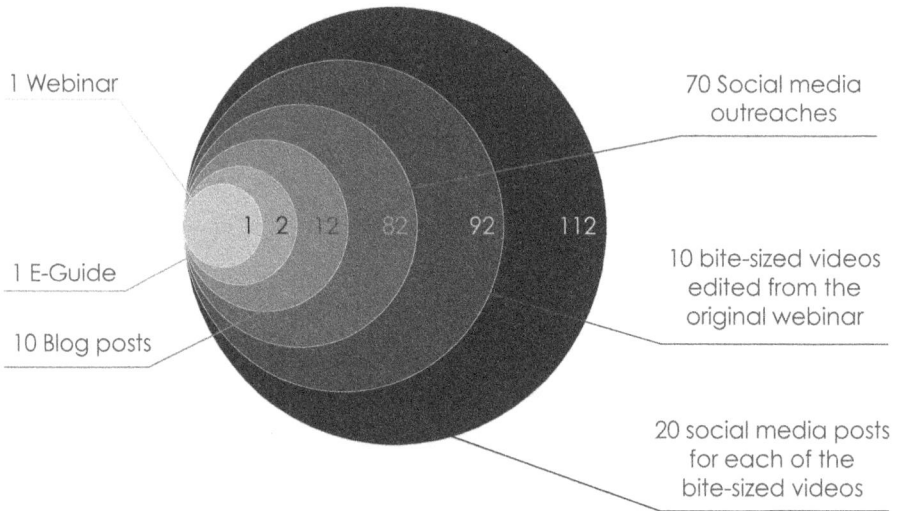

| 1 Webinar | | 70 Social media outreaches |
| 1 E-Guide | 1  2  12  82  92  112 | 10 bite-sized videos edited from the original webinar |
| 10 Blog posts | | 20 social media posts for each of the bite-sized videos |

Content Extensibility from One Pillar Piece

Just like that, with one well-designed piece of content, we now have one hundred plus outreaches, through various channels.

Marketing professionals are being asked to do more with less, all while increasing our cadence, quality, value, and impact. Repeatability is a fast, cheap way to do this. But it should be well thought out for maximum results. Look at your exiting content and program outputs, and see where and how you can reuse them. Think about the content and programs you already have planned and how you can extend their life. And then add your ideas to your content strategy and editorial calendar.

Imagine going to your manager (Shelly) and saying you have an idea for a piece of content that you'll be able to turn into twelve other pieces of content for use in top-of-funnel and middle-of-funnel campaigns and programs. "Oh, and did I mention, it will help get prospects to their aha moment more quickly, likely pushing them over the wall to purchase in less time?" Then show Shelly how extensible it is.

Remember, start with your customer's journey—the who, what, and when. Who are they, what information do they need to move to the next phase or to purchase, and when do they need it? From there, talk to your sales team to see what is working for them and where there are gaps. Once you have all that info, go do your content audit. Leverage this to define your content strategy and marketing programs for the quarter and year. Think how you can and will repurpose, repackage, and reuse. Just as you did with your influential touchpoints, add this information to your Map of Influence, especially if you are a visual person or want something to refer to or share quickly. Now go implement.

Remember my story of the three thousand useless pieces of content? Oops, sorry. I meant the 2,850 useless pieces of content. I took the top fifteen that were being consumed on any sort of regular basis and repackaged them, developing comprehensive programs around them. Some ended up in Resource Kits that we then did an ad campaign and nurture email campaign for. We took one of the how-to on-demand webinar videos and chunked it up into fifteen one- to three-minute pieces that we pushed on social media. We took a white paper a partner had developed, got their permission to market it with them, and then used each theme presented in the paper to build our twelve months of programs, all slotted into our overall plan. And we didn't even write the piece in the first place. This is how you continue to build influence and trust, with your managers, sales team, partners, and company executives.

I'm reminded of a scene in *Iron Man,* where Tony's nemesis Obadiah Stane says, "Tony Stark was able to build this in a cave . . . with a box of scraps." Just pretend you are Tony Stark. In a cave. With a box of scraps. And now go make something amazing out of it.

Go ahead. Call yourself a badass marketing genius while you're at it.

# CHAPTER 11

# Let Me Predict Your Future

Have you ever played the game Twister? Classic party game for ages 6 to 101? (Seriously?! 101? Not on my watch!) There was the magic spinner board, where the needle always got stuck on the same color and body part. And the cheesy plastic mat that never stayed put and was starting to smell a bit funky.

This is how marketing feels sometimes. Remember the "If I had a million dollars . . ." question? Do you sometimes feel as though you're just taking a spin on the Twister board? "We're behind on revenue by $300K? Um, let's see. Oh, look, right hand on red. Let's try that." In other words, $10K on digital ads, and hope we don't fall on our ass. Or maybe you're the kind of person that will move your left foot when no one is looking to make sure you don't fall.

Now imagine you are playing chess instead. There is no randomness—or even chance, really—in chess. It's a game of strategy. No one is spinning a goofy little board where the needle will land on "King, 1 square vertically" (although this might be an interesting game, called Chesster). There is no guesswork or luck involved, just some strategy and thoughtfulness. And in chess, it's helpful if you know your opponent as well. You want to have a sense of your next move, your opponent's next move, and potentially a few moves even further out. If Player A moves this piece there, what are the potential moves Player B can make, and what are the potential moves from there?

Now let's put this example of a chess game into marketing terms. You need to know your audience well enough to understand what their next move, or need, will be. Then you need to develop a path to help them, seamlessly and without friction, make that move (okay, maybe not so much like chess). This results in the ability to forecast the outcome accurately. I like to call this "predictability." By understanding your audience and customer journey, and defining your touchpoints of influence, you should start to see patterns. With this information, you'll be able to identify specific programs, content, and flows that are working for specific segments of your audience, as well as identify the how, what, when, and where of pulling levers. By observing the patterns of your target audience, you can build better, more predictable customer journeys for them, which will likely shorten the sales cycle and encourage hitting revenue numbers in a predictable manner. (And it will help you gain a tremendous amount of influence.)

In this chapter, I'll show you why predictability is important in building prescriptive campaigns and programs, what it means to you, and how it will impact your influence even more. I'll discuss how to understand your programs better, so you can pick and choose the right ones or adjust them appropriately. (We'll talk about measuring all this in the next chapter.) I'll walk through how to build out scenarios; you can do these "on paper" at first, but eventually considering programs through this lens will become more natural and effortless. By focusing on predictability, you will be better able to prioritize and prepared to answer the one-million-dollar question. Get ready to play a better game of chess, and win it.

## LOOK INTO MY CRYSTAL BALL

There are multiple "types" of predictability I want to cover here. One type involves knowing the customer journey an individual will take. The other involves knowing how your programs will perform. Both of these are based on what you know about your customers' behavior, and in some cases, their company. Both are critical to prioritizing programs effectively, proving yourself, increasing the value of your programs, and building trust and influence.

Remember my "17,000 leads, please" story? Lovely board member saying my team needed to bring in 17,000 leads? Good times. Thing is, he had no idea what he was asking for. Was the end goal to achieve a specific revenue number? Were we looking at expanding into other markets, and we wanted to test these new market segments? Were we behind schedule for achieving a revenue target and needed to do something to get there fast? Turns out, in the case of "17,000 leads, please," it was the former. We were trying to reach a certain consistent, sustainable revenue goal so the company would be in a better position to be acquired. Well, why didn't you just say that? The random leads number was just that—random.

A better approach would have been to give me a revenue number we were trying to reach and how long we needed to stay on that trajectory to be acquired at the right price. Very different from the original ask. Once I have the full story (again, reason #34,653 why marketing needs to be involved in the overall corporate strategy planning), I can start looking at what my team has and needs in order to accomplish those goals in the right time frame. I can look at our programs and their conversion rates. Did one program perform better than the other? Did one program net out leads that ended up consistently having a shorter sales cycle? Did one persona or size company close bigger deals on average? Did one industry perform better than others, and maybe at different times of the year—in other words, is there a seasonal or cyclical factor involved?

Give me a set number of leads, and I'll give you a snarky answer. But give me the endgame, and I can work backward from there. Because I can predict the behavior of my prospects and my marketing programs. And you can too.

Understanding predictability enables you to build your programs and content with a clear and concise path, or funnel, in mind. What are your audience's predictable behaviors? The customer journey isn't as neat and linear as the image we use, for simplicity's sake, to talk about it. There are many forks and loop-de-loops people take. Not everyone will have the same length path. People from the same company will come in and out of the journey at different times and for different reasons. What you need to do is use your sense of what's predictable to then guide prospects to the path of least resistance, while making sure to provide the right information to them regardless of which direction they take. Sounds easy, right? Admittedly, it can be a bit tricky setting it up the first time, but it should be easy to maintain once it's in place and the process has been automated.

Let's say your target audience is CTOs. You have an amazing report you just produced and need to get into their hands. You send out an email campaign to all the CTOs in your target company list. The open rate is great, but you notice they aren't downloading the report. Instead, you see that folks from your targeted companies with the title executive admin signed up for the report. Your first thought might be that this was a bad campaign, since conversion for your target contact, the CTO, was low. But what you can probably assume is that the executive admin downloaded the report on behalf of the CTO. Now who knows where that report will end up? Printed and sitting neatly in a pile with other exciting articles? Forwarded on to the CTO? Forwarded to the CTO's right-hand person? Maybe tossed in the recycling bin?

All hope is not lost. Why not send the CTO a follow-up email? "I noticed that someone in your organization downloaded our amazing new report. I can only imagine your time is crunched, so I've created a Cliff's Notes version of the report for you here, with the most salient information. Blah, blah, blah. Four short bullets of cool info here. You're welcome." You may even recommend to the CTO who they should forward the article on to, knowing that person will likely not have the time to read the full report either. Then, with the Cliff's Notes, that next link may even forward it on to yet another person in the organization (preferably another influencer in the decision-making process). "We have found this information to also be of importance to your security engineers. Feel free to forward this link to them." Be careful you don't let the CTO off the hook too soon, but give them some alternatives and an easy way to share. If your systems allow it, add a forwarding tracker on your email, which will grab the forwarded email address and add it to your system. And why not implement an automated email drip campaign that does all this for you? The more you can automate, the easier your life will be.

Now, instead of your sales team saying they don't have enough qualified leads, they will have multiple points of contact within their target account. They might even be able to shorten the sales cycle, because you were able to ensure everyone in the buyer's journey and decision-making process has what they need. Look what you just did there. You built up some trust and cred with the sales team. But to do all this, you need to understand your audience, including all roles in a company that are involved in the decision-making process and their predictable, specific behavior.

From the standpoint of your programs, the importance of predictability is even more critical. Knowing, or having a sense of, how your programs will "behave"—what the predictable results and outcomes are—is essential to building consistently performing programs, prioritizing, and having the ability to pivot quickly when necessary. This includes knowing when to modify your marketing campaigns and when to fold 'em. Trust me, it's much better to divest early and reallocate resources elsewhere if a program is not performing as expected.

# Know Your Target Audience

It seems obvious, but do we always really understand our target audience? Do you really know who your target market is—which accounts and which roles within those targets? Do you know their pain points, overall needs, and goals? Do we have clear, concise ways of segmenting our prospects? Did we take the time to actually build out personas? And if we did, have we reviewed and updated them recently?

When was the last time you looked at your total available market (TAM), service available market (SAM), or serviceable obtainable market (SOM)? If these terms are new to you, simply defined, TAM is the total market demand for a product or service. SAM is the segment of the TAM that is targeted by your products and services and is within your reach. SOM is the portion of SAM you can capture. Sometimes this information hasn't been shared down through the ranks. Most likely it just hasn't been updated in a long time. But it's key for *you* to know so you can build programs with appropriate goals.

I once worked for Company B, which had a goal for marketing to bring in ten thousand qualified leads annually. This number came about by working backward from the company's target revenue, the monthly recurring revenue (MRR), and conversion to close rate. Not a bad strategy. Work back from the revenue you want to attain to define the number of customers needed. Take into consideration the conversion from lead to customer, and voilà, you have your marketing goal. So I'm in this meeting, nodding in agreement that the calculation itself is correct, but in the back of my head I'm thinking, *Hmm, I don't think there are that many of our target leads in existence in the world, let alone in our target region of North America.*

So I started asking questions and had everyone focus on the numbers. Turns out when this goal was established, someone had been looking at the total number of *people* working within the target company, not the number of target companies. Oops. These people also made up the conversion rate to what they wanted to see—what would get them to their revenue goal—not what it was or could be. Big sigh. We didn't have a good sense of our TAM, SAM, or SOM. We had to go back and recalculate based on true market numbers in our space and what we thought we could convert. Needless to say, the maximum revenue was a heck of a lot less.

Once you have a good sense of your audience, you can build out personas and specific targets. In general, you don't want to have more than a few personas you are going after. It's usually better to think in terms of depth versus breadth. First, does your product really serve more than three to four distinct targets? I get that there are multiple people involved in the buying decision, but think about who is buying and who they are buying for. Second, do you want to have that many different messages, pieces of content, programs, and so on? Sometimes you have to put a stake in the ground and pick your top two to three. Then, once you have a stronghold, you can look at adjacent markets and targets. But you need to have a main focus.

Take this book, for example. The main target is marketing managers early in their career (three to five years) and marketing directors trying to figure out how to add value, get credit for their work, gain influence, and get promoted. Would a VP of marketing gain knowledge from reading this book? I certainly hope so. What about your favorite salesperson? Absolutely. The CEO of your company? Oh yeah, definitely. But each of those has slightly different needs and goals, so I would likely need to have multiple messages and campaigns. Not insurmountable, but I would rather be laser-focused on my target. (I had pictures of folks representing my target all over my office while I wrote this book to remind me to keep you all front and center.)

It's critical you understand the different pains, motivations, needs, and goals of your targets, as this will help you be a more effective marketer. How do you get this info? Well, some of it exists online. Or maybe you inherited a super-organized deck from your predecessor. But you always need to be listening to make sure you stay relevant, both as a marketing

*continued*

professional and as the company you represent. In addition to looking at any available market data, I recommend connecting with targets themselves. Call them up to check in. Do a survey addressing their current needs and pains. Hop on a sales call or a customer support call, or at minimum, peruse the support tickets.

## KNOW YOUR POOP–*PS* OF PROGRAM PREDICTABILITY

Admittedly, I have been doing this for so long that knowing how well a program will perform is second nature to me. I have a deep understanding of my audience, how long different personas from each channel and program take to close, the journey to get them there, how many leads programs will bring in, and the conversion rates. Throw some information at me about your solution, how you sell, your audience and your programs, and I can estimate number of leads and conversion rates with phenomenal accuracy (which might make for a fun Ask Me Anything webinar). But I understand this is likely not the case for most folks. So here are some foundational things to think about when predicting the behaviors of your target audience and marketing programs.

I like to call these the new four *P*s, those of predictability: People, Programs, Pulleys and levers, and Period of time.

## People

People—otherwise known as your audience—are a critical component of your go-to-market and marketing strategies. Kind of a no-brainer. They are why you are here. But in general, this section is about why understanding them is critical to predictability. As I mentioned previously, understanding the path your audience will take lets you design your programs and content significantly better, thereby making your programs more predictable too. If you look at your customer journey, you can identify some of the flow and customer behaviors, but you will need to look at data from your marketing automation and analytics tools as well.

Google Analytics can tell you a lot about your website's content and how well your programs are doing. Where are people coming from? What page do they land on, where do they go next, where do they go after that, and so on? For a simplified overview, go to Google Analytics, click the Behavior drop-down, and select Behavior Flow. Voilà, you can drill down and see where people enter and exit your site. If you click the Site Content drop-down, it literally has a section for Content Drilldown and Exit Pages.

This isn't a book on Google Analytics. There are plenty of those out there already. But this gives you a sense of the information available. Think about how you can use that data to predict the behavior of your audience to help define the programs and content you should have in place—which you can then predictably measure.

How many times have you received an email, clicked on the link, and arrived on a landing page that goes nowhere? Wow, there's a missed opportunity. There should always be a next step for your lead. Another CTA. I'm not saying add in an exhaustive, meaningless path. But if you have someone's attention and they are hungry for more info, give it to them. If you notice people come to your home page and then go to pricing, this usually means you've been able to show them your solution has a minimum of what they were looking for—enough to find out how much it will cost. Whoo hoo. If the lead goes to and then exits the pricing page without signing up for a trial, you might not have shown them the *value*, or maybe your price wasn't what they were expecting. You may need to think about the information you have on your pricing page. On the other hand, if the lead goes to the pricing page and signs up for a trial right then and there, you nailed it! You provided a path that helped them understand your solution and the value, enough that they were comfortable moving to the next phase of their customer journey.

Whatever you do, please, please, please set up your acquisition conversions in Google. And use UTM parameters. These are easy to set up and cost you nothing. And if you don't know what I'm talking about, Google it.

## Programs

Your programs, and marketing mix, are another component to consider when seeking to build predictability. You want to get to the point where you can answer the "if I had a million dollars to invest" question quickly while articulating what the expected return should be: for every dollar you invest, you will get X dollars out in revenue. (Hopefully, the return is higher than the cost; otherwise, you might want to reconsider that program.) But to get there, you need to understand your programs. Which programs are working and for which audiences? Which programs are pushing the prospect over the fence to purchase? When do other influencers in a target company come into the picture and how, and through which programs?

You want to build programs that convert faster and bring in more revenue. What's working now and what isn't? Can you optimize programs that are performing well to do even better? Or continue to build on those programs to keep the momentum going? Remember last chapter, when I talked about reusing and extending programs and content? Consider that e-book you created that performed insanely well. Dust that bad boy off, update it, recycle it, and see if it can produce similar numbers again. You need to really understand how well your programs and content are performing so you can leverage that information to build a predictable plan.

Think of how your programs perform (or will perform) for each of your audience segments and personas. For example, I know a certain type of product webinar for my prospects in a trial performs differently than that same webinar would perform with my top-of-the-funnel leads. A product webinar digging deep into how to use features might be too granular for that audience at that point in their journey—they might instead be looking for general information on the solution and value propositions. In contrast, those later in the sales cycle who might be ready to buy but still need validation might be more impacted by a webinar featuring customer use. A webinar around best practices and tips and tricks could help current customers engage and use more, leading to higher renewal rates. Then I might have a thought leader webinar that would work across all of these. Clearly, you should have different webinars focused on the different phases and stages in the customer journey.

Having a sense—ideally, grounded in real numbers—of how your programs perform with different people should enable you to know which levers to pull, when and why, and what the predicted outcome will be. That's why you selected the program in the first place, after all. Did it meet your goals?

## Pulleys

Pulleys—because it starts with *P*, but otherwise known as levers—are the programs you can quickly put into place to have a certain effect, usually to quickly increase leads generated, conversion rates, or revenue. Think of these as the tools in your back pocket. You may have heard of *lift*. Essentially, this is the difference between the before and after when you run, or have optimized, a program. You want to build out programs that will bring visible lift in whatever it is you are measuring.

Now is as good a time as any to dive deeper into conversion rates, because you'll want to be aware of these when thinking through your pulleys. The conversion rate is the percentage change between one phase of your funnel and the next. Too often marketing professionals get busy and only look at the minimum, and likely easiest to find, conversion rates, such as MQL to SQL and then SQL to Closed. By doing this, you miss a lot of critical and valuable information.

What you really need to be looking at is conversion between the points of contact you have, the multitouch attribution. This is a way to evaluate the impact of each marketing touchpoint as a prospect moves through the customer journey. We know it takes more than one touch to get a prospect to convert to a customer. Even with folks self-educating, it still takes seven to ten touches before they even engage with your company. Wait, wait. Don't toss this book across the room. The great news is you already have a list of all these multitouch attribution points. It's your Map of Influence. The touchpoints you identified for your Map of Influence are likely the same touchpoints you need to consider from your audiences' perspective, since you followed the customer journey when selecting your touchpoints, and you have determined the conversion rates of the touchpoints between the phases and stages. And touchpoints can become levers.

Let's consider Prospect Pamela. She sees an article in *Inc.* about your solution—touchpoint #1. (Good job getting an article in *Inc.*, BTW.) Then Pamela goes to your website and views a few pages—touchpoint #2—but has to run off to a meeting. Several hours later, Pamela has completely forgotten about you—sorry, nothing personal. She's on Facebook several weeks later looking at cat videos when an ad for your product is displayed with the option to download an e-guide—touchpoint #3. She totally ignores your ads (she's busy with cat videos, after all). Then she sees another ad pop up when she's searching for something on Google—touchpoint #4. She doesn't click there but instead types your URL into her browser and goes to your website—touchpoint #5. A chat bot pops up saying, "Hey, we've got this amazing e-guide. Would you like to see it?" (Touchpoint #6.) She clicks "Yes, please," gives you her name and email, and downloads the e-guide—touchpoint #7—and touchdown! Whoo hoo, you finally have her contact information, so you put her through your email drip campaign and invite her to an upcoming webinar (touchpoint, touchpoint, touchpoint). And on and on.

By optimizing even one of those touchpoints, you can potentially increase lift and conversion rates. Let's focus on chat, a touchpoint we talked about early when we were building out your Map of Influence. Pamela came to your site and was cookied, then you retargeted her on Facebook and Google with e-guide ads. When she came back to your site, having the chat bot once again offer the specific e-guide she was looking at provided continuity and consistency. That's the beauty of a chat solution. You can set them up the way you want, for automation and effectiveness. Not only that, but you gave Pamela the frictionless journey she was hoping for, based on what you knew she would want and expect. You anticipated and predicted her moves.

Imagine if your chat bot had said, "How can I help you today?" instead of "Hey, Pamela, would you like to download this e-guide?" Which one is going to sway Pamela to engage? The former would likely not be as impactful, and your conversion rate and lift would be lower. With the latter, not only do you likely have higher conversion and lift; you now have a much more qualified lead, as she's read an article about your company, been to your site several times, might have seen your ads through all of the cute kittens, engaged with your chat bot, and hopefully downloaded that e-guide. By simply understanding your customer and following their journey, you have led them down a path that is meaningful to them, helped them self-educate, and reduced the effort on the part of sales. Just remember to look at conversion between *all* the points of contact you have, the multitouch attribution. This is a way to evaluate the impact of each marketing touchpoint a prospect has as they make their way through the customer journey. By doing this, you will have created a seamless and satisfying experience for Pamela.

I know that was a lot with conversion rates, lift, multitouch attri-bution points, and more, but hopefully it's all coming together. Now, getting back to pulleys and levers, chat is just one touchpoint you can pull to make a huge difference. Leveraging chat will likely get you a higher volume of leads and higher quality of leads, which will lead to more closed-won deals and more revenue. Just by changing the interaction of your website's chat bot from a generic "howdy" to a more targeted conversation, you can potentially bring in millions of dollars in revenue. This example shows how you can predict your audience behavior and flow through the funnel, then put in place cer-tain programs—pull those predictable levers—where you will be able to predict their positive outcome.

Now you can see why I suggested implementing just a few of your magical touchpoints at first, one at a time. Even one could have a significant impact. Imagine what you could do over time if you continued to focus on implementing your Map of Influence and touchpoints. Think of the millions of dollars (depending on the aver-age deal size for your product or solution) you and marketing could help bring in. You could literally double or triple your company's revenue. Or even more.

## Period of Time

The final $P$ is for period of time. What is the length of time from lead engagement to capture, through nurture, and to a closed customer? How do you predict this, and why do you care?

To understand the period of time, you can look at when a contact came into your funnel and when they closed. I say that as if it's easy to determine exactly when a lead became a lead, but I know it's not. For example, they might have been anonymously visiting your website for a while. Or there might have been multiple people from the same organization researching your solution, as in the earlier example with our referral Bob. Should you count the first touch of the first person you can identify? Or should you look at the first touch of the first person that matches your persona? For the sake of not having to write an entirely different book, let's just say it's when you capture the first name and email address of a lead from a given company.

Now you spend some time nurturing them. Sometimes the lead will see your email, sometimes they'll read your email, and sometimes they'll take action from your email. How long does this take? Days, weeks, months? Is this different depending on what lead source they came from? Leads usually take longer to nurture when you capture them from a live event, such as a conference, versus when they come to your site organically and sign up for a trial. For example, one time when we participated at Dreamforce we brought in 1,200 leads. This may seem like a lot of leads, but these leads will convert differently depending on the level of attendee participation and engagement with us at the event. In other words, swag hounds versus looky-loos versus demoers will likely have different periods of time before conversion.

Can you tell when others from the same company become engaged, either via email forward notifications, website data, or just a general influx of leads from the company? This is usually a sign of interest in your solution. Do these folks have different roles in their company, and are they looking at different content or programs? Does one specific role like blogs, while another fancies webinars? And how much weight do you give each of those roles? Say a person in a manager role likes webinars, while the person with a director title likes ROI reports or use cases. Knowing how much influence each of these roles will have and at what point in the process is critical. If the manager has no say, or is no longer involved in the buying process, why spend time and money building a webinar for them? The sales team can help you better understand the influence different roles will have on a sale.

Let's say a company has now purchased your amazing product or solution. Cha-ching! Can you look back and piece together who did what, when, and what the final tipping point was? Knowing all this can help you predict someone's journey so that, again, you can put in place a meaningful path for each prospect, role, and rank within a company. You want to look at not only the customer journey but when, how, and how quickly prospects move through the phases. Do some channels or programs perform better in terms of closing more quickly? You are looking for patterns you can act on. You can see these patterns in your marketing automation system and CRM. You can look at traffic on your website. You can also ask your salespeople at what point in the sales process your original contact brings in others (e.g., IT, CFO, etc.).

I worked for a company that essentially sold technical computer infrastructure to large SaaS companies. There was an average twelve-month sales cycle. The flow usually started with an IT person responsible for storage, or a software engineer making sure they had what they needed (redundant systems, zero downtime). At some point in the conversation, the CTO was brought in—after all, it would go under their budget. Ultimately, the CFO was brought into the discussion, as they would need to sign off on the purchase.

There was almost always a point where conversations stalled. Usually this happened when the original contact/champion (IT person) needed to bring in their manager and CTO, but the champion felt as if they were going out on a limb. They needed validation that they were making the right decision before they brought in their boss and their boss's boss. So we gave them just that. I took a case study and ROI doc and repurposed it (changed the title page to say something like "Use Case of Industry A for Company Z"), showing the success other companies in their industry had by using our solution. Now we had a champion who had the tools they needed to bring in the next level of decision makers and who could show proof of why one solution was better than the other.

But wait, that's not all. The next point of friction was getting the CFO onboard with this large purchase, which may or may not have been in the budget. I needed a reason to bring the CFO into the discussion sooner. Note, this was early on in the SaaS style of selling, where infrastructure, blades, storage, and so on were still amortized and thought of as capital expenditures (i.e., categorized differently in the accounting books). So I simply coached the sales team to start talking about the purchase as an operating expense from the beginning. After all, it was a SaaS purchase, so as an operating expense it wasn't thought of as one big-ticket item. Rather, it was considered a monthly expense. It's like the difference between buying a car and having a lease. Even if it was paid as an annual fee upfront, it could still be considered an operating expense. Guess what? These two simple steps—reusing content we already had and changing the talk from capital expenditure to operating expenditure—shortened the sales cycle by 10 to 20 percent. While that may or may not have brought in more revenue, shortening the sales cycle certainly freed up several months of our sales team's time to focus on closing other business. So period of time matters.

If you think about the "one dollar in" equals "X dollars out" premise, then add the "by when" component, you will be able to answer the million-dollar question more easily. "If I had ten thousand extra dollars, I would spend it updating our content to enable our champion prospects, and training the sales team to obliterate any objections the CFO might have. By doing these things, we should convert to $2.3 million in sales by June, shortening the sales cycle by two months."

Damn, you are a genius!

Pro tip: I have a "magical" formula to tell when a company is likely to pull the trigger on a purchase. It's when there are multiple people from the same company visiting various pages of my website on the same day or in the same week. When I suddenly have a deluge of traffic from one company, they are likely getting serious about buying. Make sure you have a trigger set in your CRM to let the sales owner of that prospect know something might be going down soon based on activity like this. Then that salesperson can take the opportunity to reach out ASAP. Again, this can be automated in most systems. "Hey, sales gal Rochelle, one of your accounts is super active, so we're bumping this up in your queue of folks to reach out to today. Enjoy!"

You should now understand why being able to predict the behavior of your prospect as it relates to a period of time is important. If you put that together with the other *Ps*—People, Programs, and Pulleys—you should be able to predict which programs to focus on and what the outcomes will be (especially if you had a million dollars). How do these people behave, and what do they want in terms of content and programs? Depending on which channel or program they came through, how long will it take them to close? And knowing all this, do you have a sense of the levers you can pull based on the requirements you've been given to decrease budget or increase leads?

Let's go build out some scenarios and see.

## "IF I HAD A MILLION DOLLARS" SCENARIOS

If it hasn't happened yet, it will. And it usually happens at an inconvenient moment. (If you must know, it usually happens when I have exactly thirty-seven seconds for a bio break after sitting in a two-hour meeting that went an hour over.) It's called "the ask." There are different categories of this: the good (best-case scenario), the bad/ugly (worst-case scenario), and the BAU (business as usual). The ask could be to you directly, or it could trickle down the chain to you, depending on your role. Regardless, below are some helpful ways of framing your response.

Always start with a clarifying question or two. The goal is to understand what the actual ask is, what the desired outcome is, what caused this change, when a response from you is needed, and in what format. Also, if you can quickly come up with a response to help the inquirer know you've captured the essence of the ask, and even provide some initial thoughts, this is helpful. "If I understand correctly, we need to reduce our budget by 10 percent next quarter because we lost a large customer this week and need to compensate in case we can't make up the revenue. I have some ideas of how the marketing department can do this, like maybe skipping blah, blah event. I'm also curious as to why we lost the customer and if there are some changes we can make in our sales process as well. Let me get back to you by the end of the day with some initial thoughts." By responding like this, you show you not only have a pulse on your programs but understand issues along the entire customer journey. And, even more importantly, you likely reduce some of the asker's angst by not freaking out (at least not in front of them) and give them hope this can be achieved without too much effort. It builds up their confidence and trust in you. Well done.

Now let's look at some potential responses to specific scenarios.

## Best-Case Scenarios

**Increase budget.** This is when someone comes to you and says there is "extra" money that needs to be spent somewhere, somehow, and asks if it were to be given to you and your organization, what would you do with it? Remember, they are looking for an answer right then and there—not just to what you would do with these magical funds but what the result would be and how that compares with what other teams might do. Invest $X into Program A. Get $Y in revenue in X months. Challenge accepted.

**Clarifying questions:**

- Is there a specific goal in mind (i.e., a specific pipeline number sales needs to reach by the end of the quarter)? Or is there a revenue number we need to hit our stretch goal or a percentage we're trying to increase by? And by when?

- When would we have access to the magical funds? Are they available now? Next quarter?

- Is this a one-time "bag of money," or will this increase be available in future quarters and reflected in a new budget number?

- Do the funds need to be used by a certain date, or are they only good for a specific period of time (e.g., this month only or this fiscal year)?

*Scenario 1*

The company needs to increase incoming pipeline by 10 percent for next quarter, which is Q3, with a goal that the pipeline, or expected revenue, will then close by end of Q4. In order to do this, an additional $50,000 could be set aside for marketing. Got it.

**Things to consider:**

- What is your current sales cycle? If it's six to twelve months, it would be hard to bring in anything that would close by the end of next quarter. Focusing on nurture programs for leads you already have is key.

- Where is the pipeline now, and is the 10 percent a stretch goal? What is needed to make numbers for the quarter or year?

- Is there anything your sales team has been asking for that you couldn't previously give them due to budget constraints?

**What would Christina do?**

(So glad you asked.)

- I would check that my current workflow is working as set up (i.e., are leads getting qualified and over to sales the way the flow was designed, and is sales following up? Are the anticipated number of leads coming in?).

- I would invest in programs that I know shorten the sales cycle, in order to usher the prospects to close in time.

- I would optimize my nurture campaigns and either focus on moving people through more quickly or focus on prospects further down the funnel. This is relatively low-cost but might require some content to be developed.

- I would develop a specific webinar to move folks through the bottom of the funnel faster (e.g., a thought leader–type webinar that will convince the naysayers to sign a contract).

- I would do a promotion that encourages prospects to close by the end of the quarter if they want to leverage the discount. I've got the budget; why not consider a discount or promo? Note: I would make sure to think through the additional money gained against the overall cost of the promotion. I can use funds for ads, the design for an ad and landing page, or 1:1 content (i.e., switching out the title page to personalize for prospects), but I may also have to use some of the funds to cover the cost of lost revenue over time. It's got to come from somewhere. So I might need to also divest of something.

*Scenario 2*

The company is behind on revenue by $250,000 for Q4, which is five months out. What could you do with a whopping $10,000 to help meet this goal? Lots. No problem.

**Things to consider:**

- What is your current sales cycle? Same potential issue as before: If the sales cycle is six to twelve months, it would be hard to bring in anything that would close by the end of next quarter.

- Do we have any big-ticket prospects in the pipeline now? In other words, are there any "whales" you can focus on?

**What would Christina do?**

Who, MOI? (See what I did there?) In addition to doing some of the things in Scenario 1, I would also do some of the following:

- I would focus on expansion of current customers. I've already essentially paid for them, so the return could be high. What can I do to help current customers better understand the value and either renew, renew early (lock in price now), or buy more seats/licenses? Are there any incentives I can give them?

- I would definitely plunk down my newfound funds on ABM. Often thought of as too expensive, ABM is one of the best ways to get qualified leads ready to buy faster. Oh, and someone else does the work for you. You just have to pay them to do it. I'm okay with that since I just got a whopping $10,000!

- I would focus on some 1:1 marketing, working closely with sales. At one company, we were trying to close a multi-million-dollar deal, a whale, but the target company was having trouble understanding what the product would look like for them. So I spent some budget developing a sandbox and landing page just for that company. Rather than having three to four people set up a trial with their own data, we created it for them, with their own brand. That way, the prospect could clearly see what it would look like. They were sold, and that deal pushed us over our goal for the year.

## Scenario 3

Extra budget. Seriously? "Yes, we found an old bag of money under Lisa's desk. We think you could use the money more effectively than any other team, so here you go." Easy peasy.

**Things to consider:**

- Are there some potential quick hits you can do?
- Can you expand or optimize your current programs?
- Can you use funds to help others be more successful?

**What would Christina do?**

So many things. So little time.

- No question. I would use the funds to try new things. Test the crap out of stuff. A/B new landing pages or ads. Come up with an innovative, experiential marketing program.

- I would try out some of those programs the sales team or specific regions have been asking me for since last year but I didn't have the time or money to do. For example, maybe I would translate pertinent case studies into different languages where those case studies might be useful, or do a webinar in a different language. (By the way, I like to repurpose older webinar slides and scripts this way. I just update them and have a native speaker do the webinar. Boom. Happy sales gal in your Asia-Pacific region. Happy prospects in the Asia-Pacific region. Easy win for me.)

*Scenario 4*

You asked for it, you got it. You submitted a plan months ago and thought no one saw it, or at the time the budget was denied. Now they are giving you all the funds you requested. (Okay, this scenario might be a stretch, but work with me.)

**Things to consider:**

- What did you ask for? Is it still pertinent? Has anything changed since you last asked for it?

- Is there anything that needs to be reprioritized, especially given goals and upcoming deadlines (e.g., quarter close)?

**What would Christina do?**

- I would do a Snoopy dance (when no one was looking).

- Then I would get serious, look at the plan I submitted, and reprioritize as needed.

- I would start implementing the plan fast so I don't lose the money. And I'd focus on some quick hits so I could go back a month later and say, "Thanks for the extra budget. We've already implemented and seen results XYZ from the first program. Looking forward to seeing how the program works out over time. Oh, and we're getting ready to launch three more programs that we think will do just as well or better."

**Increase in headcount.** Congrats, you are now the proud owner of a brand-new headcount. Time to determine who (title/role) to hire, what will they do, and why to prioritize this particular role.

**Clarifying questions:**

- What is the budget/salary range/grade for this headcount? I want to create a role and job description appropriately and hire the right-level person.

- Are there any skills in particular that management thinks would be beneficial to hire immediately? While it is my job, or my team's, to determine where the skills gaps are, it's always good to understand management's perspective.

- Are there any specific goals we need to consider when hiring for the right role? For example, are we planning on doubling events and so should focus on bringing in an amazing events coordinator?

- How many people can I actually hire? Is it a budget constraint or an actual headcount constraint? That is, can I use the budget for consultants and specialists, or does it have to be a headcount?

- Is this for realsies? Or is this headcount going to go away or be given to another team if I don't move fast enough, like within a month?

## Scenario 1

You get one headcount, they will report directly to you, and you have enough budget to hire a mid-level person. Yay!

**Things to consider:**

- What programs do you have coming up where there is a skills gap?

- How long will it take to fill this gap?

- Do you have folks on your current team who might be a good fit or would like to try a new role?

- What level would you hire? Should you bring in an expert or someone who is hungry to learn?

- How will this person impact your goals over the next six to twelve months? There will be a learning curve in addition to the hiring and onboarding time. So what do you need now, and what do you need going forward?

**What would Christina do?**

- I would likely already have in my head, or even in a document somewhere, what roles I need, in order of priority, based on the goals we have for the next twelve months.

- I would likely already have someone in mind. I can see if they want the job, or I can use them as a representation for who I want to have.

- I would get someone hired ASAP. I can't tell you how many times I have been "given" a headcount, posted the role, and interviewed applicants, only for the headcount to go away. Poof! Just like that.

## Scenario 2

Your team is getting a new headcount! They will report to your manager, likely one grade above you.

**Things to consider:**

- What programs did you not recommend doing because the skills or resources didn't exist? Can this new person help fill the gap? For example, if doing thought leader webinars would be key to increasing sales pipeline, but you've had to focus on top-of-the-funnel lead-gen, can you push the hiring manager to take the skills or roles you need into consideration?

- Is this a role you might like to present yourself as a candidate for?

- Do you know a great candidate you can refer—someone you know would do a good job and would like to work with?

- Can you help the hiring manager formulate the job description based on some of your needs? For example, you write a lot of short-tail pieces but would love someone who can write long-tail—so can you suggest bringing in someone who can write longer pieces to complement your skills?

**What would Christina do?**

- I would make sure my manager and the hiring manager know my skills, even if I am not going after that job. This way I can ensure whoever is brought in will complement and not overlap my skills.

- If I wanted the role, I would talk to my manager about the best way to go after it, and get some honest feedback as to whether I would be qualified and considered. If they laughed at me, that would be a clear sign that not only would I be a bad fit for the role, but maybe my own manager doesn't know my worth. Just putting that out there.

- I would articulate the various programs I'm running and areas where a headcount would be able to have impact.

## Worst-Case Scenarios

You might not actually have any headcount reporting to you, and you might not have any budgetary authority. So your goal here might be to influence those who do have budget and headcount. Can you help your manager understand where it's best to divest or shift focus and priorities? Can you guide them to make impactful decisions? What from your Map of Influence can you pull in here to help?

**Decrease budget.** Sometimes this comes as a dollar amount. You need to slash your budget by $100K. Or it could be a percentage. You need to trim your budget by 20 percent. Or, um, yeah, you no longer have a budget at all. Been there. Done that.

**Clarifying questions:**

- Is this a universal cut across all departments? Try to get an overall sense of what is going on, as this will help you decide how to downsize as effectively as possible.
- How does this impact current goals set for the company, the marketing team as a whole, and me? It's critical to understand if you and your team are being asked to achieve the same goals with less money, if the goals have been reduced too, or—the worst worse case—if you're being asked to do more with less.
- Is there a possibility of more decreases?
- Is headcount impacted, or might it be soon?

*Scenario*

Your budget is being decreased by 25 percent for the remaining fiscal year, which has eight months left, but by all means, please maintain your current goals for number of leads, pipeline, and revenue. Bring it!

**Things to consider:**

- Double-check your goals, and make sure they're even still attainable. If they are not, make it clear what you *can* do within these constraints and what the likely outcomes will be with the reduction in funds.

- Prioritize. Goes without saying, but it's a good opportunity to reflect on current programs and see if you need to shift things around.

- Are there others in your organization or company who can help? Who can maybe let you use a person 25 percent of the time? Can you piggyback off of someone else's PR budget? Quid pro quo?

**What would Christina do?**

Ha! I laugh in the face of adversity. Seriously, though . . .

- I would refer to my Map of Influence. For net new leads, what can I reuse and repurpose? Can I rerun an on-demand webinar? Can I have a Q&A session going on in my community either concurrently with the webinar or as a follow-up?

- Who else in the company can I work with to get shit done? "Hey, amazing partner in product. How about I produce a webinar you can leverage and market to as well, but I need you to pay for the designer and ads? Such a deal." By the way, this should be much easier now, because you have built up trust and influence with them.

- For revenue, I would focus on expansion of my current customers. What nurture campaign can we run, and how can we help with customer satisfaction? I would look at the touchpoints on my Map of Influence. What can I pull in here? I worked for a company once where there was a high correlation between customer satisfaction (which was going down per NPS) and churn (which was sadly going up). I asked the customer support team to identify the top five issues they were seeing with customers. From there we built out a FAQ that we made easy to find and use. Churn went down 20 percent in the first three months. Part of the dissatisfaction was that customers had to call someone to get what they thought were easy answers to frequently asked questions, so we removed that friction. Less friction = happy customers. Go figure.

**Decrease in headcount.** This can come in the form of needing to let go one or more current employees, which sucks on all levels. But you have to now ask, how are you going to shift your programs to accommodate for the downsized team—that is, if you weren't the one to get cut?

**Clarifying questions:**

- Is there a universal headcount reduction across all departments? In other words, will other organizations be as strapped as mine, or will I be able to leverage them?

- How does this impact my current goals? I assume they will change too, since my headcount is going away.

- What is the justification for this, as it may impact other programs I have running?

*Scenario*

You have been asked to decrease your headcount by 10 percent, or the equivalent of one full-time employee. This needs to be done immediately, but you're expected to maintain the current growth level. Good news is you don't have to go for your stretch goal. Gee, thanks.

**Things to consider:**

- Based on your current programs and strategy for the foreseeable future, who on your team has the most skills and capacity to help see it through?

- What can you divest of or put in maintenance mode (i.e., what can you let run as is, without any headcount)?

**What would Christina do?**

- If I needed to choose who to cut from the team, I would likely keep those bringing in the biggest results based on our goals. Or those who have the potential to step up and help us through this hump. Or those who are generalists that I can shift from one program to another.

- If I was not the person managing headcount for our team, I would definitely make sure my manager knows what I am bringing to the table, what my contributions are, and what results I bring. Hopefully I will have made myself indispensable and built up enough trust and influence that my manager and others know my value and potential.

**Increase in expectations and goals.** Congrats, you still have a job, but we need double the leads or 30 percent more revenue. Oh, and you get zero dollars more to spend until you can prove yourself and your programs.

**Clarifying questions:**

- What is prompting this shift or demand?

- How were these numbers determined?

- For what period of time does this cover? This is important, because your programs likely run for months at a time and possibly even longer.

*Scenario*

More leads, please. Not the first time you've heard this, whether it's from sales, your manager, or executives. Just assume they always want more. Here, you have been asked by your manager to increase leads volume by 20 percent.

**Things to consider:**

- Going back to a previous example, why do they want more leads? What is the ultimate goal? More revenue? More opportunities in the pipeline? More net new customers? All of the above, please. Now, please.

**What would Christina do?**

I'm pretty sure you can guess where this is going . . .

- I would use my Map of Influence to see where I can optimize my programs and content to be more effective, bringing in higher-quality leads, more of them, and ones that close faster without any sales intervention. Imagine, not only are you bringing in more leads (by repurposing, understanding your audience better, etc.), you are bringing in more revenue, and sales are converting faster. Genius! Your manager will love you.

- I would front-load my programs. In other words, I would invest heavily now and implore the marketing goddess that I can show value added in time to get more revenue. Again, this goes back to having trust and influence. Trust me. If you go tell your manager about a program you ran to help bring in the new higher goal of leads, that they're already converting at a higher rate in less time, and that you need more money to continue down this predictable path, I can almost guarantee someone will find the money for you. But you have to take a leap of faith in yourself. Just follow your Map of Influence. You already vetted all of that anyway.

In building out these scenarios, it's critical to understand the overall goals of the change in budget and headcount, for better or worse. Is it because there is a change in the budget (good or bad)? Is the goal to increase revenue or hit a certain revenue by a specific date? Is it to hit a certain number of leads or quality of leads for a given quarter? Is it new accounts? Reduction of churn by X percent? Increasing multiyear contracts? Retaining X percent of customers? All of these will likely lead to different scenarios. Remember those mix-and-match books, where you had three things you could interchange? Head, shirt, pants, for example? That's a good way of thinking about scenarios and building programs.

Ultimately it comes down to knowing your four *P*s well enough to know how to shift and pivot based on different scenarios.

## How It Helps with Influence

In case you didn't see a pattern in the scenarios, I'll sum it up. In situations like these, building trust and influence helps you make smart decisions quickly and with confidence. This leads to still more trust and influence. Congratulations, you are now on the influence gravy train. By being able to respond quickly on your feet, you show you know your programs inside and out and have a clear sense of which ones perform better under different circumstances. You can also more confidently say what you would do, why you would do it, and predict the outcome. This is especially helpful if you have to "put a stake in the ground"—in other words, commit to something you can't back up 100 percent just yet, but you have enough confidence in it that you are willing to go out on a ledge.

You are able to give numbers for your ideas, backing them up with data. This is about the time someone will say to you, "Really? How do you know this? Are you certain?" Don't be bullied. You know your shit. Either show them your data or tell them to go . . . on second thought, just show them the data. Always have numbers in your back pocket to demonstrate your reasoning.

You should also have a good sense of how to predict and plan for best-case, worst-case, and BAU situations. And finally, try and get to a point where you feel confident telling someone at a higher level that what they are proposing is a bad idea. Be able to explain why, as well as tell them what a better idea would be. For example, if someone were to tell you that you need to bring in 20 percent more leads for the next three months, tell them that while you could potentially do this, if the ultimate goal is more revenue and your sales cycle is six months, it would be better to focus on expansion campaigns with customers.

CHAPTER 12

# Infinity Is Measurable

once heard someone say that trust is highly contextual. I would take it a step further and say it's also highly subjective. So what can you do to build trust in context for your different audiences? And how can you make trust less subjective? Well, looky here, it's your old frenemy—data. Data usually has the magic power to take subjectivity out of the equation, allowing you to confidently demonstrate all that you have accomplished. That said, it's important to still be mindful of your different audiences and how they see, and want to see, the data to back up and support decisions.

I know I keep talking about showing results—proving yourself and backing it up with data to develop trust and influence. This section of the book, the *M* in RPM, is all about measuring. What should you be measuring? How and why? Who are you measuring it for, and how do *they* want to see it in a way that is meaningful to them? How can you present results to them so they understand?

When I started my role at Wells Fargo, I was tasked with understanding and building a contact-management strategy for their thirtyish-million-person database. At the time, I was working with sixteen different business units (BU), including mortgage, auto and student loans, credit cards, business accounts, wealth management, and more. That was at least sixteen people I needed to share my plans and results with every month, quarter, and year. Each BU had their own goals, their own email campaigns, and their own perceptions and biases. And each BU leader wanted to see the data for how these email campaigns performed in their own way. Sixteen different reports. Every. Month. One person liked seeing it with a graph. Another person liked a lot of numbers. Yet another person only read the prose. One poor guy was actually color-blind and couldn't follow along until I reformatted my reports. And so on (and on and on).

It was so crazy I could literally spend the entire month creating sixteen reports from the previous month and never catch up. Not only that, my job was to develop a *strategy* for the list of thirtyish million, not to develop reports all day, every day. Oh, and did I mention I would then have to have sixteen different meetings to present the information? The same information, shown differently, sixteen different ways, in color and gray scale.

So what the heck did I do? I met with each BU—not just the leader of the BU, but other stakeholders in those units. I wanted to understand what their goals were, from a BU level and from an individual level. I wanted to understand what information these folks needed to send up their management chain to build trust and grow influence with their bosses. What were some of the business issues they were struggling with? For example, were they behind on revenue or net new customers? Was there high churn? Might they possibly be dealing with a mortgage crisis, from the bank's perspective? (Pro tip: During a mortgage crisis, sending out an email to soon-to-not-be customers about a great new referral program you have is frowned upon.) By having conversations and gleaning this information, I was able to better understand what these units needed to accomplish and why. Turned out 80 percent of what these folks needed to see, and then share out with their own unit, was the same across all units. Imagine that. Now I can build one report that gets me 80 percent of the way there. I get to reuse and repurpose one report. Now we're getting somewhere.

I rebuilt the report to represent everything, yet kept it short and digestible. Then I added one slide per BU that addressed their specific needs. Initially they were more tailored from a look-and-feel stand-point to what the individual BU leader liked, but over time I was able to morph it into a slide with the same look and feel. Then, instead of sixteen different meetings, I cut it down to one, showing the overall data and then specific outcomes for each business unit. In addition, sharing one, consistent report helped everyone get on the same page, which made discussions and resource deliberations so much easier, because everyone was looking at the same data.

Altogether this freed up about 75 percent of my time, so I could focus on developing better email strategy and campaigns. (More on that a bit later.) What had previously been missing was an under-standing of what the different audiences wanted to see and how I could convey the results in a digestible manner for each of them.

In this chapter, I want to lay out some ideas on what to measure, how to measure it, and how to present the information, all based on your different audiences. And remember, this is going back to your Map of Influence—picking out those specific touchpoints, imple-menting them, and measuring the lift. You need to understand your data. Where is it coming from? Is it inclusive of everything you need? Are the systems you're pulling from functioning as intended? Were the workflows implemented properly across your MarTech stack so that you're measuring the right information? Can you replicate your reports consistently month over month so that you're always compar-ing apples to apples? Because, even if they don't trust you yet, people need to be able to trust the data.

Why does all of this matter? Maybe you aren't responsible for the overall development and dissemination of monthly, quarterly, or annual results. And maybe you are. Maybe you only need to look at and share results from specific campaigns and programs you own. Regardless, if you want to have more trust and influence, you need to become familiar with and understand the data available to you. It will help you share your results, both successes and areas for improvement. It will help you show the value you bring to customers and the impact you have on overall company performance. It will make it easier to ask for, and obtain, resources. It will also enable you to pivot quickly if needed, as you will have your finger on the pulse, so to speak. And if you are intentional about how you measure and consistent with how you report results, people will have confidence in you and the numbers you are sharing, which will enable you to gain more trust and influence.

This is even more important when you think about your overarching goal of creating significant change. Whether it's through developing or owning more of the go-to-market strategy; having a different approach to how you go-to-market; shifting focus to different programs, campaigns, or even audiences; or driving the direction of the product itself, change is hard. Really hard. It's going to be hard for you. But now you are asking others to get onboard with your change, which is their change too. If they trust you, and the data, it will be much easier. You are essentially becoming a disrupter, in a good way. But to do it effectively, you need to know your internal audiences.

There are generally three main audiences you need to think about when measuring results and developing outcomes and reports. The first is the executives and company leaders, which would include the board of directors. The second is your own marketing organization and adjacent teams, if you work with them. This includes your manager and others on up the chain. The third is the sales organization, from reps to partners, at all different levels. Then there is everyone else. Not to minimize them, but your target audiences for measuring your programs and providing results are essentially the first three.

Other folks you should consider are product teams, the customer success organization, and anyone else you work cross-functionally with. While they are important, they aren't as critical, so we'll focus on them less.

I'll walk through who these audiences are, what they care about, what they don't give a shit about, and areas they think they should give a shit about but really don't. I'll cover what to measure and how to present it to them, both graphically and verbally. I'll also give you some suggestions on what to do if you don't have access to this—or other, or any—data. (Run.) And I'll close out with not only how to use all this to show value, results, and impact but how to leverage it to influence strategy and build business cases for funding and resources.

## EXECUTIVES

We've already mentioned at the beginning of this book that one of marketing's key issues is that executives don't get what marketing does, and that we as marketing professionals might not fully understand where they are coming from. Just as we do with the target audience we market our products to, marketing professionals need to think about the audiences they need to convince within their company—in this case, the executive. Sounds super ominous. This group would include the C-suite, CEO, CFO, CTO, CRO, your CMO if it's not you. These are the folks tasked with gathering all the company information and making sure the business is moving in the right direction to meet its goals and obligations. These goals and obligations include maintaining or growing a specific share of the market, meeting revenue targets, ensuring customers are happy, and making sure shareholders are really happy. There is a lot on their plate to make this happen. Hopefully a lot of what you have identified with your Map of Influence and touchpoints are things that can help these executives meet their goals, as well as the overall corporate goals.

So what do they care about? Well, as you can imagine, that depends. It depends on their specific role, the structure of the company, the product, and extenuating circumstances, like pandemics. But likely what they care about most is revenue and how the company is going to get there. From a role perspective, the CRO focuses on the overall revenue and *always* how to get more of it. The COO makes sure everything is running as it should, from people to production. The CEO cares about revenue, especially as it relates to the overall goals (IPO, hypergrowth). And remember, the CEO likely has a boss too, called the board of directors. And, if you work for a public company, the company has millions of owners in the form of shareholders the CEOs are held accountable to. (You thought you had it bad!)

To get into the mindset of an executive, let's think of leading versus lagging indicators. Leading indicators are predictive measurements: Where are we going and how are we going to get there? They measure the activities necessary to achieve goals. Lagging indicators look back to measure past performance. Leading indicators can influence change, while lagging indicators are simply a record of what has happened. Fundamentally, a leading indicator equals action (what are you doing to achieve your goals?), while lagging equals results. Guess what? The executive is concerned with the leading indicator. They don't really care how you get there; they only care about the results. Keep this in mind as you are measuring and presenting your data to executives.

What do they care about most when they think of marketing? Revenue. Um, yeah, that's about it. I'm being hyperbolic, but seriously, that is what they care about and understand. Remember the story of the webinar I did that had eighty thousand plus views, and how the very next day I was asked how much revenue it brought in? They care about revenue, so you need to show them what revenue is attributed to your programs and campaigns. They also care deeply about the ROI. They gave you a budget, and they want to understand what you spent it on and the revenue it will bring in. This can be tricky for marketing professionals, as our programs take time to implement and for outcomes to be realized.

Also recognize that there might be a different cadence for when you need to present your revenue results. For example, with a startup, the CEO might be meeting with investors on a monthly basis and need to show progress. More established companies might need to show impact on a quarterly basis, which means you do too. Whatever schedule the executives are on for showing results to their "boss," that should be the same schedule you work toward to share your own results.

What executives don't care about? Well, sorry to say, they don't care about your marketing funnel as much as you do—in other words, at all. What executives do care about is the overall company performance—revenue—and what you and your programs are doing to help the company as a whole reach these lofty goals. This includes securing net new accounts, expanding contracts for current customers, and retaining customers. They don't care that you brought in 50 percent more leads at an event than were brought in the year before. What they care about is what that lift of 50 percent equals in terms of revenue. In their mind, it should be a 50 percent lift in revenue too (so be careful what you say). Forget Marcia from the *Brady Bunch*! "Revenue, revenue, revenue . . . I'm tired of being in revenue's shadow all the time."

| Funnel | How marketing professionals see the funnel | How an executive sees the funnel |
|---|---|---|
| **Top of Funnel/ Awareness** | Whoo hoo, we have 1,000 leads from the event we just went to. High five. | How much did that cost? When will we see the revenue? |
| **Interest** | Wow! 13% of the folks (130) from the event turned into SQLs! Thank you, nurture campaigns. That thought leader webinar did wonders. We rock! | Wasn't that event three months ago? And 13% seems kind of low. Our trials on the website are converting at 27%. Why is the conversion so low? And what will this all equate to in terms of new accounts and revenue? And when? And wait—sales just *now* got these leads? |
| **Consideration** | Saaaweeeet. 15% (20 of the initial 1,000 leads) of the SQLs from the event signed up for a trial! That's a 2% conversion so far. Awesome. That's a bit higher than industry standard for an event. | OMG, are we still talking about that event from six months ago? Have any of those leads closed yet? WTF does marketing do all day? All I hear from sales is that they don't have enough qualified leads! Why are you hoarding the leads? |
| **Intent & Evaluation** | OMG, we knocked it out of the park with those webinars and the e-book. We really helped nurture those leads even more. I think they will end up buying 25% faster now with all this cool stuff we are working on. | Blah, blah, blah, Ginger. I want my money back. And wait, now you want $25K as a deposit for this event for next year when we haven't seen a single close yet from the event this year? Are you punking me right now?! Am I on *Candid Camera*? What kind of an idiot do you take me for? |
| **Purchase** | Coolio. Six of the leads from the event we did nine months ago turned into closed-won deals. That's just about 27% conversion from trial. And they closed 20% faster and at a 23% higher average selling price (ASP)! Yay, that's above projections. Snoopy dance! Fist bump. Um, you're welcome, sales. Sales? Bueller? Bueller? Well, whatever. I've got to go produce another three events and two webinars. | What event was that? Oh, right. Well, it's about time. How much did that event cost us? Why did it take so long? It's been nine months, and why didn't we have more closed deals from it? |

So what do you do? What do you tell executives to allay any big fears they have about how much was spent, what the return might be, and when? Well, just recognizing that revenue is what they really want to hear about is step numero uno. Next, you need to make sure you always set proper expectations with executives. "Hey, Executive Sharon. As you know, we have a big event coming. It will take up a considerable amount of time and money. But we have seen good conversion of 1 percent year over year for this specific event. That might seem lower than other channels, but the ASP is usually higher with this audience, as it is our main target. That, combined with our very focused nurture campaigns, should shorten the sales cycle by 25 percent, from twelve months to nine months. I know this is a long way away, especially to show breakeven and a good ROI. But it should result in four to six closed deals, with an average sale of $85,000, which equates to $510,000 versus only $340,000. This is 15 percent higher than other channels. And we should start to see them close in nine months. We'll let you know if there is any significant movement." By saying something like this, you have set expectations that the numbers will look low but revenue will be higher per sold account, and you've made it clear when you think these sales will come to fruition.

Okay, now imagine you, or your manager, need to put all of this into just a few slides for all the executives to see, communicating what you do and your impact on the bottom line. No problem. I can do it in two slides. One slide would literally just have a revenue number on it: expected revenue by projected date (i.e., whatever date is significant to them, whether quarterly or annual). You've got to put a stake in the ground in terms of how much your programs and campaigns will contribute to the overall revenue generated. The slide could just be a number:

### Revenue = Huge
### Projected by mm/yy

Or it could show growth month over month to help executives visualize the progression. (Check the Resources section in the back of the book to access a sample slide.) And, for the love of Philip Kotler, show this slide to them first!

Okay, next slide, if you must: I would quickly and succinctly show how you plan on getting there.

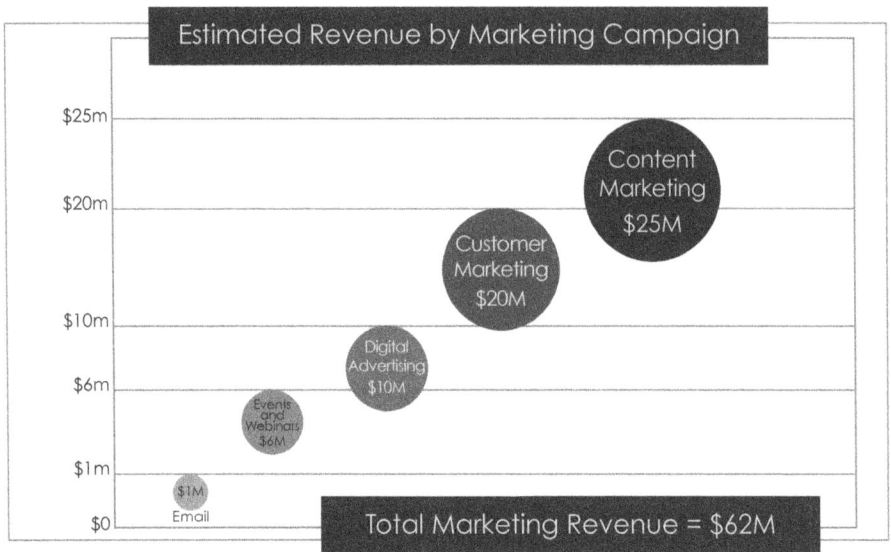

Estimated Revenue by Marketing Campaign

- Content Marketing $25M
- Customer Marketing $20M
- Digital Advertising $10M
- Events and Webinars $6M
- Email $1M

Total Marketing Revenue = $62M

Executives on Projected Revenue from Marketing Campaigns

Just like that, they can see what your focus will be and approximately how much each channel or bucket of programs will bring in. And, if you add the lift in there, it (1) shows you are focused on optimizing programs, (2) shows they're having a positive result, and (3) opens things up for further conversation.

That's it. That's all they care about. Okay, you will have to have all the data to back it up in case they ask you to dive deeper into how you got to these projections. But over time you will build enough trust, by delivering on what you said you would, that they will just accept it.

Also, because you have been focused on optimizing your programs and increasing influence, you are now likely exceeding your goals, bringing in more leads (of higher quality), shortening the sales cycle, and doing things to ensure a higher ASP. Wow, you really do rock.

Now is a great time for me to remind you that marketing really is a revenue center, not a cost center. So act like one. While it might appear that we are only focused on top-of-the-funnel leads, we are an integral part of the entire customer journey, all the way through, and past, the sale.

Where to find these magical numbers to help you establish your goals and projections in the first place, and to measure the outcome and impact? Your own backyard. That's right. Which takes us into looking at the numbers you and the rest of the marketing organization care about.

## MARKETING

You need to measure a ton of stuff for yourself, your team, your manager, and others you work closely with. You need to think about the different programs you have running, from content to events to nurture campaigns. You need to know how all your programs are performing, and by channel. Heck, by target and role. And why not by region while you're at it? You need to think about what your partners might need or want to see. Think about the different levels within your organization. Are there things you need to share up the chain, to your manager? Are there things you need to measure and share with your peers or employees? Yep, you bet you there are.

Again, you need to think about who your audience is and what they need to do their job better and show their own impact. Let's say your manager is the CMO. They have a weekly meeting with the CEO. Good news, you already have two handy slides you can share with your CMO to pass on up. But you also need to provide your CMO the context and backup data that shows how you came up with the information on the slides. If the CMO goes into a meeting and tells the CEO their team is going to bring in $X revenue this quarter, you need to supply your CMO with information to support this. The CEO might ask the CMO how they got to this number and what plans are in place to reach it. Great, you've already given that to your CMO. You're doing a great job making your boss look good.

If you are reporting out to your employees, what do you need them to take away from the conversation? Is everything on target, and if not, what can be done about it? (Oh, oh. I know. Have them check out their own Map of Influence and see what levers can be pulled.) You may need to show your partners, value added resellers (VARs), or other marketing teams in your company what you are working on and what the projected outcomes are. This helps them understand what you might need from them.

Everyone in your marketing organization, regardless of role or level, is going to need to understand the goals, plans to get there, impact, and results. It's best if you, or someone in the organization, can establish what numbers will be measured, how they'll be reported for the sake of consistency, and the cadence in which the report will be created. This can be done simply, on an ongoing basis, by creating dashboards in your systems and tools. For example, there are several numbers I want to see first thing every day: the number of "open" leads still sitting with sales (i.e., SQLs) that sales has not yet touched, closed-won deals and the amount of the sale, and a chart showing where we are in relation to our forecasted revenue goal. If I see an anomaly or a note that we are behind forecast, I can dig deeper, see why that is, and look at what we can do to fix it. But if I don't see that initial number in the morning, I'm flying blind, and likely spinning wheels.

I have no doubt you are already measuring a lot of things. The key is to focus on analyzing and evaluating the factors that help you understand how your campaigns are performing against the outcomes you forecast, so that you can show your impact. Remember, you need to measure and share meaningful results and data from your programs that clearly add revenue and therefore show your value add. Doing this enables you to build trust and influence the future of the company.

Let's look at data we can gather to use within our marketing organization (which we can then extend out everywhere). When helpful, I'll note out how some of it falls into buckets of leading versus lagging, as we talked about earlier. Marketing wants it all. These buckets, though, will help us organize around what might be most useful to other audiences too.

Remember, leading data points to where we are going and how we are going to get there, and lagging data shows how we did.

- Website traffic. Do you see cyclical patterns? Are Mondays better or worse than Thursdays? July sucks for most industries (except maybe tourism and hospitality), but in December do things really pick up? Are there pages on your website that seem to convert better than others? Website traffic is a key indicator for who is coming to your site, where they are going on your site, and how they are converting.
  - » Leading: website conversions, trial sign-ups, blog sign-ups
  - » Lagging: revenue
- Bounce rate. The industry standard bounce rate average is 50 percent. But it's best to aim for 25 to 40 percent.
  - » Leading: low bounce rate (in other words, people are finding what they expected to find on your site)
  - » Lagging: website conversions, time on site
- Your funnel and all the conversion rates associated with the prospect moving through the funnel.
  - » Leading: number of MQLs and SQLs, conversion rates

» Lagging: revenue by channel and program

- Sales team numbers. How many calls have they had? How many meetings have been set up? How many untouched leads are there? What is the conversion of an SQL to a sale? Are there salespeople who sell better? Leads from channels that close faster? (Magic tip #265: If there are leads from channels that close faster, put more focus, energy, and money into those channels.)

  » Leading: number of calls, meetings, opportunities

  » Lagging: deals by channel, time to close (through various points in the journey)

- CAC. Sometimes this is just a straight marketing program number ($567 spent on programs and ads to acquire an average-sized customer), sometimes that number includes marketing personnel ($787 spent on average, including marketing personnel's time to produce and implement programs), and sometimes it even includes your sales team and expenses ($1,285 spent in terms of overall costs to acquire a customer). Regardless, having a goal for this number and measuring against it are important.

  » Leading: cost per click, CAC

  » Lagging: revenue, deals by campaign

- CLTV. This number is often developed at the corporate level, but you need to understand how much your programs cost and whether there are ways to reduce churn and increase ASP, both of which should increase your CLTV.

- Conversion rates. I know I've said this already, but this is key. If you know what conversion rates are, and you know what levers work to improve rates (cause you have a nice and tidy

Map of Influence you can look at), then you can implement a new process or program to help. For example, you know the conversion rates for people who engage with chat are 20 percent higher than for those who don't engage. So what can you do with chat to help get people engaged? Hmm, I don't know, maybe have the chat bot pop up with something relevant to them, like an e-book? Here are some examples of the rates you should gather.

>> Website conversions

>> Email open and click-through rates

>> Conversion rates by channel, program, salesperson, organic versus paid

>> Both stage and status conversion rates

- Content performance. This is tough unless you have content management and systems implemented that enable you to measure. But if you don't, you can always look at how the content is performing as it relates to a specific campaign. Say you have an e-guide you offer as a bonus for attending a webinar. Did people download it from the email you sent? Campaign-specific performance is a heck of a lot easier to measure than looking at more general content performance over time, especially if it is an ungated piece of content or collateral that technically isn't being tracked.

- Program ROI. Yep, everyone wants to see this. How much revenue did this create, how much did it cost, and just for fun, how long did it take?

Remember, you could measure just about anything and everything. The key thing is to look at only what is relevant to you and your audience. You are trying to show the lift from your programs and optimization. This is where dashboards come in. All marketing automation and CRM systems have a dashboard of some type. A lot already have built-in templates for best practices. Start with these and tweak as needed. I would highly recommend having one dashboard for each of your audiences. At minimum: executives, sales, and of course, marketing.

## SALES

Let's face it. There is always going to be some friction between sales and marketing. But the more closely you can work together, and the more empathy you have for one another, the easier it will be. You know that revenue question you get a lot? Sales gets it a hundred times more than you. Working with them and better understanding their goals, their process, and their needs will help you tremendously. As I've known ever since my experience with the salesperson at Oracle ("data sheet straight to trash" man), marketing professionals need to engage the sales team to build better programs and content that will help sales sell faster, better, and more.

There are potentially different sales teams and structures within your company. You may have sales development reps (usually focused on inbound) or business development reps (usually focused on outbound), and these folks may even report into the marketing organization. You might have sales engineers, who know the product inside and out and partner with the salesperson who owns the account. You may have a direct sales team or a named accounts team. And you also might have a partner channel or VARs. You could also have an account management team that focuses on customer expansion and renewal. Or your company may be very transactional, and the focus might be on a more streamlined, low-touch sales process.

There are also multiple layers of management within a sales organization, with assorted VPs and maybe even a CRO to own it all. All of these could be reporting into one or many different organizations. And, to make it even more complex, they all have their own goals. Luckily for you, they are mostly revenue based. But they also want to have high conversion rates, in the shortest amount of time, with the highest possible ASP. No problem.

So at the end of the day, what do salespeople want to see in terms of your results? What data does sales care about? Well, sales cares about pipeline growth, in terms of both number of opportunities and the potential revenue from these opportunities. And sales cares deeply how you, amazing marketing professional, are going to help them accelerate this. Sales also cares about the time to close, or in other words, the quality of the leads you send them.

I worked for a company where, on a weekly basis, marketing would give an update via conference call to sales on where marketing was against our goals—month-to-date leads, conversions, top of the funnel, programs we ran the past few weeks, and upcoming programs. On a monthly basis, this would be an in-person meeting. My team created a lovely colorful PowerPoint that went through the entire funnel—graphically pleasing, and full of great information about how many leads came from this or that event, how much website traffic was up and bounce rate was down, and so on. Then the presentation went through the funnel, the conversion rates, blah, blah, blah, all the way through to pipeline, opportunities, and closed-won sales. Sound familiar? It's a normal report out on the state of marketing to constituents and stakeholders, in this case, sales. But I noticed the sales team became less and less engaged as the presentation went on. Phones came out of pockets to look at the latest cat videos or see what might be for dinner. Other people made excuses to leave. Some salespeople were on their laptops "taking notes." This went on for about two months, and I really struggled to understand what the issue was. After all, the numbers we had to share were awesome!

Then one day I was talking to a salesperson at my cube. He kept looking over my shoulder, and I could tell he was getting more and more agitated. I asked him what was going on, and he said, "I hate your whiteboard." Wow, not sure what my whiteboard ever did to him, but it definitely made me wonder. So I turned around, and on my whiteboard I saw the same funnel that was in the presentation. Only this funnel I updated daily. It showed the number of leads marketing brought in at the top of the funnel. IN BIG GREEN NUMBERS! Whoo hoo! It was a good reminder to me and my team how we were doing against our goals. And yet, it was literally pissing off this sales guy. I asked him what specifically he disliked. Turned out the whiteboard was a beacon for executives to bitch about how crappy the sales team was doing. What? How the heck did that happen?! I was just trying to pump up my own team's spirits.

Turns out, executives walked by my board every day and saw a huge green number (remember, these are top-of-the-funnel, newly acquired, haven't been nurtured or qualified, don't-even-know-if-they-really-know-who-we-are-yet leads). Then, unbeknownst to me, the executives would use this to ask sales why they didn't have more closed deals. After all, "marketing is claiming they brought in two million leads" (I embellish). Oh shit. No wonder the sales guy, and likely the rest of the sales team, hated my whiteboard. I literally erased it then and there. The salesperson visibly eased up. Phew. But it got me thinking: That was the same number we started our monthly report-out meeting with, which was coming up the very next day. And I had just approved the slides for that meeting. Ugh. I went to the person on my team who was going to be presenting the next day and told him to flip the slides. Say what? Yep, you heard me. Flip the slides. Literally start the presentation from the last slide, which shows how many closed deals came in and how much revenue it equates to. And then work the slides backward from there.

Truth is, sales didn't really care about how many leads we brought in. They didn't really care how many leads marketing was nurturing, or which programs the leads came from. What the sales team cared about was opportunities marketing created for them through our programs, how much pipeline marketing brought in, and what leads we sent over that had converted far enough along so they were likely to close. They also wanted to know what we were doing to accelerate more leads to pipeline (i.e., how marketing could move leads through more quickly so that sales would get them more quickly, and then what marketing could do to help sales nurture the leads even more). And finally, they wanted to know what we were doing to grow quality leads. Um, yeah, that's our funnel, just backward. Well, how do you like that?

Just like the executives, the sales team wants, or needs, to see certain information. And it would appear salespeople prefer to see numbers pertinent to them, at least initially. Flipping the order in which we dispensed the results immediately helped them see how marketing contributed to their success. Oh, and because the meeting wasn't such a slog, we were able to cut it down from one hour to thirty minutes and actually accomplish more. It also made the sales team want to collaborate more on upcoming campaigns. It was a total win-win. We turned mistrust and contempt into an opportunity to build trust and influence.

Just like the executives, this audience doesn't really want to hear all the details about how we got somewhere—they want to know how we're helping them, and how they can help us become even more efficient. I would keep the results you share with them to a minimum and cover the following:

- Opportunities created: pipeline, leads

- Closed-won opportunities by month and quarter

- Pipeline deals by projected close date and current stage

- Traditional funnel (sure, go ahead; just don't focus on it)

- Top ten pipeline list (I also like to build out seek lists, or queues, that help prioritize which contacts/leads/prospects should be followed up on, and update in real time. Seeing the contact's score change based on activity can help the salesperson identify moments that might be pivotal.)

- Open opportunities by created date (This one may be more for marketing than sales, but it's a great discussion point.)

- Conversion rates for opportunities, both closed-won and lost

- Deal price, however it is measured for your company (e.g., ASP, annual recurring revenue, etc.)

If you were to do a one-slide presentation to this group, it would have just a few numbers on it. (Check the Resources section in the back of the book to access a sample template.)

## Quarter Results

| Pipeline | Revenue | Closed Won |
|---|---|---|
| Q3 $ 13,784,445 | Q3 Revenue $ 6,456,453 | 134 |
| 17% above Q3 Target | 123% of Q3 Target | 15% above Q3 Target |

Example Slide for Sales

# EVERYBODY ELSE

I don't mean to minimize anyone else in your organization that is a stakeholder, collaborator, or contributor to your work. It's just that, as in a good marketing campaign, it's better to have just a few target audiences. Everyone else is sort of ancillary when it comes to effort, resources, and focus. But that doesn't mean you should ignore them. You just need to spend less time thinking about, measuring data for, and developing specific reports for them.

I worked for a company that did an hour and a half weekly update to the entire team of 150-plus folks. While it might seem efficient to have one meeting and get everyone on the same page, unfortunately it had some negative effects. In general, only about 10 to 20 percent of the information being shared was pertinent to any given person. That meant that for 150-plus people, at least an hour of time was wasted, weekly. I calculated it out (probably in the middle of one of those meetings where the presentation had nothing to do with me), and it was about $1 million annually of wasted time. It really goes back to knowing your audience and then measuring and sharing out data they care about.

For me, this usually means sharing information with the product, engineering, and customer success teams. I create a standard report or presentation, usually leveraging the presentation I did for the sales team. Instead of presenting to everyone all at once, I have team-specific meetings; even though I just said there's no need to customize, it's still beneficial to highlight specific areas that impact them. I usually do this as a lunch-and-learn on a monthly basis. And, while I might make the entire presentation available to everyone, during the meeting with a specific team, I only touch on points I need them to understand.

It is important that folks on these different teams understand everything in context. With the product team, for example, I need to convey that the reason our ASP was higher for the deals that closed that month was because of the amazing features and functionality they had added to the product. I need engineering to understand why I pushed so hard to get a product out by a certain date, by demonstrating how we were able to take advantage of the huge press and prospect presence at that event to launch our new product. And I could show customer success how conversion rates increased while the time to close decreased because of their efforts around developing how-to videos for our trials.

Deciding who to share what successes with will depend on you, your role, what your company does and the structure, and so on. But you should be able to take your handy Map of Influence and identify several areas where you can measure and demonstrate other teams' positive impact. Helping teams understand things in context and how it impacts them, or how they impacted the outcomes, is key. It opens more opportunity to collaborate and facilitates a more cross-functional organization moving toward one, or a few, main goals.

During one of my lunch-and-learns with the engineering team one day, I shared a case study we had just completed, where customers shared their successes and ROI based on a new feature. Yay, engineering. Nice job developing that useful solution that is saving our customers money and giving them a competitive edge. Suddenly, one of the engineers spoke up (which surprised me, because it actually looked as if he hadn't been paying attention). What he said was "You know, we have anonymized, aggregated data that can show what the industry standard should be for customers like this. Could you use something like that? Would that be helpful?" Wait, what?! Are you kidding me? I would kill for that information. Turns out, our engineering team had access to a plethora of industry data based on the ten years our product had been out in the ether. Gold. Mine.

Why didn't I or any of my predecessors know about this? Well, no one had ever shared results with the engineering team before so that they understood the impact they had and could have. They all became very excited and said if I could help them better understand some of the programs we were working on (e-guides and articles, infographics, and more), they could provide us with some cool data. They even agreed to write some blog posts for us. Wow, over a one-hour lunch, we helped engineering better understand their contribution to the overall company performance and how they were helping marketing achieve our goals. They were practically giddy (I mean, as giddy as software engineers can get) and planned to go off and think about other areas where they could help us, and thereby the company. Another win-win, and a great trust builder.

Always be thinking about your different audiences, what their goals are, and what data you can measure and share with them in a way that is meaningful.

## OH SHIT, WHAT IF I DON'T HAVE THAT DATA?

All right, some of you might be thinking this is all fine and dandy, but you don't actually have some, or any, access to this data. It could be because you don't have systems in place to capture the data. Or maybe those systems were implemented so long ago they make the data questionable or meaningless today. Maybe you have data, but you have no way of knowing whether it's spot-on or total shit. Later in the book I'll talk about tools and systems you should have in place to make this a bit easier.

But if you don't have the data you need now, there are a few things you can do. First, take a class on Excel. While I don't recommend it as part of your MarTech stack in general, if it's all you have, at least learn to use it to its fullest extent. You can look at industry data and benchmarking to get a sense of where you should be. Then do what you can to establish a baseline for yourself that you can measure against. Make sure you document how you are building out reports. That way, you will always be looking at your data from the same perspective—so even if the data sucks, you'll still see trends, patterns, and hopefully lift.

Leverage free tools like Google Analytics and Google Data Studio. Jerry-rig things by using UTM parameters, and capture the information via Google Analytics (which is actually a really strong tool if you know how to use it). You can also, as I mentioned before, set up your conversions in Google Analytics or using a Floodlight tag. Or use Google Tag Manager, which helps you manage tracking codes.

I feel pretty comfortable using my gut (i.e., thirty years of experience) to know what the outcomes will be. If you know the industry well, feel free to estimate your goals via your gut. Just make sure you can measure this. Regardless, you might have to throw a well-aimed dart at some numbers so at least you have some goals to work toward.

Over the last few chapters, we've covered how to develop programs and content we can effectively reuse and repurpose. Doing this extends your ability to deliver, and it builds consistency across your channels. And you can now predict the behavior and outcomes of your programs and content. The final component is to measure the results and present the right data to the right audience. Always put yourself in the shoes of the person receiving the data, and consider what you can share to make it easier for them to see your value and impact.

Now that you know your RPMs, you might want to go back and reprioritize your touchpoints on your Map of Influence. That thing just keeps getting better.

# CHAPTER 13

# Um, Yes.
# That Was My Intention

How many times have you been in this situation? You work hard to define a goal, set in place an amazing plan to reach that goal, then once you reach the goal, people think it was some weird anomaly. "Wow," says incredulous company leader. "You coincidently hit the goal you forecasted and budgeted for. What are the chances of that happening? There must have been some outside force that made that happen. Seriously, what was it? Magic wand? Pixie dust? The sales team?" Arrrrggggghhh!

Unfortunately, it's not enough to develop a good forecast and solid plan, execute seamlessly, and accomplish the goals set out. You need to market with intent and show everyone that what you are doing is executed with that intention. Otherwise, people will think achieving your goals was mere coincidence, or magic.

Simplified, an *intention* is the plan you aim to execute and the goal you try to accomplish. If you are being intentional, you have a goal or purpose in mind. Doing something with intent is doing something you mean to do, whether you end up pulling it off or not. This isn't something you hear at work often, if ever: "What are your intentions?" But it's something marketing professionals should consider in order to be as effective as possible. You also need to *show* others that your outcome, and the impact, is a direct result of your being intentional. It wasn't dumb luck or magic. It was pure grit.

In this chapter, we'll cover how to take your go-to-market strategy and align it with your customer journey path, your Map of Influence, and your repeatable and predictable programs; and then put it all together to develop marketing programs with intention. From this you can show how you intentionally impact company performance through measuring and sharing results with your different audiences. We'll discuss how you set goals and deliver results in a way that leaves no doubt as to your contributions, thereby building more trust and influence. I want you to be able to show the intention behind your decisions—what programs you ran, what content was created, which webinar you produced, and why. You want to convey your results so it is clear the success of the programs was intentional, because you are a marketing genius.

## GOOOOOOOAAAAAAAAAALLLLLL(SSSSSSS)!!!!!!!!!!!!!!!!!!!

In order to drive forward with intention, you need to understand the overall purpose, vision, and goals for the company as a whole and the organizations within it. Luckily, you should have a much better sense of this after having gone through the Map of Influence exercise. It all layers together. Understanding the overarching company goals, short term and long term, allows you to mindfully and purposefully develop impactful programs. Knowing your external audience allows you to be prescriptive with your programs so the customer's journey is seamless, resulting in a positive experience. You can identify touchpoints throughout the customer journey, and you can leverage your Map of Influence to be intentional with the programs and content you develop.

We talked a lot about what to measure and how to measure in the last chapter. And we keep talking about building more intentional marketing programs based on goals (both company and department). But what does that mean, and how do you do it? First, you need to understand the goals and why and how they were established. Also, dare I say it, you need to develop your own professional goals, or as I like to call them, MAP, for MOI Action Plan. That's French for My Action Plan (kind of). Heck, if we're going to have yet one more acronym to learn, why not make it something you can get your hands around? Like a Treasure MAP. Okay, I know it's corny, but it has a nice ring to it.

Let's start with the company, though. You should have a good sense of what your company's overall goals are. What's their purpose? Their North Star? Think about it in terms of understanding their intent. For most companies, this will be revenue based, but why? What is the endgame? Is it to get funding or go public? Maybe your company wants to be acquired. Maybe the company needs to pay off debts or investors. Maybe keeping the shareholders happy is the goal. In order to be as effective and intentional as possible, you need to understand these high-level goals.

Let's say you work for a mid-size business that has a few rounds of funding under its belt. The company needs to have significant revenue growth to get the next round of funding, which will be used to expand into other regions and update the product itself. The company hopes to close this round in the next twelve months. From there, the goal is to IPO in the next thirty months. Seems straightforward, and your CEO has likely talked about it at company all-hands. So now you know that short term, the company goal is more revenue. Great. Mid-term, the company needs enough revenue growth to entice and excite current and new investors. Nice. Long term is an IPO. Yeah, baby, that's why I'm here.

What can you as a marketing professional do now, knowing

everything you know, to help grow revenue and scale the company? This is a great opportunity to either leverage your Map of Influence or use this information to shape your Map of Influence. If nothing else, this information can help you prioritize or reprioritize. You might bump up efforts for faster-converting channels to bring in more revenue in the short term, or increase the pipeline, which would show investors growth opportunity. To entice investors even more, marketing might focus on some key case studies or a momentum release, to show progress. Or you might focus on having some positive press or high-performing article in the *Wall Street Journal*, which would help investors see the significance of your company in the market. All of these should already fit nicely into your very intentional marketing plan, and you might have some programs and content you can repurpose if needed.

Now let's say the product needs a complete overhaul due to extenuating circumstances in the world. What the company thought was a clear path to an IPO is now experiencing a bump in the road, and therefore the company needs to go after another round of funding *now* to fix the product issue ASAP. The timeline is now truncated, from twelve months down to six months for the midterm goal of getting another round of funding. "No problem," says enthusiastic marketing professional, with Treasure MAP in hand. "X marks the spot! If we shift our event budget to activities for our account management team, we can focus on expansion of our current customers. This should bring in $majordough by the time our company has its next meeting with potential investors. We will be able to show the investors that our customers are not only loyal but growing significantly. You're welcome." Investing in events seemed like a good idea when you had more time to nurture the leads, but now amazing-marketing-professional-to-the-rescue you can quickly pivot to expansion of current customers with some programs and tools we discussed earlier.

You should always know what your company goals are, as they will help you plan, prioritize, and be intentional about how and what you develop and implement. As your company goals change (which should not be that often), you too should be able to pivot quickly to accommodate these changes.

# TOOOOOUUUCCCHHHDDOOOWWWNNN!

We're so close. You're in the final stretch to becoming an influential marketing leader. While it's super easy to say "I've got this" and to know you really do (by now, hopefully you can see that you really do have this), not everyone is going to have the same confidence in your programs just yet. You'll need to focus on which programs to run and then tell people what you are projecting in terms of outcomes and by when—in other words, share your key performance indicators (KPIs). And you need to have a timeline and milestones established, if only for yourself and your team.

Projections and KPIs are critical, not just for your own sake but because they show your company leaders you're serious about the programs and confident in the results. You are putting a stake in the ground. Doing this will show people you're capable of understanding the situation, capable of making decisions based on that situation, and committed. And that you'll follow through on that commitment. We discussed it earlier, but I want to be clear here. It won't, or shouldn't, be just you working to develop and implement marketing programs. You should collaborate where you need to in order to ensure success. By all means, ask for help. Leverage the heck out of whoever you can. The key here is that you come up with a solution to resolve a problem or get the company closer to a goal.

Your KPIs are the components of your plan where you convey what you expect to achieve and by when—what you will measure, what the goal is, where you will find that data, and how often you will report the results. With KPIs you want to have four to seven indicators you can measure and track the progress of, with associated goals that are attainable. In the earlier example that involved switching funds from events to programs with account managers, your KPIs might look something like this:

- Number of expansion contracts signed by X date
- Dollar value amount of these expanded contracts
- Percentage increase of that contract from the previous one
- Average time for upsell
- Net sales in dollars or percentage growth

These are all things you should be able to measure from your CRM. You might even be able to set up a dashboard and automate it. That way, on any given day you can see the progress and measure it against where you thought you would be.

Speaking of, milestones or checkpoints are key to any plan you develop. Whether you share these with others or not depends. Usually you will do your projections for the ultimate end date, but milestones help keep you on track throughout the process and show the incremental lift or results. Having milestones will let you see if you are above or below your intended plan, helping you adjust as needed. I like to have milestones for my team to establish my expectations with them. The milestones you come up with can include information on who owns the task, what the budget is, and when it's due.

Finally, make sure you set goals that are attainable! Remember, while you want to achieve great things, base your goals on data or past experience. If you're looking at best-case and worst-case scenarios, assume the worst and plan for that, at least externally. You might have some stretch goals in the back of your head, and you might have shared these with the immediate team, but do not put them in writing to set expectations. The only thing executives will see is your stretch goal, and they'll try to hold you accountable for that versus the lower, agreed-upon goal. Push yourself and your team to go beyond the "minimum," while also being realistic about what you can achieve.

## FOR THE WIN

I started off this book by telling you there was a way you could have more influence and sway in your organization, that marketing should own the overall go-to-market strategy, and that marketing really is the hub of a company and should be thought of as a Revenue Knowledge Center. We know which programs and areas we should be investing in and divesting from. We know when to pivot. When a company is behind target, who do they go to for help? When there aren't enough leads or pipeline or revenue, who gets called in to fix it? Who knows which programs and channels perform the best, or worst? Who can influence touchpoints throughout the entire customer journey, adding value and having huge impact? Who knows which levers can be pulled, why, and when? Who knows how to flip a huge in-person event into a virtual event without missing a step? Who you gonna call? Marketing!

We know and own a lot of this. We just need to help others understand the significance of our role and the intentional impact we have (as we also add even more value).

## THE CASE OF THE MISSING REVENUE (A MARKETING MYSTERY THRILLER AND SUSPENSE SERIES)

Once upon a time I was working as the VP of marketing for an e-commerce platform company. When I started, I had many conversations with the sales team about which channels were working for them. Turns out they loved Etsy. We were getting an average of one hundred sign-ups a week from that channel. Amazing! Each week it was generating a high number of leads that were converting to trials, and the sales team loved them. The leads pretty much closed themselves. Win-win-win. What could go wrong? Er, what's that you say, customer success? You hate Etsy customers? And when you say "hate," you mean "HATE." Interesting. This wasn't the first time I'd seen disparity between sales and customer success, but I definitely wanted to investigate.

First, I looked at the overall goals for the company, then the teams' goals. Then I looked at how the Etsy leads performed against these. And then I went all Sherlock Holmes:

- Hitting our revenue targets? Hmm, we seem to be behind here with this channel. How can that be? Conversions from trial to sale are really high. Something is amiss.

- Good profit margin? Wow, this channel seems to have a bad profit margin ratio. It seems as if it's bringing the rest of the company's ratio down, which is bad. Interesting.

- Cheap top-of-the-funnel leads? Check. Yay, marketing rocks.

- High conversion rate to trials? Check. Whoo hoo, we all rock.

- High conversion rate from trial to customer? Check. Outstanding rate. Much higher than other channels. So why are revenue and profit margin down?

- High MRR? Not so much.

- Easy self-serve onboarding? If by "easy self-serve onboarding" you mean that what should take a prospect thirty minutes max to do themselves now takes our customer support team twenty hours to do for each, which is now a monthly and annual loss for us, then yes. But that's not what we were going for. Onboarding for this particular channel is not easy.

- Low churn? Holy shit, these people drop off like it's no one's business. Wait a minute. What is their business? Ah, side hustle, fun-to-do-on-the-weekend creation of FIMO dough beads that don't actually sell. Oh, and "I have no idea how to run a business. Can you help me do my accounting and marketing too? Oh, and I didn't know I actually had to *pay* for this service. I'm out."

That's right, turns out the Etsy folks were shocked—even after they signed up and technically *bought* the solution, onboarded, and started using the service—to find out they actually had to *pay* for it. With our thirty-day guarantee, we would spend the time and effort to onboard them, train them, and teach them how to run a business, and then they would leave before the thirty days and demand a full refund. Well, no wonder customer support hated them. The Etsy leads were costing us about five to ten times what they were worth. Not a typo and not a good ROI. And the profit margin sucked. What is a marketing person to do? How can you delicately tell sales you are going to altogether stop leads coming in from this channel?

Actually, it was fairly easy. I knew what our company goals were (revenue, high MRR, and low churn). I knew what the sales team's goals were (high conversion rate to close, revenue, high MRR). And I knew what customer success was hoping for (the right customer, easy onboarding, and low churn). How could I build a campaign with the intent of fixing some, if not all, of these issues and influence the outcomes? In looking at my Map of Influence, I found lots of options and knew some combination would work. It's kind of like being in a test kitchen. You have a pretty picture of a dish, the recipe, the ingredients, and the oven. Then you play—what things can you do to impact the flavor and presentation for a different effect or audience?

In this instance, these were the options I came up with, based on touchpoints in my Map of Influence:

- Set better expectations around pricing on the website and app description content.

- Do a better job explaining who the solution is intended for (i.e., folks with a high volume of sales, both from a revenue and a number-of-transactions perspective).

- Stop advertising on Etsy or ditch the Etsy channel altogether, and spend the money on other channels that perform better and meet our objectives.

- Train sales to qualify quickly (e.g., ask prospects, "What's your volume of monthly sales?" If it's low, send them to marketing for long-tail nurture. If it's a high volume, work the lead).

- Incorporate chat onto the site to help automate the process of determining the prospect's volume.

- Focus on a better self-service onboarding, working with product and customer success.

- Score leads differently, based on which channel they are coming in from, so they don't SQL until we know their monthly volume.

Some of the options required working cross-functionally with other organizations, such as sales and product. In other cases, there were things marketing could do to directly change the trajectory of the current path. And, with the exception of changing the actual onboarding of the product, all of these were super easy and fast to implement. We changed the content on the website and sales channels to be clearer about who the intended audience was, the price, and the value proposition. We implemented a variety of ways to determine the monthly volumes being transacted to determine just how much of the salesperson's time should be devoted to working a lead. We changed the scoring on the backend to make sure that if we did not have volume numbers, it would take more nurturing to get a lead truly qualified. And we completely ditched the Etsy channel—not only stopped advertising on it but removed our listing from the site.

With the budget we saved, I moved funds to more lucrative channels. The first month was rough. We saw a huge drop in leads and trial sign-ups, which we knew would happen and had warned everyone about. But we also saw a significant decrease in churn and the equivalent of a full-time equivalent (FTE) reduction in the amount of time customer success spent on support tickets, all of which we also told sales and executives to expect. Eyebrows were raised, but I told them to trust the process. We had a plan, it was built with intent, and it was playing out as we'd anticipated. We were on target. The following month, even fewer leads came in, but those that did were more qualified. They closed more quickly and with a higher MRR, because sales could focus their energy. Sales was no longer wasting time with tire kickers.

By marketing with intention, you can make a huge difference in how you develop and implement programs and content, and how you show the impact you are having. It only took a few hours to implement most of these bullet items, but the outcome was significant, with a 30 percent increase in overall MRR in a very short period of time. There was a significant decrease in the number of support tickets. Both sales and customer success were thrilled. Developing and running programs without purpose and intent can lead to disaster, so always think about your goals, then build or restructure from there. Even if you can only influence one thing, it will have an impact.

# CHAPTER 14

# Totally Awesome Tool Time

You are so close to having grit! Stay with me just a little longer. The *T* in G.R.I.T. stands for the tools and technology marketing professionals can, and should, have in place as part of their MarTech stack. This might not be the sexiest topic, but these are all the tools and systems you need in order to accomplish your job.

The main goal of a MarTech stack is to provide a single, unified view of the customer journey from the marketing professional's perspective. As you know from the Map of Influence, that covers a lot! These tools will help you build and run your programs, as well as manage your content and contact strategy. And it's through these tools that you will be able to measure the impact your programs have and the value you bring. They'll facilitate building influence—helping transform you into that badass, influential, thought-provoking, industry-leading marketing genius. No pixie dust required (just a shit-ton of tools and systems).

Throughout the book, we've talked about ways to build influence, design more effective programs, and show impact, and I want to make sure you have what you need to put it all into action. In this chapter, I'll walk you through which marketing tools are must-haves versus nice-to-haves. I'll take you through what types of tools and systems I recommend based on the kinds of programs and channels you focus on, which will vary based on your product offering and industries served. I will mention some vendors, but I would rather concentrate on the *type* of tool you need instead of a specific product. I do this for a variety of reasons. First, there are over five thousand plus marketing tools available for you to choose from, and this book is already getting pretty long. Second, there are so many factors that go into selecting the right tools for you and your organization, such as the size of your team and company, skills gaps, industry and channels, budget, and more. Third, technology is evolving so fast that by the time this book gets published, new tools and technology will have been developed, and existing tools will have morphed or grown obsolete. And finally, you are likely coming into a marketing organization or company where there is already some kind of MarTech stack in place, and your options to switch or add on top of it might be limited.

No two MarTech stacks are the same, but they all need to cover the fundamentals. At minimum, I recommend having a marketing automation and campaign management tool, such as Marketo or HubSpot, and a CRM tool, such as Salesforce. Oh, and the two tools need to be integrated with each other. Google Analytics is a great supplement to these tools. You can do a lot with Google Analytics, and it's free, while other systems can be costly to buy, implement, and maintain. These three—marketing automation tool, CRM, and Google Analytics—are the essential components of your MarTech stack. From these three tools, you can build and run programs, see how they are performing, route leads to sales, and at a basic level, measure everything we looked at in previous sections. There are many options out there with different price points, features, and other systems they integrate into, and there are infinite ways you could set these tools up. You don't need five thousand tools, but you do need to think about your overall programs and company goals to ensure what you have is adequate.

## THE MARTECH STACK

There are tools for video marketing and tools for content marketing and interactive content marketing. There are personalization, optimization, and website-experience tools. There is a whole slew of advertising tools, from display and programmatic advertising to social media advertising to PR and print (yes, that's still a thing) advertising. Don't forget the social media realm. There are tools for influencers and advocates, tools that help with social media monitoring and reputation, and ones that focus on conversational marketing like chat. Channel marketing has grown significantly over the past five years, and there are tools to manage all the different channels you might have, from e-commerce to partners to affiliates. There are business intelligence (BI) solutions to specifically help collect, aggregate, manage, analyze, and understand data. There are also some common tools that are useful to marketing, like collaboration tools, project management, budgeting, and so on. You can go to martech5000.com to see all of them in a really big infographic they managed to shrink onto one 8½ x 11-inch page. In other words, bring your magnifying glass, and maybe a glass of wine while you're at it.

Here, I'll cover the tools that are essential for marketing professionals, especially those in B2B and SaaS organizations. To be clear, a huge chunk of your overall budget will go to your technology, from licenses to implementation to maintenance. So, if you are going to spend that kind of money, you should ensure you have the right tools in place and the workflows are set up properly, both of which will make your life easier in the long run: easier to run and optimize campaigns; easier to collect and analyze results; easier to go from marketing follower to marketing leader, and from leader to influencer. We, as marketing folks, often leave the task of selection up to the IT and operations teams. While they should certainly be involved in analyzing and deciding, the choice should be yours, as these are your tools to help you do your job and show your impact and value.

When thinking about your MarTech stack, you need to understand your company's and organization's strategy. You also need to understand the customer journey. Sorry, had to beat that dead horse again. Your marketing automation tool will be the foundation of your stack. If you don't have one already, there are several things you need to think about before purchasing (besides your strategy and customer journey). You need to understand the features it offers and if those features are what you need (versus want). What is your budget, and when do you need the tool to be operational? What other tools and systems do you need to integrate it with? Is it going to meet your specific needs based on your requirements? Pricing, scalability, onboarding, training, and ongoing support also need to be considered.

If you do have a marketing automation tool, you should count your lucky stars. Then go find the leaks in it. All the things we have been discussing up to now—customer journey, Map of Influence, measuring outcomes—will need to go through your marketing automation tool. This includes programs, content, leads, chats, conversion information, closed deal's size, and revenue amounts. You know the old adage "Garbage in equals garbage out"? That holds true here. Remember my example from Chapter 1, where I found out the company I had just joined wasn't even collecting the name of the prospect? How can you tell if you are attracting your target or how your program is performing—let alone if it's meeting your goals—if you are not collecting essential information? In addition to the systems themselves, you need to pay close attention to the workflows (or, if you have a marketing operations person, work with them to look at and set up workflows) and make sure the flows are functioning as intended for your goals. Even a small thing, like a score being wrong, can alter your entire workflow.

I had a fellow marketing friend, Sharon, who was trying to understand why her campaigns seemed to be producing great-quality leads, but the conversion rates were crap. More alarming, sales wasn't even complaining that the leads were crap. That right there should have been her clue. I had her dig deeper into her workflow. Were leads coming in with the right tags? Were they getting scored properly? Were the leads getting to sales but just not converting? Maybe the leads weren't really great-quality leads after all. But Sharon couldn't find the "leak." I took a look at her flows, and it turned out there was a trigger in her system that reset the behavioral score of the lead to zero every time it got to a certain point in the flow. So the leads were technically SQLing in the system but never making it over to sales for follow-up. That's right, because their score kept resetting, the leads never "left" the marketing automation tool. Instead, they were just recycled for nurture, then went directly into an automated flow from there. Good news, that was super easy to fix, but you must be able to recognize when something is amiss, as Sharon did, to even start look-ing for what might be broken.

I remember when I used to code HTML by hand, back in the day. It didn't take much for the whole program not to work. With one simple period missing or in the wrong place, the code would not run. Marketing automation tools are very similar. It only takes one small thing to throw every subsequent step out of whack, and it can be hard to find the glitch if you are not familiar with your workflows and systems. You need to be mindful of what you are inputting and trying to get as output. This is particularly important if someone else is managing those workflows, like your operations person.

Most people use Salesforce for their CRM. It's pretty com-mon and integrates well into most marketing automation tools. Regardless of which systems you have, the CRM tool usually "takes over" the lead once you pass it to sales. The marketing automation tool is focused more on marketing, whereas the CRM is focused on the sales side of things. But there are still things you need to work on within your CRM. For example, in Sharon's situation, the trigger that reset scores could just as easily have been a trigger set in the CRM system. And often you will build programs, campaigns, and their budgets in your CRM and then sync it over to your marketing automation tool.

You need to understand and influence how the CRM is set up. The system needs to benefit you, your programs, your goals, and the data you need to get out of it. It's a little-known secret of mine—although I suppose now that I am writing it here, the cat is out of the bag—that I am a certified Salesforce Admin, and I know how to code. I'm not saying you have to have these skills, but the more you know about the systems you depend on for data, the better off you will be. The CRM is usually where the master record of the prospect or customer will live, as well as the revenue generated from your programs, and the ROI of those programs. Marketing professionals need to make sure what shows up in the CRM ties back to the information in the marketing automation tool, especially the lead source.

Sometimes the lead source is not "carried through" the workflow; therefore, when the contact shows up in the CRM, it does not have the lead source associated with it anymore. I've worked with many companies where the website was also the application or solution. This can make it hard to capture the lead source, push it through these backend systems, and then have it populate into the CRM. If the workflows from the marketing automation tool to the CRM are not set up to have the proper flow, it can be a manual process to determine where the lead came from so you can attribute revenue to that program you launched. In other words, without the flow of information working properly, you will not get credit for the lead, and you will not have the fuel (revenue numbers and ROI) to prove the value of your programs. I spend a fair amount of time in pipeline reports making sure a lead source has been attached. I'm like the Nancy Drew of marketing, trying to piece together the clues to figure out who done it—in other words, which program the lead came from. "It was the thought leader program, in the Resource Kit, with the webinar that pushed them over the edge."

While your marketing automation tool and CRM focus on breadth—everything in and everything out—the rest of the marketing tech stack focuses on depth: the tools that help depending on what type of programs you're running, the target audience, and how that audience buys. In general, the main categories are advertising and promotion, social and relationships, content, commerce and sales, data, and management.

Here are some of my favorite tools in these areas, and what the tech stack might look like. This next part might feel like a technical blur of brief notes on various options, but I want to give you some broad context on what's available. So bear with me. This stuff is pretty fascinating (especially if you are a nerd like me) and game changing once you try it. So grab a big cup of coffee, and let's check it out.

## Advertising and Promotion

I do a lot of advertising around content, display ads, search, and social media ads, but I rarely do any mobile advertising or print. The solutions I need to manage my advertising may be different from what works best for others. For example, since I do more B2B enterprise marketing versus retail or e-commerce, there might be a display ad solution that is better suited for what I am doing (LinkedIn) compared to what someone more focused on D2C transactional sales is doing (AdRoll or Criteo). There are tools like Taboola that help you manage paid content and pay-per-click programs, but also help with retargeting campaigns. Video advertising is starting to bubble up for some companies, and there are many tools out there to help produce, and manage, marketing programs around video ads.

If you do a lot of advertising, it is helpful to find a tool that will allow you to manage your programs. It should also provide significant analytics on your programs. Pro tip: Find a tool that is multipurpose if you can. It will be less of a hassle to implement and manage, as well as cost less.

## Social and Relationships

This one is huge for me, as it includes ABM, chat, communities, event and webinar management, social media marketing, and reviews, as well as our lovely CRM tool. Depending on the size of your standard deals, ABM can be vital to the success of your programs and company performance. If focusing on a few big potential named accounts is your company strategy, then ABM is essential, and having a solution like Demandbase or Radius to help manage ABM is key. Believe me, the ROI is there.

I am a firm believer in leveraging your entire customer base as much as possible. One of the best ways to do that is to set up a community that allows both your customer success team to provide more support and your customer base to collaborate (or even commiserate) together. It also provides a platform for marketing professionals to disseminate information and learn more about your targets' pain points. While I feel these tools should be owned, maintained, and populated by customer success, marketing can play a role in how they are set up and used. Therefore, marketing should be involved in the decision-making process for determining which system to implement, how, and why. I look for tools that allow for customer reviews and collaboration, as well as for the community itself to rank content on the site.

I've given a lot of examples on how chat, or conversational marketing tools, can help all the way through the customer journey. These tools can help product understand feature requests and issues, and they can be great for top-of-the-funnel, general website interaction, and nurturing by marketing and sales. Sales can leverage chat to answer questions as the customer makes their way along the journey, as well as build the relationship. And customer success uses chat for tickets, maintenance, education, FAQs, general messaging, and more. Done right, and with some planning, chat is an extension of many organizations in your company. I look for chat systems that integrate nicely across all my websites and channels and that have a higher degree of automation capabilities, with a little AI thrown in, such as Drift and Intercom.

There is no end to the tools you can leverage for events and webinars—from tools like sli.do that let you share surveys with your audience during keynote sessions at in-person conferences, to webinar platforms like ON24 and Webex, to registrant and attendee management tools. The key is to make sure these tools integrate seamlessly into your marketing automation tool and CRM. Pro tip: Check the integrations page of your *primary* tool (e.g., marketing automation or CRM), and see if it integrates into what would be a secondary tool, versus the other way around. The likelihood of a more seamless integration will be higher. For example, if you use Marketo and are looking for a webinar solution, look on Marketo's integration pages to see who they integrate with.

Social media should be a huge channel no matter what your company's focus and industry. That said, you should think about which channels are best suited to your audience and concentrate on those. And don't be manipulated by the marketingsplaining out there. There's nothing more irritating than having someone in your company (not in marketing) marketingsplain to you about social media. "Hey, marketing gal, I don't see a lot of posts from us on Instagram. What gives? There's some cool stuff on there. Like of cats and sunsets and stuff." You can nicely, or not, respond, "Our target audience is not on Instagram. Oh, and we don't sell sunsets and kittens. Our audience is on LinkedIn, so that's where the majority of our efforts and budget go." Diatribe aside, you certainly will want to have a mix of social channels and try new things, but focus on those where your target audience is looking for information related to what your company does.

To that end, there are tools out there to help you manage and measure all your social media outreach. Some tools automate your daily postings, like Hootsuite and Buffer. Others help you better understand your impact on social media through analytics. Some tools offer predictive and trend intelligence that help determine virality and key influencers. Some tools will help you understand and optimize your ranking in social media and look at your social reputation. And on and on. The key tools for me are ones that can automate postings, monitor engagement, and provide analysis of performance. Beyond that, there are always new and fun things to check out in this space if you have the time (after you have spent the time to build out your Map of Influence).

## Content

Content is a fun one, at least for me. So much of what we've talked about in this book centers around content: what to create, what medium to create it in, and how and where to use it and measure it effectively. There are tools in this space to help you plan, create, and disseminate your content. There are numerous solutions to help you then manage and measure it, like BuzzSumo and Contently. These tools help you drive pipeline, revenue, and even customer retention by automating the delivery of engaging content experiences all along the customer journey. We talked about how important it is to know your audience and personalize the content (or at least give them the content they are seeking), but tools like Uberflip help you personalize the actual experience, not just the content.

Some tools out there, like Turtl, help you create interactive content. Instead of PDFs, the viewer can select what to see next as part of the experience. For example, on the web page, a visitor might be able to respond to a survey question, and we can share the cumulative results immediately. Then there are tools like Vidyard, Bonjoro, and Snagit that help you personalize videos. Think about your audience and the channels you are driving content down. Look for automation and tools that integrate seamlessly into your current tech stack.

Finally, asset and digital asset management tools—such as Bynder, Canto, and Capterra—are really helpful if you have a large quantity of assets you need to manage.

## Commerce, E-commerce, and Sales

These are tools that help you, your affiliates, your partners, and VARs sell your product. Whoo hoo. Who wouldn't want that? If affiliates are a channel of yours, then having a solution to help onboard, train, track, and sell will help your company in the long run. Affiliates are great if you have a product that sells a lot at a lower price point. You, as a marketing professional, probably won't own this specific piece; however, you need to be part of the buying decision, as you need leads flowing through to the marketing automation and CRM systems.

Your company might have a different channel strategy, focusing on resellers and VARs, especially if you have a longer sales cycle with a bigger ticket price. These partners need a place to hand over leads and track the progress, and they need to understand the long-term status of closed-won customers. Salesforce has a decent partner tool, but there are others out there, such as ChannelAdvisor, that focus on companies in the e-commerce space.

Then there is a plethora of solutions for your e-commerce and retail store selling platform—everything from Amazon to BigCommerce and Shopify. Finally, there are systems that provide quote-to-cash solutions, such as Apttus.

Again, the point here isn't that you would select, implement, and fund any of the selling solutions in this section. It's just that you should be involved in the selection and implementation to ensure the right information is going into your marketing systems.

## Data and Management

Data and management round out the tools that marketing professionals might find in their MarTech stack. A lot of the data you need can be found in your top three tools: marketing automation tool, CRM, and Google Analytics. Anything above and beyond that, and it's likely out of your realm. You might have a marketing operations or sales operations person who owns this piece, or you might be lucky enough to have a data analyst on your team, or at least have access to this person.

Data tools allow you and the company to dig deeper into the data, more from a business side of things. These solutions let the company evaluate and project where things will be in twelve months, and if things are on track. The person on the team who handles this data should quickly become your best friend, because they likely have at their fingertips a lot of the numbers you are trying to measure. If this person can give you the measurements you are looking for, it will be much easier than if you tried to find them yourself. You probably didn't get into marketing because you loved deep-diving into business intelligence and insights.

From the management side of things, what you as a marketing professional should care about are tools that help you collaborate with product and project management. Collaboration, as we have discussed, is key. Tools like Slack and Zoom (which can double as a webinar platform) help with both internal and external communication and collaboration.

Remember earlier when we talked about how you can influence the product strategy by understanding what customers are saying about your solution and how they are using it? Well, technically, ticketing tools such as Atlassian, Wrike, and Productboard are for the product team, but you need to understand what they do and how they complement and integrate with the rest of the marketing stack.

Finally, project management tools, such as Asana, Monday, and Airtable, provide visibility and transparency into the process and the status, in addition to being, well, tools to project-manage your programs.

As I write this book, more and more AI-based tools are becoming available for marketing and sales. I spoke about this at South by Southwest a few years back. Technologies that leverage artificial intelligence and machine learning will continue to automate the more mundane pieces of your job. These AI-based tools will no doubt transform the way we do things, but for the better, in my opinion. AI tools will reduce your effort in determining the workflows, for example. Instead of you spending time to figure out which path website visitors might take, tools will be able to predict those paths and guide folks down them. Yes, please! We're not quite there yet, but there are a lot of predictive tools that can help you now.

There are tools such as Send2 that determine what type of communication to send to folks, as well as the channel (e.g., email, SMS, etc.) and what time to send it. Click360 looks at your website traffic and information in your CRM to determine when someone is ready to purchase. Your marketing automation tool likely already has components of AI incorporated into it and can help with dynamic content and personalization. There are several tools out there that look at what the right mix of collateral and content is to help develop more effective campaigns. And there's so much more on the horizon. Keeping in mind your specific role and what your plans are for the next twelve months, do a quick search to see if there are other tools out there that can aid you.

As you can see, there is no end to the options you have for your MarTech stack. And while you may not own some of these, you do need to understand how they might overlap and integrate with your systems, how you can influence the decision-making process, how the solutions are set up, and how the workflows are developed. Also, not everything you need will cost you. Some of these are free or have a free option that could work just fine for you and your company. And again, if an integration already exists with your primary MarTech stack tool, it will be easier and less expensive to implement everything. And it will take less time to get it up and running.

## MARTECH STACK EXAMPLES

Remember, your precise MarTech stack will depend on your goals, the tools you already have available, your budget, your target audience, and the skills you have on your team or that are available to you from another team. That being said, here's a standard MarTech stack for a B2B company:

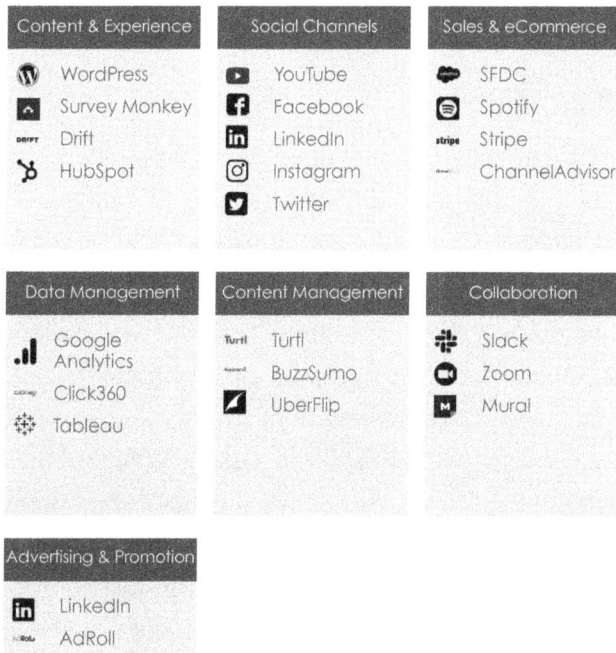

| Content & Experience | Social Channels | Sales & eCommerce |
|---|---|---|
| WordPress | YouTube | SFDC |
| Survey Monkey | Facebook | Spotify |
| Drift | LinkedIn | Stripe |
| HubSpot | Instagram | ChannelAdvisor |
|  | Twitter |  |

| Data Management | Content Management | Collaboration |
|---|---|---|
| Google Analytics | Turtl | Slack |
| Click360 | BuzzSumo | Zoom |
| Tableau | UberFlip | Mural |

| Advertising & Promotion |
|---|
| LinkedIn |
| AdRoll |

MarTech Stack Example

Per the same categories just outlined, you might use LinkedIn, Google Ads, or AdRoll for advertising. For content dissemination and engagement, you might use Drift to chat or SurveyMonkey to do surveys. You probably already have several social media channels—such as Twitter, TikTok, and Instagram—to interact with your target audience. From a sales standpoint, you might have a tool that deals with payments, and you likely have a CRM in place that can track where folks are in the sales process. At minimum with your data, you can use Google Analytics. But your marketing automation tool and CRM, as well as all the other tools you might have, allow you to capture and analyze performance, conversion, and more. Finally, you may have some tools like Google Workspace, Slack, or Microsoft Teams to manage day-to-day internal interaction. All of these systems need to be able to talk to each other, and most important, you should have one tool that acts as the master record, that all these other tools "report" into. This will usually be your CRM.

## IN ONE'S BACK POCKET

If you think about all the touchpoints on the customer journey, your very own Map of Influence, and all the tools and technology we have touched on, the key piece of technology needed to bring it all together is already in your back pocket. That's right. It's your very own website. We are so focused on some of the other tools, technologies, programs, and channels that we often overlook, or downright forget, what is likely our most impactful and easy-to-control tool—the website.

We use it to share our brand and messaging, distribute content, and publicize upcoming events and programs. The website is usually the tool in which people buy from us too. It is likely that everyone who has ever purchased and used your product has visited your company's website. Mind blown. We also use our website to run our programs and capture leads. Product, sales, and customer success all use the site too, through chat, content distribution, the community and knowledge base, and support tickets. There are so many touchpoints you can influence that pass through the website, which you, or someone on your team, already owns.

Your website is way more than just traffic and bounce rates. It's a powerful tool. If you've had a chance to start building out your Map of Influence, take a quick peek at it (or the version floating in your head). How many times did you think specifically about how you could use your website for some of these touchpoints? Now think about how many non-website-specific touchpoints you considered, such as reviews, ROI calculators, promotions, and chat. Oh, wait, they all flow through the website. Well, how do you like that?

I like to separate the website as a tool into three distinct areas of focus: navigation, content, and conversion—all of which can be optimized and A/B tested.

Starting with navigation, have you set up your website to guide your targets down the appropriate path seamlessly? Are visitors navigating as you intended, based on their persona? Have you provided the visitor with only what they need and removed the noise and distractions? Do you have CTAs where needed to help visitors continue the journey? At minimum, when you launch a new program, you should consider the navigation on your site. I'm not talking about doing an entire revamp. Just make sure that if you are introducing something cool, like a new e-book, it is reflected across your visitor's website journey, including the home page.

How many times have you downloaded something, then ended up on a landing page that either didn't go anywhere or took you to a place that seemed completely unrelated? There are times when I literally have to think, *What the heck did I type in to get to this page?* That's where the journey ends for me, and usually leaves me annoyed. Or maybe you make it a page or two into the website, but then nothing. No path to go down. No more content to read. This happens to me at least once a day. Cool new shiny object. I get all excited and click a link that takes me to a landing page. I download the shiny object. My mind is blown. And then nothing. Er, now what do I read next? I may look around for the next step, but because I have what I came for and am super busy, likely I'm gone. See ya! You've lost the opportunity to have me continue the journey right then and there. Sure, you will email me later, maybe even later that day. Or you'll have a sales rep reach out. But you already had me on your site. Why not try and keep me there longer by providing a series of actions I intuitively want to take?

In addition to looking at navigation for specific programs, it's good to evaluate your website quarterly. Look at it with your conversion rates in mind—both what you had forecast and what is actually happening with your rates. Then it's always good to assess the site on an annual basis as well. You've spent the last twelve months adding content, changing navigation by programs, and so on. Your site might be a little jerry-rigged at this point, so make sure it still has the right paths your prospects are looking for and is providing that seamless experience.

Content is the next area I like to focus on when it comes to the website. We already talked about how you can reuse and repurpose content. In terms of the website, we often struggle with a balance between not enough and too much content. Really, the consideration should be about quality, not quantity. You want to keep your visitors engaged and educated and guide them to take the next step. But it doesn't need to be an exhaustive, circuitous journey. It's one thing to try and keep people on your site for the sake of moving them through the nurturing process and customer journey. It's quite another to throw useless content at visitors just to keep them there. It makes you look like a delusional ex-girlfriend. "Please don't go! Just walk through one more infographic with me. For old times' sake." If the end goal is to have your visitor sign up for a trial, instead of crazy ex-girlfriending it, determine the shortest route to get the prospect there. Make sure your content is meaningful, is concise, and moves people through their journey seamlessly. Not sure if you are doing this now? Go check out your user flows in Google Analytics. Pro tip: You can apply a "Segment" to your flow view in Google Analytics. In other words, you can set it up to look at the flows based on your personas. Whoa.

Making sure visitors convert along their journey, hopefully to a positive end result, is your ultimate goal. You should have data that shows the conversions of form fills and trial sign-ups. You may have even set this up in Google Analytics as a Goal. But you also need to look at the conversion along the entire journey your website visitors take. Note pages that have a high exit rate. Is it because the visitor got to a page and didn't find what they were looking for? Or maybe they didn't trust what was there and left. Or maybe you sent them off site. Oops. You should see patterns. And if you leverage "Segments" in Google Analytics, you will see patterns by persona. This is especially true if you've recently launched a new program and want to see if visitors are behaving the way you intended. For example, if you just completed a webinar and have sent out a follow-up email that leads people to a landing page where you want them to take an assessment and then sign up for a consultation, is that what happened? You can usually see this within a few days of sending out the follow-up, although other programs might take longer.

Some website platforms give you the option of A/B testing. This can be great if you really don't know which way your visitor is going to go. Will they choose what's behind door A or door B? Do they prefer looking at an infographic or an e-guide? Does it depend on their persona? Most likely. A/B testing is great for seeing if your navigation is working as intended. It's also a great way to determine what messaging most resonates (e.g., do people respond better to "Buy Now" vs "Try Now" on a button?). Pro tip: Don't use A/B testing as a crutch because you don't know your audience, or because you don't have the confidence to make a decision. The goal of this book is to help you get to a point where you are confident in your decisions, and for others in your company to trust the decisions you make. Take advantage of A/B testing for what it is, but recognize it as a small support in your growing arsenal of resources.

Your website—now, that's a big one. A magical tool. Don't forget to use it, optimize it, and truly own it!

## A WORD ON WORKFLOWS

Workflows are an essential part of implementing and running your tools and systems effectively. If you were making pizza, you wouldn't drop some pizza sauce on a half-shaped pizza crust, add some cheese, cook it, then add some raw pizza dough on top. Okay, that might be extreme, but you get the point. You need to think about what outcome you are looking for, what ingredients you need, what you already have, and then what the right steps in the right order are to accomplish this.

Your workflow is a way to systematize the key steps in getting a lead from top of the funnel all the way through to happy, reference-able customer, essentially automating your customer journey on the backend in your tools and systems. This ensures consistency in how leads are recorded, routed, and worked by sales, all while removing administrative effort through automation. It allows you to simplify complex tasks, streamlining your process.

Your workflow also gives you visibility into where your leads came from, where they are now, and how they are performing. What stage is the prospect at in their journey, and what is their status? It helps you identify conversion rates and, by doing so, helps you see the levers you can potentially pull. You will likely have different workflows for each program—events, webinars, social media, email campaigns, and so on. But the majority of the workflow will be the same in terms of when they get pushed to sales for follow-up, since you likely have a score-based method of converting leads.

Continually improve and iterate on your workflows. Definitely set them, and "forget" them for now. But always make sure they work—and work effectively—for you. Look at updating them when new personnel or roles come onboard, if need be (e.g., when you hire a content marketing manager); when new programs launch; and when new sales processes begin (e.g., going from a named accounts lead distribution process to a round robin or territory-based process). Always think about the results you are getting (or not getting) and adjust accordingly.

Some marketing automation solutions and CRMs come with either default or suggested workflows, which are a good option if they work for what you need. Otherwise, you may have to customize your workflows, which can be cumbersome, especially if you don't have an engineer assigned to maintaining the CRM. The main components for you as a marketing professional to consider are the lead stage (MQL to SAL to SQL) and then the lead status (Marketing, Open, Converted, Opportunity, etc.).

It's always good to work directly with sales to define some of these workflows. You need to make sure sales agrees to the flows and that some of the SLAs are put in place (e.g., follow-up on trial leads must happen within four hours). Then you will likely need to train sales and anyone else involved on the flow. It's also important that sales management supports this workflow, as it's easy for everyone to point fingers when things get out of whack.

A colleague of mine, Mary, was having trouble showing the value of her programs. The main issue was that there was an agreed-upon process between marketing and sales for documenting the journey the prospect took once it was "owned" by sales. But in the rush to get deals closed, the sales team was not completing the contact record by pulling over the lead source. So while the leads Mary and her team were bringing in were closing, she couldn't prove it.

Granted, pulling in the lead source was an extra step for sales, so they just started ignoring that part of the process. It's a bit of a vicious cycle for marketing professionals. If we can't prove success of a program, we can't get budget for it. And if we can't get budget for it, we simply can't do the program. And if we can't do the program, we don't get leads, which sales then complains about. We need sales to follow through with the processes in place to understand the performance of the programs. Sound familiar? To stop this cycle, I recommended to her a tactic I have used in the past. Get leaders and executives, especially the sales leader, to agree to reduce the amount of commission given to the salesperson if they do not complete the records. If you have tried everything else, and you have the influence to make this happen, it can be very effective. As a matter of fact, the one time I had to implement this type of drastic move, it worked like a charm. One salesperson refused to update the contact record and didn't receive his entire commission for that sale. After that, he and all the other sales folks updated all the information marketing was asking for, giving us the data needed to make better decisions.

That might be an extreme example, but you have developed workflows for a reason, and you, hopefully, have agreement from the sales organization. Make sure to train folks on the workflows and help them understand the significance of them. Also, make sure you set expectations with everyone involved.

You should now have a good understanding of all the tools and technology available to you to automate as much of your programs and flows as possible. Defining and implementing your MarTech stack could be a make-or-break move to measure your results and show your impact and value.

As with most things, it might take a while to build out the perfect MarTech stack, potentially up to a year. The first step is to assess your current stack, or at least the essential three—marketing automation tools, CRM, and Google Analytics set-up. Then determine if you need to refine any workflows (usually done with your sales and marketing operations people), negotiate contracts, and implement all the pieces (working closely with IT). Remember, you will likely have to continually iterate on your workflows. As you look at touchpoints from your Map of Influence you want to employ, think about the tools and technology you need to pull it off, and be able to measure your impact.

# CHAPTER 15

# What's the Forecast for Tomorrow?

I know you are itching to finish this book so you can go refine your Map of Influence and develop amazingly efficient, repeatable programs and content, built with intention. And you know what tools you need and how to use them to measure and communicate your awesome results, becoming a marketing influencer with sway. You are a rock star! But you still have more to do. You also need to forecast out the anticipated results from your campaigns and programs.

When I first started out in marketing, there wasn't a good way to measure, let alone forecast, how our programs would perform. Nor was there a solid way to measure against the forecast. All of that changed when I went to work at Oracle. Oracle was a database company, after all. Surely they had data, right? In fact, they did. It was the first time I could see in black and white the impact I was having. We need data to both measure and forecast.

"Wait, why are we building a forecast?" you ask. A forecast shows what you agree to do in terms of lead numbers, conversion rates, and revenue, and how you will get there. It shows you have a plan to reach the numbers you have either been given or projected.

A forecast provides transparency and visibility for how you are trending between forecasted and actual at any given time, and it will help you determine quickly if you are on the right course or if you need to pivot. For instance, if for the second straight month there are fewer leads coming in, or trials are converting at a lower rate, you can identify this and see if you can fix it. Is it a pattern, cyclical, cause for alarm? On the other hand, if conversion rates are off the charts for one campaign, should you invest more in that campaign?

Even more importantly, a forecast will hold you accountable: to your manager, your leaders, and yourself. Yes, with influence comes great responsibility. But if you have gotten this far, in this book and in life, that responsibility doesn't intimidate you.

Because things change quickly in marketing, I build forecasts that allow for flexibility, as well as ones that help me understand the goals the marketing organization needs to aim for. I also make these twelve-month rolling weighted forecasts. That way, I am looking at how the leads convert over their lifetime, and I am always looking a year out, not just at the year-to-date for the fiscal year.

When building out the forecast, I always work backward from the overall revenue goal of the company. You as a marketing professional may have a revenue target, or maybe your marketing organization as a whole does, but here I want you to work all the way back from the overall corporate revenue goal. That is ultimately what everyone in the company is driving to and what you are trying to influence. If the company has a stretch goal—the this-is-our-actual-corporate-goal-but-we're-afraid-to-tell-the-board-in-case-they-hold-us-to-it goal—use that as your starting point.

From there you should forecast your website traffic, top-of-funnel leads by program, lead stage conversion rates expected (and therefore your leads converted over to sales for follow-up), pipeline estimates, closed-won/lost, churn, and expansion programs—in other words, conversions along the customer journey and your Map of Influence. If you have a good sense of conversion rates between these different phases and stages, you can forecast the next outcome in your funnel along the customer journey. And because you have a good understanding of the different levers along this path (touchpoints), you can build out a more accurate forecast model. In addition to the stages, you need to decide if you are going to forecast out by campaign (a specific program, maybe based on a theme, that has multiple tactics and components), by lead source (advertising, events, etc.), or by each tactic.

Your forecast toolkit should have, at minimum, three components to it. First, you need to estimate leads by lead source and, if you can, by stage in the customer journey. Second, you need to add up these estimates so you can track actual against what you forecast. Third, you need to create a slide you can share with just about everyone that shows how everything is trending, month over month, quarter over quarter, and year over year.

## FORECASTING FUN

Okay, let's get into the nitty-gritty. Again, start with the overall corporate revenue goals, understanding the different phases a lead goes through and the conversion rates from one stage to the other. Next, decide how you want to track your results, either by lead source, tactic, or campaign. Your company might have a portfolio of products you are responsible for, but for now, I'm going to focus on just one product. And because I am a glutton for punishment, I like to build out best-case (or stretch goal), worst-case, and business-as-usual forecast models. Luckily, you can use a simple formula to change these up, but remember to start with your stretch goal, since that really is the overall company goal.

As I just mentioned, you need to know your customer journey and have defined stages based on that. These should map to the same stages you have been thinking about for your Map of Influence. For example, with the buyer's journey, we referenced the following: trial & evaluation >> discovery >> nurture >> negotiation >> closed-won.

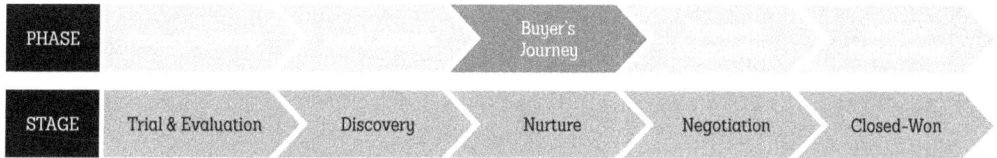

| PHASE | | | Buyer's Journey | | |
|-------|--|--|-----------------|--|--|
| STAGE | Trial & Evaluation | Discovery | Nurture | Negotiation | Closed-Won |

Buyer's Journey Phases and Stages

You should know what the conversion rates are between these stages (unless you are a new company that hasn't been through a full sales cycle yet, in which case use industry standard or benchmark conversions). What percentage of trial sign-ups move on to a discovery call with sales? And what percentage of those folks stay with sales to be nurtured and are considered pipeline? (Remember, we defined pipeline as the number of deals expected to close in a given period and the dollar value of those closed sales.) Then what percentage of prospects who have made it this far go on to a negotiating phase? What percentage go from negotiation to close? This is usually a lot higher than the other conversion rates, since by this time, it's really just a matter of cost and value (and maybe a competitor or two). I like to look at the overall conversion rate within this part of the customer journey. What is the overall conversion rate of prospects that went from trial to closed-won? I look at lead to closed, phase over phase and within phases, stage over stage, at least for the programs that are part of my Map of Influence.

The only other missing piece is your ASP. With this information, you should be able to build your forecast. You should be able to affirm that if your goal in revenue is X and you have conversion rates of Y, this is how many leads you need to bring in for your various programs. I like to use this simple equation: (Leads x Conversion Rate) x ASP = Revenue.

**Example 1:** forecasting number of leads needed to hit revenue goal

Leads = ?
Conversion rate = 15%
ASP = $1,000
Revenue goal = $200,000
(1,333 x 0.15) x 1,000 = $200,000
Leads = 1,333

Or let's say you don't know your revenue target, but you do know how many leads you have or are projecting, and that sales converts leads to revenue at 15 percent. Now you can estimate revenue.

**Example 2:** estimating revenue

Leads = 1,000
Conversion rate = 15%
ASP = $1,000
Revenue = ?
(1,000 x 0.15) x 1,000 = $150,000
Revenue = $150,000

Hopefully this isn't the situation you are working with (i.e., not knowing your revenue target). Just know that if you have three parts of the equation, you can always figure out the missing numbers.

Next, you need to decide whether to base your forecast on primary lead sources, specific tactics, or campaigns. Which you choose will depend on a few things. How granular do you want or need to go? And what can you capture, measure, and analyze from your tools? The easiest way is probably by lead source, which is easily tracked via every marketing automation tool. But as our tools and we as marketing professionals become more sophisticated, forecasting by campaign is more effective, as it's a real measurement of how your *strategy* is working. Don't forget, the goal of all this is to build trust and influence, so think about your audience and what would be helpful for them to see and understand. Let's look at forecasting by campaigns. With these forecasts, I look at the different themes we will have throughout the year and specific targeted campaigns (e.g., an ABM program, a program on expanding our current accounts, etc.). Unlike the other two ways of forecasting, this method incorporates many different tactics and lead sources. This is my preferred method, as it really captures the entire scope of my intended campaigns.

While forecasting by campaign will provide you more accurate information in the long run, it can be cumbersome, as each of these campaigns likely includes multiple lead sources *and* tactics. In addition, some tactics might overlap and be used in multiple campaigns (i.e., reused and repurposed programs and content). This makes implementing programs easier but forecasting and measuring a bit trickier. Your marketing automation tool can help here.

Working toward your revenue goal, think about conversion rates in the different stages, and combine all this with your programs to develop your forecast. Since I haven't been able to find a suitable tool to do forecasting for marketing (most of them start with sales and pipeline but skip the first essential step), I have built out my own spreadsheet (yes, sadly, we still need to use Excel for some things). You can find information in the Resources section in the back of the book or on my website at www.christinadelvillar.com. Here's what it could look like if you view it for one month, using lead sources as your measurement:

**PRODUCT 1**

### January

| | Marketing Lead Lifecycle | | | | | | | |
|---|---|---|---|---|---|---|---|---|
| | Lead and prospects | Conv Rate | Interest and engaged (MEL) | Conv Rate | Nurture | Conv Rate | Consideration (MQL) | Conv Rate |
| **LEAD SOURCES** | | | | | | | | |
| Webinars | 900 | 0.42 | 378 | 0.8 | 302 | 0.23 | 70 | 0.35 |
| ABM | 50 | 0.85 | 43 | 0.9 | 38 | 0.75 | 29 | 0.75 |
| Email | 3000 | 0.1 | 300 | 0.5 | 150 | 0.1 | 15 | 0.1 |
| Website | 45000 | 0.02 | 900 | 0.75 | 675 | 0.23 | 155 | 0.35 |
| Advertising | 4500 | 0.85 | 3825 | 0.55 | 2104 | 0.15 | 316 | 0.1 |
| Content | 12500 | 0.75 | 9375 | 0.75 | 7031 | 0.21 | 1477 | 0.35 |
| Trade Shows/ Conferences | 1200 | 0.5 | 600 | 0.25 | 150 | 0.23 | 35 | 0.3 |
| Regional Events | 75 | 0.7 | 53 | 0.5 | 26 | 0.5 | 13 | 0.5 |
| Outbound | 900 | 0.2 | 180 | 0.2 | 36 | 0.23 | 8 | 0.2 |

| | Sales—Buyer's Journey | | | | | | | |
|---|---|---|---|---|---|---|---|---|
| | Evaluation/trial (SAL—Sales Accepted Lead) | Conv Rate | Discovery (SQL) | Conv Rate | Negotiation (Opportunity and pipeline) | Conv Rate | Closed-Won/ Lost | Conv Rate |
| **LEAD SOURCES** | | | | | | | | |
| Webinars | 24 | | | | | | | |
| ABM | 22 | | | | | | | |
| Email | 2 | | | | | | | |
| Website | 54 | | | | | | | |
| Advertising | 32 | | | | | | | |
| Content | 517 | | | | | | | |
| Trade Shows/ Conferences | 10 | | | | | | | |
| Regional Events | 7 | | | | | | | |
| Outbound | 2 | | | | | | | |

Example: Measuring by Lead Source

I just threw in some potential lead sources, estimated how many leads we'd bring in for each of those lead sources, and added the conversion between the stages. Right away, you can probably see some areas of opportunity, as well as optimization. For example, if you look at webinars versus ABM, it takes eighteen times more leads with webinars to get around twenty-two qualified leads to the sales team. The ABM program might seem like a dud—fewer leads, higher initial price—but if I were to play this out more, we would see that the ABM leads will likely close at a higher rate and much faster. Also, industry average deal size for ABM leads close 171 percent higher than other lead sources. That's because ABM is all about identifying high-intent accounts: prospects within a target that have a high propensity to buy and use the product.

With the webinar lead, you might get four leads that close at an average deal size of $1,500, while the ABM will close ten of those at an average deal size of $2,600. That's $6,000 for the webinar versus $26,000 for the ABM campaign. That's significant! Two more things to think about here are your ROI and CLTV. If a campaign cost more than the revenue it brought in, you need to determine if it was worth it. Just remember, you might work for a company that is selling large, multiyear enterprise deals that will have an average customer life of five years. So your CLTV might be $150,000, while the cost was $33,000 for those ten deals. That's a 1:5 ratio, which might be a good ratio for your company. Regardless, you will sound like a super data marketing rock star having these numbers handy.

- *Company executive:* You want how much for a program that is only going to bring in fifty leads?!

- *Shiny marketing rock star:* Yes, but these are quality leads that close faster with a deal size that's an average of 171 percent higher than our standard leads. While the program might seem expensive, if you look at CLTV, we'll end up with three times the revenue.

- *Company executive*: Well, when you say it like that. Here, take my wallet.

Not only will forecasting help you understand the value of your different programs; it will help you further define your programs, inform others why you are investing in your chosen programs and campaigns, and show what the revenue outcome will be.

That's a lot of numbers, so now is probably a good time for a story. I worked for a company that needed to do some downsizing in terms of budget and headcount. Double whammy. Upper management had discussions with all the organizations, trying to get a sense of where cuts could be done with the least impact. When it came time to look at marketing, I had my handy forecast ready to go. I was able to show the number of leads we planned to bring in and how that equated to revenue; where the team was to date on leads, pipeline, and revenue (which was ahead of target); and what it had cost us so far. Then I showed them how much revenue would be lost if we took away a headcount, some of the budget, or both from the marketing organization. It was a significant loss, close to 30 percent. My forecast allowed me to easily show not only that we were on target but how much we would lose if we didn't maintain our current budget. Guess what? They made cuts in every organization except marketing! And even with headcount being cut from other teams, marketing continued the momentum, and the company ended up hitting its revenue targets.

The next piece of the forecast puzzle is to look at how you are performing against your forecast. Are you on target? If not, why, and what can you do to course correct? I'm using Excel spreadsheets for this example, but you may have tools that can automate this process and push data into an analytics or BI program. It's best to capture this information monthly at minimum. That way, you can see where you are trending and if you are on target or need to adjust. Plus, if an executive comes to you and says you need to cut something, you can show you are on the right trajectory and suggest the executive look elsewhere for budget to cut.

| PRODUCT 1 | January 20XX | | February 20XX | | March 20XX | |
|---|---|---|---|---|---|---|
| | Forecast | Actual | Forecast | Actual | Forecast | Actual |
| Total Lead Volume | 68125 | 66296 | 64610 | 36794 | 70750 | |
| Actual vs Plan | | 97.32% | Month-to-date February 15, XX | 56.95% | | |
| | | | | | | |
| Lead Sources | Forecast | Actual | Forecast | Actual | Forecast | Actual |
| Webinars | 900 | 1156 | 950 | 650 | 1450 | |
| ABM | 50 | 53 | 60 | 43 | 75 | |
| Email | 3000 | 1597 | 3000 | 1453 | 3500 | |
| Website | 45000 | 43789 | 42000 | 23546 | 46500 | |
| Advertising | 4500 | 4567 | 4500 | 2250 | 4500 | |
| Content | 12500 | 13423 | 12500 | 7654 | 13500 | |
| Trade Shows/Conferences | 1200 | 785 | 550 | 673 | 0 | |
| Regional Events | 75 | 25 | 150 | 75 | 25 | |
| Outbound | 900 | 901 | 900 | 450 | 1200 | |

Example: Forecast by Lead Source

If we look at the forecasting by lead source from earlier, there are several takeaways. First, marketing is hard—but you already knew that! Seriously, though, marketing is truly a combination of art and science. Let's break this example down.

For the month of January, this team came close to hitting their target. They fell short by 3 percent, give or take a lead. Webinars brought in more leads than expected, but more importantly, so did ABM. Email and tradeshows were way off, so I would look at that.

Was the tradeshow we went to a flop, not the right audience? Or maybe we weren't visible enough at the show, or we had a crappy booth space on the floor. For emails, did we have good click-through rate but fell flat once the customer got to our site? Website traffic was down by 8 percent. Significant? Significant for January, maybe, since that's usually our biggest month. But that could be because email leads were down.

For February, we're halfway through the month and trending to hit our target. Yay! Content programs are doing great, which could be why website traffic is doing well. And we seemed to hit a chord with our webinars, since we've only done one out of three so far and are well on course to hit our target. Can we capitalize on the previous webinar even more? Maybe follow up with a cool video use case or customer testimonial? Maybe that would be a better use of our resources than doing three webinars this month. In March we aren't doing any tradeshows, so we need to bump up our reach with other programs to hit our lead numbers. Maybe we move that third webinar and video follow-up to March to capitalize on it here instead, since February is doing fine? That's a strategic question you should consider. All that said, I still think it's better to go for more leads now. Don't hold back campaigns and programs just to make sure you hit a certain number of leads in a future month. I mean, have you ever heard a sales team complain about too many leads?

Forecasting, and the subsequent measuring to date or month over month, helps illustrate what you are doing, how programs are performing, and if you need to pivot. And now that you have your January actuals, you can dump them back into your forecast to see how everything is trending and if you need to divest in one area, invest in another, or ask for more funding overall.

Sometimes you will use the data to guide you, to help you make decisions and then make better decisions. Other times, the data will be there to prove you were correct. Either way, if you want to build

**PRODUCT 1**

### January—Actual

| | Marketing Lead Lifecycle | | | | | | | |
| --- | --- | --- | --- | --- | --- | --- | --- | --- |
| | Lead and prospects | Conv Rate | Interest and engaged (MEL) | Conv Rate | Nurture | Conv Rate | Consideration (MQL) | Conv Rate |
| LEAD SOURCES | | | | | | | | |
| Webinars | 1156 | 0.42 | 486 | 0.8 | 388 | 0.23 | 89 | 0.35 |
| ABM | 53 | 0.85 | 45 | 0.9 | 41 | 0.75 | 30 | 0.75 |
| Email | 1597 | 0.1 | 160 | 0.5 | 80 | 0.1 | 8 | 0.1 |
| Website | 43789 | 0.02 | 876 | 0.75 | 657 | 0.23 | 151 | 0.35 |
| Advertising | 4567 | 0.85 | 3882 | 0.55 | 2135 | 0.15 | 320 | 0.1 |
| Content | 13423 | 0.75 | 10067 | 0.75 | 7550 | 0.21 | 1586 | 0.35 |
| Trade Shows/ Conferences | 785 | 0.5 | 393 | 0.25 | 98 | 0.23 | 23 | 0.3 |
| Regional Events | 25 | 0.7 | 18 | 0.5 | 9 | 0.5 | 4 | 0.5 |
| Outbound | 901 | 0.2 | 180 | 0.2 | 36 | 0.23 | 8 | 0.2 |

### February—Forecast

| | Marketing Lead Lifecycle | | | | | | | |
| --- | --- | --- | --- | --- | --- | --- | --- | --- |
| | Lead and prospects | Conv Rate | Interest and engaged (MEL) | Conv Rate | Nurture | Conv Rate | Consideration (MQL) | Conv Rate |
| LEAD SOURCES | | | | | | | | |
| Webinars | 950 | 0.42 | 399 | 0.8 | 319 | 0.23 | 73 | 0.35 |
| ABM | 60 | 0.85 | 51 | 0.9 | 46 | 0.75 | 34 | 0.75 |
| Email | 3000 | 0.1 | 300 | 0.5 | 150 | 0.1 | 15 | 0.1 |
| Website | 45000 | 0.02 | 840 | 0.75 | 630 | 0.23 | 145 | 0.35 |
| Advertising | 4500 | 0.85 | 3825 | 0.55 | 2104 | 0.15 | 316 | 0.1 |
| Content | 12500 | 0.75 | 9375 | 0.75 | 7031 | 0.21 | 1477 | 0.35 |
| Trade Shows/ Conferences | 550 | 0.5 | 600 | 0.25 | 69 | 0.23 | 16 | 0.3 |
| Regional Events | 150 | 0.7 | 105 | 0.5 | 53 | 0.5 | 26 | 0.5 |
| Outbound | 900 | 0.2 | 180 | 0.2 | 36 | 0.23 | 8 | 0.2 |

Example: Actual vs. Forecast by Lead Source

trust and influence, you will need to follow the data. And having a forecast will give you a benchmark by which to measure your programs. In some cases, someone else may have already developed the forecast. That's okay. Just make sure you know which pieces you are responsible for. And if you have opinions about the validity of the numbers, speak up and make note of it. For example, if the webinar conversion number is 25 percent from lead to closed won, you might want to find out where that number came from, because that conversion rate is high for a webinar. Remember, if you're not sure what the conversion rate is for your company for this type of program, go with industry standards.

Whether a forecast originates with you or another team, it's always better to build it collaboratively and share with the rest of your marketing colleagues. But at minimum, you need it for yourself.

## MARKETING IS THE REVENUE KNOWLEDGE CENTER

Yep, you've heard me say it before, but I don't want you to forget it. Marketing really should be thought of as the company Revenue Knowledge Center. We have insight into the hundreds of touchpoints along the customer journey, which are essentially levers to be pushed and pulled to reach our goals and beyond. We can project company performance by lead source, campaign, programs, even down to the specific tactic. We know how much revenue can be generated from specific programs. We can see trends and cycles and take them into consideration when building out a forecast, and that forecast can provide the necessary visibility and transparency for everyone to work together and adjust when needed.

Not only do we hold the answers to ensure we hit revenue targets; as we've seen with the Map of Influence touchpoints, there are many things marketing can do to grow and exceed company revenue, not just meet it. ABM can increase revenue three times.

Optimizing the website can bring in more qualified leads (both in numbers and degree), which can lead to shorter sales, generating revenue more quickly and freeing up salespeople's time to sell more. Working with customer success and developing programs for current customers can lead to expansion of those accounts for more licenses, longer terms, and more revenue realized. Helping the product team prioritize features leads to more, and happier, customers. Revenue, revenue, revenue. You get the point. Not only can marketing meet our goals; we can exponentially increase the overall revenue by a significant factor.

Marketing professionals really do hold the key to a company making or breaking it. There's a reason we can and should be indispensable. And now you have the tools and confidence to start building more and more influence across your company.

# CHAPTER 16

# Swashbuckling Swayer, Full of G.R.I.T.

want to end where we started, with 17,000 leads (please!). That story of the board member who randomly asked for 17,000 leads was the true start of my journey with this book. It was the first time I truly saw that a lot of folks just don't understand marketing and the value marketing professionals bring to the table. I've been instilling the G.R.I.T. Marketing Method in my teams for years to try to change that, and this book puts it all into a formalized framework. You already have the skills; now you have the tools and mindset to change your trajectory, have more influence, and show the value and impact you bring.

In the beginning of the book I went through the sad details of how marketing professionals are currently undervalued, underappreciated, and villainized as a cost center. We have to take some responsibility for that, because most of us haven't been able to educate our audience about what we do and how it fits into the grand scheme of things—the overall company goals and performance. We have been the invisible corps. Basically, we failed to market ourselves.

I created this book to show how you can take this concept you know well—building and implementing a marketing strategy and plan—and apply it to yourself. You are a marketing machine when it comes to your company products and solutions. Now spend some time building, developing, and implementing a similar plan for yourself. I guarantee it will help you build trust, increase influence, add more value, and have exponential impact on the company revenue. The framework and methodology in this book enable you to build better, more effective programs; be smarter about how you spend your time and budget; and show people what you do, why you do it, and the impact you are having, framed in a way that is meaningful to them. You now have the framework to break the cycle. You know what to focus in on. Go-to-market strategy. Repeatability, predictability, and measuring. Intention. Tools and technology. You have grit.

You know marketing needs to participate in the go-to-market strategy development process more, if not own it in its entirety. We looked at the entire customer journey through this go-to-market lens and walked through each of the phases, from the product blueprint to the lead lifecycle, through the buyer's journey, and ending with customer engagement. In each of these phases of the customer journey, we dissected the various stages and identified the many areas marketing touches and how we can influence these touchpoints. All of this allowed you to build your Map of Influence, which should identify every place you can add value and have more impact. What are all the levers you can identify and pull? This map—prioritized by short- and long-term goals, potential impact, attainability, and value—is your own North Star, always guiding you and providing agility as you pivot through chaos.

Another key component of G.R.I.T. is the concept of RPM—repeatability, predictability, and measurability. By applying the concept of repeatability—reusing and repurposing programs and content you have already created—you can develop and implement "new" programs more effectively. You probably already have way more content than you need, so why not leverage it better? Some of your content might need a little touch-up or modification. Some of the content could be chunked up for use in multiple ways on multiple platforms. By building repeatability into your strategy, you provide consistency for your prospects too. Recycle, reuse, repurpose, rinse, and repeat. This enables you to get to market more quickly, be more impactful, and build predictability right into these programs.

With predictability comes the ability to know the outcome and impact you and your programs can have. No more playing Twister with your marketing programs. In order to have influence, you need to know not only how your programs will perform but how your customers will behave. All of this makes it easier to build the right programs and to measure and report your impact, which is essential to showing the value you bring.

Not only is measuring key; you need to know what to measure and why. How much revenue your programs bring in, directly and indirectly, yes. But what else? You need to think in terms of audiences and tailor reports and data around them in a way that is effective (e.g., not creating and dispensing sixteen different reports, in sixteen different formats, sixteen times every month). You need to use your newfound influence to guide the conversation. Show the weight of your data, and show how it ties into the overall company goals and performance. This should lead to people recognizing that your strategy, plan, content, programs, and results were all intentional.

Ah yes, intention. This is a cornerstone of the G.R.I.T Marketing Method. Marketing professionals don't have the luxury of extra time or resources, so we need to be intentional and strategic about everything we do. Doing things intentionally garners respect and also allows for focus, easier assessment of progress, transparency, and visibility.

The final piece of the G.R.I.T. Marketing Method is the tools and technology you need to help run, measure, and adjust your programs quickly, from foundational tools such as your marketing automation tool, your CRM, and Google Analytics to all the other five thousand plus options you have to integrate. With these tools, you can test and implement new programs, optimize everything (programs, content, website), and pivot when needed. And, speaking of, don't forget to leverage your website more. It really is the hub of all your programs.

Just like G.R.I.T. is the foundation of your influence.

And when you have that foundation set, you can build out your forecast. The forecast gives you, and others, visibility and transparency into your goals and where you are to date. A forecast can validate your decisions, which will continue to help you build trust and influence.

How does this look when we put it all together? Well, how awesome would it be if for any given scenario, you could save, revive, grow, boost, or expand your company? That's what it looks like.

Let's close it out with some examples, shall we? (Disclaimer: These are fictional portrayals of not-so-fictional people. Any resemblance is probably not a coincidence.)

> **CXO:** Sales is behind on their numbers for the fiscal year. With only three months to go, I'm not sure we'll hit our target. If we don't hit our target, we'll have to wait another year to go public. We're doomed. DOOMED!

> **You with your internal voice:** Oh, hell no. I haven't worked this hard for the past three years to not go public for another year.

> **You with your external voice, full of grit, figuratively holding your Map of Influence and forecast:** Fear not, favorite CXO. For the past two years, sales has closed the majority of deals in the last quarter and currently seems on target to do so again (forecast), based on the

types of leads that were brought in (intention, pre-dictability) and where they currently are in their cycle (customer journey). That said, I can think of three things we can do to ensure we hit our target numbers. First, we can divest time and money from ads and move those resources to programs that will quickly expand our current customers (MOI). Next, we can take the wildly successful webinar with complimen-tary e-book campaign we did last year and run it again (repeat, reuse). Finally, we can shift funds from one of our planned events to ABM, as those leads close fast and at a rate 170 percent higher than our other leads. Doing these should ensure we hit our target on time. While the event is critical to our long-term success, event leads take a lot longer to close (trust, forecast, measurability, predictability), and focusing on shorter-term programs will be more impactful (influence).

In less than a minute, you have given several options that could ensure the company can meet its revenue goals, leading to a successful IPO. Whoo hoo. Isn't this fun? Shall we do another one?

**Sales exec:** My team doesn't have enough leads. We won't meet our numbers. We're doomed. DOOOMMMED.

**You with your internal voice:** I call bullshit. Er . . .

**You with your external voice, full of grit, figuratively holding your Map of Influence and forecast:** I noticed that several of the marketing campaigns did not bring in the number or quality of leads we had forecast and aren't converting at the rate we had planned for (measurable, forecast). Here are three things we could do that would have an immediate impact. First, we can populate the chat with some bite-sized how-to videos, to help people in trial move more quickly and successfully through the evaluation (MOI, reuse, repurpose, intention). We can also provide sales with a testimonial quote sheet, with quotes from our advocates (MOI). Next, we can adjust the leads score, scaling back those that are not as qualified (MOI, predictability). I recognize that your initial concern is too few leads, but if we can get the sales team focused on highly qualified leads, the sales team should be able to close more deals, more quickly (trust, influence, MOI, measurable). Finally, marketing can develop a series of emails with best practices, ROI case studies, and invites to "exclusive" webinars, which sales can send out to help nurture the leads (repurpose, MOI, forecast). Oh, and I just thought of another option. We can work on a promotion to close out the quarter. How does that sound?

**Sales exec:** We're saved! SAAAAAVVEEDD!

Even if these are not the programs you ultimately develop, just being able to spout off three or four potential options shows you know your programs, understand the company goals, recognize what's at stake, and can offer a solution. Back when I started out in marketing, I thought it was better to listen, analyze, formulate a plan, come back, and present my findings and solution. But that actually reduced people's confidence in me, as it appeared my response was delayed. Don't be like that. You should now understand how to quickly offer an option or two. Then go back and figure out which one really is the best solution.

One more example? Sure, why not?

**CEO:** Holy crap! We spent how much per lead for ABM? What the hell is that anyway?

**You with your internal voice:** Okay. They probably know what ABM is. They just don't understand the value yet. I got this.

**You with your external voice, full of grit, figuratively holding your Map of Influence and forecast:** Account-based marketing, also known as ABM, provides some of the biggest returns of all programs and campaigns in marketing. You can see from our forecast that while we are bringing in few leads and the cost per lead seems high, they are much more qualified, coveted by sales (MOI), close more quickly, and bring in an average of 170 percent higher deal size (forecast, predictability). In other words $mega revenue (measurable), or 25 percent of our overall revenue (Revenue Knowledge Center). In addition to that, we have been working with customer success for the best adoption experience and already have two customer testimonials from it (MOI, influence). Because of all this, we have also seen faster expansion with customers coming from the ABM channel. And churn is lower for them. So technically, overall CAC is lower and CLTV is significantly higher (measurable, predictable, MOI, forecast, etc.).

**CEO:** Holy crap! Why aren't we spending more on ABM programs?

**You with your internal voice:** Sigh. Because when we presented it at the beginning of the year, you said no. But I see now I have some cool data to back it up, you are a believer, and you trust me (measurable, trust). So . . .

**You with your external voice:** I guess now is a good time to ask for an additional $50K to do more with our ABM programs. I believe we can increase revenue by 20 percent with these (forecast, measurable, predictable). I'll have a business case over to you this afternoon (trust, influence).

**CEO:** Amazing. Why don't we set up some time next week to discuss your future here at Company IPO and what you would like your career trajectory to be?

Hopefully you can see, with all the touchpoints marketing can influence, that marketing professionals like you truly hold the key to attaining and growing revenue. In the end, marketing already has a lot of influence on what the company does and how successful it is. We just need to be more strategic about what we do, and we need to help people within the organization recognize and appreciate it. What has been missing is your voice (and data, forecast, MOI, you know the drill) to prove this.

I have no doubt in your ability to see this to fruition. I've given you the framework and tools necessary to start your own journey to building trust, having more influence, and guiding your company to success. I know you can do it. You are a badass revenue-generating marketing influencer, full of grit. You can sway anyone. Now grab a chair, pull it up to the table, crack your knuckles, hunker down, take command of your future, and go save your company. You've got this!

# Acknowledgments

I'll try to be brief, which if you know me or have gotten this far in the book, you know will be difficult for me. It might be easier if I create an infographic. But until then, here we go . . .

First and foremost, I would like to thank my partner, Ken, who has stood by me in all my work and business endeavors (including over fifteen start-ups), shenanigans, and wild adventures. His steadfast and unwavering belief in me has been the rock that has allowed me to build my business, my life, and of course this book. His optimism always helps me see what is possible and gives me the strength I need to carry on. As he likes to say, albeit, completely stolen from Monty Python, "Always look on the bright side of life." Phwwwh-phwwwwwwhht. Phwwwh-phwwwwwwhht, phwwwh-phwwwwwwhht, phwwwh-phwwwwwwhht.

My career has been a lifelong research project culminating in this book. Well, hopefully it's not *the* apex of my career, but rather a crest, with another fun hill "just around the corner." For all the opportunities I've had over the past decades, I am forever grateful. While not all experiences were stellar, I definitely learned a lot from each and every single one (see chapters 1–15).

To all of the marketing professionals I have ever worked for, with, and managed, thank you! You inspired me in so many ways, and it's because of you that I wanted to write this book. I heard you loud and clear, and I feel your pain. In particular, I'd like to thank Jessica

Macintyre, for not only helping me get this book off the ground but always being an amazing soundboard. Of course, there are so many more (in no particular order, I swear)—Sheree Storm, Brenda Li, Jessica Ly, Becky Knecht, Rachel Knight, Amy Goldfine, Ellen Gomes, Charla Session-Reed, Richard Dym, Josh Han, Sabrina Ricci, Kirsten Cameron, Jeanne Mankinen, Jocelyn Moffat, Audrey Sullivan, April Rassa, Sharon Conour, Leah Walling, Misty Megia, Katie Carlson, Lisa Lang, Josh Henry, Moe Min. Oh man, this is a long list. And I didn't even get to everybody. I could go on. I also want to add thanks to all of the marketing professionals who took the time to read this book. I hope you found it useful and inspiring. And to all of the up-and-coming marketers, you were my muse.

Thank you to those not in marketing that put up with my crazy ideas, programs, and demands. To all of the amazing sales people, product managers, engineers, finance and accounting peeps, designers, web developers, and sales ops, you are an integral part of marketing's ability to be successful. If you read this book, and I hope you do, presumably, it will help you understand where I was coming from, and help guide you as you work with your internal and external marketing organizations.

I would like to thank four individuals who have been so important in not only keeping me sane, but successful while at work and beyond. But first, a story. A marketing professional, a publicist, a product leader, and a biz dev guy walk into a bar together. Okay, just kidding. No joke. To Eileen Conway, who has been with me for I don't know how many companies, always ensuring the best media coverage. But more importantly, thank you for convincing me to tell this story in my own words versus hiring a ghostwriter. I forgot how much I love to write. To Rob McGrorty, an amazing product leader and executive, I appreciate all of our honest conversations about business and life. You have been an amazing advisor, collaborator, and friend. To Abbie Tuller, for always keeping it real, laughing with me, and sticking with me through multiple companies. If it's going to be a shit show at least go through it with someone who shares your—potentially twisted—sense of humor. To Christopher Sinnott, who not only helped onboard me at Autodesk, but worked collaboratively with me to ensure we would be successful together. To all of you, I am forever in your debt and truly cherish our friendship. I hope we get to work together in the future in some capacity.

To all of my managers, good and bad, thank you. You helped define who I wanted to be, and in some cases who I didn't want to be. Ultimately you helped me become the marketing leader I am today. And hey, you put up with me. That says a lot about you. Kudos and thank you for your leadership, mentorship, and guidance.

To the influencers in my life, especially those who have helped me with this particular quit-my-day-job-book-writing-going-solo journey, I appreciate your valuable time and guidance. To Pat Casey, my high school business teacher, thank you for showing me my true calling and getting me involved with Junior Achievements. To my dad, who encouraged me to be better in business than everyone else. To Sonia Foss, my college advisor, thanks for your teachings, and for encouraging me to be true to myself. To Al Bruno, at Santa Clara University, the toughest professor I ever had, but also the best at helping me understand the meaning of teamwork and collaboration. To Promise Phelon, thank you for always pushing me to do more and to do it better. To Michaela Alexis, John Nemo, and Ann Handley, whether you know it or not, your content has been significant in helping me build my platform. To David Meerman Scott and Matt Heinze, your advice has been invaluable. Thank you for sharing it. And finally, at least for this section, to Elon Musk. I had the privilege of working with/for him back in the Zip2 days. He always emphasized that nothing is impossible, even commercial space flight to Mars. I have kept this insight with me—albeit sometimes in the back of my head when sometimes it should have been at the forefront—for over twenty-five years. It has truly guided me and given me comfort.

Let's see, who else? (Are you still with me?)

I am indebted to my book coach Stacy Ennis, who kept me on track during this journey. Thanks to my amazing editors and proof-readers, especially Robin Bethel and Marianne Tatom. You helped me shine. To the entire team at Greenleaf Book Group, from Tyler to Justin, Sam to Emily, Lindsey to Neil, and everyone else behind the scenes, thank you! I could not have done this without you. I look forward to a long and successful partnership. To my team at Christina Del Villar LLC, Jessica Macintyre, Jessica Seto, Kristen Elsworth, Jules Reifkind, and Marcela Stellmach, thank you for always showing up and making a huge impact.

I am also grateful to my friends who have stood by me through thick and thin and, at times, told me the truth (even when I didn't ask or want it). Thank you for being my social directors; crafting, cycling, and travel buddies; sounding board, and more importantly, the source of much laughter. Here's to many more years of friendship, Shirley, Shari, Patrick, Sharon, Abbie, Anne, Aaron, Rob, Christopher.

Last, but not least, (far from it in fact), I would like to acknowledge my family. To my mom, Pamela, you raised me to be the strong, independent-minded individual I am today. Thanks for encouraging me to read, get an education, and persevere. To my big brother Tom, sister-in-law Delanie, and niece Beatrice, thanks for always including Ken and me in your adventures. To all my extended family of nieces (Ashley, Jessica, and Andrea), and nephews (Christopher, Peter, and Parker), thank you for all of the love, support, and game nights. I hope I have inspired you in some way. To Edd, Donna, Dianne, Jim, and Harold, my "it takes a village" family who have stood by me and encouraged me from when I was but a wee child—thank you. To my Hawaiian Ohana, Kalmia, Lisa, and Jim, thank you for your friendship and love. Through good times and bad, you are always an inspiration.

This section seems like having a kid. With the first one, there is always so much to record. By the second one, there are fewer "moments" captured and a lot less photos. All that to say I promise to keep the Acknowledgments in my next book a bit shorter.

We're at the end. But before I go, I want to encourage everyone to think about how you can give back. Maybe you can become a mentor and help others over the bumps in the road; maybe you can volunteer or donate to directly help those in need. Think about it as your personal Map of Influence.

Now go do epic shit!

Christina Del Villar

# Index

# About the Author

**Christina Del Villar** is a Silicon Valley marketing executive and go-to-market veteran who geeks out on helping companies transform, grow, and scale. With over 25 years of executive-level marketing experience at Fortune 100 companies and more than fifteen startups, Christina has worked alongside some of tech's best and brightest.

As Founder and Chief Marketing Strategist at Christina Del Villar LLC, Christina is on a mission to help marketing professionals be more effective; help companies grow exponential revenue; and show leaders, executives, and boards the significant impact marketing brings to the table.

Christina has spoken internationally for years at conferences such as Dreamforce, SIGGRAPH, and SXSW, speaking on behalf of companies like Autodesk, FedEx, Intacct, Stanford University, Nike, and others, and makes frequent appearances at marketing conferences, webinars, vlogs, blogs, and podcasts. She has also written articles that have appeared in *Fast Company*, *Forbes*, *HBR*, and NBC *Grow*.

Her love for all things marketing also extends through her philanthropic work. Christina is passionate about mentoring social entrepreneurs about go-to-market strategy and marketing, through her efforts with Miller Center for Social Entrepreneurship at Santa Clara University.

Christina has a BS from the University of Oregon and an MBA from Santa Clara University. She splits her time between the San Francisco Bay Area and the Reno-Tahoe area.

You can learn more about Christina and her offerings at www.christinadelvillar.com.

www.ingramcontent.com/pod-product-compliance
Lightning Source LLC
Chambersburg PA
CBHW030456210326
41597CB00013B/687